An Encyclopedia of
Quotations About Music

An Encyclopedia of Quotations About Music

compiled and edited by
NAT SHAPIRO

A DA CAPO PAPERBACK

Library of Congress Cataloging in Publication Data

Main entry under title:

An Encyclopedia of quotations about music.

(A Da Capo paperback)
Reprint of the 1978 ed. published by Doubleday,
Garden City, N.Y.
Includes indexes.
1. Music—Quotations, maxims, etc. I. Shapiro,
Nat.
[ML66.E6 1981]   780   80-29200
ISBN 0-306-80138-8 (pbk.)

This Da Capo Press paperback edition of
An Encyclopedia of Quotations about Music
is an unabridged republication of the
first edition published in New York in 1978. It is
reprinted by arrangement with Doubleday & Co.

Published by Da Capo Press, Inc.
A Subsidiary of Plenum Publishing Corporation
233 Spring Street, New York, N.Y. 10013

CONTENTS

Part Six THE UNIVERSAL ART

Part Seven MUSIC FOR THE MILLIONS

Part Eight METAPHYSICS, METAPHOR, AND MISCELLANY

INTRODUCTION

Writing about music—about what it is and what it means—is akin to describing the act of love. Somehow, the reduction of the experience to an unblushingly detailed exposition of how, where, when, and why who does what to whom, from prelude to resolution, loses everything in the translation. The other extreme, the one wherein the writer, in desperation, resorts to metaphor (with or without benefit of meter and rhyme), most often results in imagery that is banal, vulgar, inane, obscure, pretentious, and almost always insufferably romantic.

To achieve good and accurate writing about music is as rare an accomplishment as expert wine-tasting, lion-taming, diamond-cutting, truffle-finding and (if one just happens to be an unconverted Mohican brave) deer-tracking. Only the intuitive, the pure, the sensual, and the intrepid need apply.

Professional musicians often evidence a fixed tendency either to rudely ignore or else to actively despise those of us who bravely try to understand, define, and describe their art. To many composers and instrumentalists, those outsiders (nonmusicians) who have the temerity to discuss anything more abstract than the digital dexterity of a fiddler, the particular vanity of a conductor, or the wage scales for overtime recording sessions are judged worthy only of contempt or—at the most—patronizing tolerance.

"Music means itself," insists one of the contributors to the collection that follows, and many practitioners of the art of organized sound would prefer to leave it at that.

But fortunately for those of us who love but live outside of music, its meaning, its mystery and its profound effect upon the individual, upon its sister arts and upon society have provoked the commentaries of an impressive number of mere word users throughout our history.

If this volume, albeit unintentionally, proves anything at all, it is that in the course of a few thousand years of attempts to write coherently about music, no one seems to have been able to come up with a universally acceptable or satisfactory definition of that astonishing and most insinuating art.

And yet, as demonstrated in the pages ahead, many have made brave and lovely attempts at "expressing the inexpressible."

It may be not at all surprising to note that the works of William Shakespeare yield the greatest number of entries from any single source represented in this volume. But then, remember the lyric beauty of Shakespeare's verse, the singing oratory of his solo passages, his miraculous rhythmic sense, the enormous, dynamic range of his emotional perception, his complex yet ever clearly defined contrapuntal themes.

Many classic poets and philosophers found an abundance of metaphoric uses in music, one of the most enduring having to do with "celestial harmonies" and "the music of the spheres." The concepts that "from heavenly harmony this universal frame began . . ." (Milton) and that "the rotation of the universe and the motion of the planets could neither begin nor continue without music" (Plutarch) have been with us as long as the pen and the pipe. They are to be found not only in the Old Testament and in the writings of both ancient Greece and China, but also throughout the richest periods of Western classical literature.

But to the poets, the relationship of music to the creation of the universe was hardly the sole source of inspiration for musical imagery. A miraculous few, among them Byron, Browning, Milton, Dryden, Shelley, Wordsworth, Tennyson, Poe, Keats, Longfellow, Burns, and Pope, discovered music in the sea, in the air, in animals, minerals, vegetables; in the curve of a breast and in the shape of a cloud, in the scent of grass, in the taste of a kiss.

Of course!

Novelists and playwrights on the other hand evidently have had severe problems in dealing with music as subject matter. The serious musician, whose primary language has nothing at all to do with words, has been a cipher to the writer of fiction and drama. Certainly, very few have tried to deal with the musical beast in imaginative prose. In searching the subject indexes in libraries—or more to the point, the critics' and academicians' lists of great books and plays—one is hard-pressed to find more than a handful of first-rate works that have dealt with music or musicians.

The best novel, possibly, is *Jean Christophe*, by Romain Rolland. But after that extraordinary study of a composer, what else? Thomas Mann's *Doctor Faustus*? James Huneker's *Painted Veils*? Not really.

A number of contemporary novelists and playwrights have tried their hands at writing about jazz and jazz players as well as about rock and popular musical personalities, but none really has been able to escape the pitfalls encountered by their predecessors, those who lost their way in a maze of subjective imagery trying to describe a Bach fugue or a Beethoven sonata.

Literate composers and musicians have fared little better. Apart from scores of dull autobiographies, only a few have attempted to write about their field, among them Wagner, Berlioz, Schumann, Debussy, Aaron Copland, Leonard Bernstein, Ned Rorem, and (via Robert Craft) Igor Stravinsky. These exceptions fortunately have been able to succeed in dealing lucidly and, on rare occasions, wittily and brilliantly with their art.

Critics too have had their problems, and most often have succeeded in writing memorably about music when in a state of pique about incompetent singers and instrumentalists, the avant-garde, noisy audiences, and poorly staged operas. Only a very special and very small group of professional music critics qualify as writers of merit, among them George Bernard Shaw, H. L. Mencken, James Huneker, Sir Ernest Newman, Paul Rosenfeld, and Romain Rolland.

The largest number of wise, witty, and beautiful quotations about music come from writers who know or knew little or nothing about its mechanics or its history. Aside from the substantial number of selections from poems, novels, plays, and standard works on music, the reader of this volume will discover that the editor has drawn upon letters, diaries, biographies, essays, histories, graffiti, interviews, news stories, program notes, speeches, textbooks, lectures, songs, sermons, motion pictures, catalogues, anecdotes, advertisements, and philosophic, political, and religious tracts, as well as a number of collections of proverbs, maxims, aphorisms, jokes, word games, and—quotations.

The organization of this book is unashamedly arbitrary and is based upon some possibly questionable categorical decisions. There are many quotations of either so general or so thematically complex a nature that they might fit easily into a number of different sections. Some may not appear to fit anywhere at all.

Thus, in order that the serious searcher for a particular gem or chestnut be accommodated, an index of key words and phrases has been provided, apart from the more general table of contents.

The particular quotation you are looking for may be elusive.

Blame it on the subject—the elusive art—music.

Nat Shapiro
New York
June 1977

There are no good books on music.

Sir Thomas Beecham (1879–1961)

Part One
MUSIC IS . . .
MUSIC DOES . . . MUSIC MEANS . . .

"Expressing the inexpressible . . ."

Music: That one of the fine arts which is concerned with the combination of sounds with a view to beauty of form and the expression of emotion.

Oxford English Dictionary
Volume VI, L–M, 1961

Music is . . . that one of the fine arts which appropriates the phenomena of sound to the purposes of poetry.

Encyclopaedia Britannica

Musicke is a chearefull recreation to the minde that hath been blunted with serious meditations. These and such like are holy and good recreations both comfortable and profitable.

Anonymous
Short Treatise Against Stage-Players, 1625

Music is the art of sounds in the movement of time.

Anonymous
Quoted by Ferruccio Busoni, *The Essence of Music*, June 1924

Mathematics is music for the mind; music is mathematics for the soul.

Anonymous

Servant and master am I: servant of those dead, and master of those living. Through my spirit immortals speak the message that makes the world weep and laugh, and wonder and worship . . . For I am the instrument of God. I am music.

Anonymous
International Musician, July 1928

Music is both itself and about itself.

> Anonymous
> *Musical Times*, London, 1932

The world's a body, every liberal art a needful member, music the soul and heart.

> Anonymous
> *Human out of Breath*, 1608

To those who are not tone-deaf the argument that music vaguely of the period *must* express that period is unsound. Unsound because we are not listening with the ears of that period. I hold that Richard Strauss gives to modern ears a better notion of the daughter of Clytemnestra and Agamemnon than any concatenation of conch, ram's horn, harp, pipe, lute, theorbo, shawm, sackbut, psaltry, tabor, and cymbals that Euripides could have heard.

> James Agate (1877–1947)
> *The Later Ego*, 1951

The entrancing phantasmagoria of picture and incident which we think we see rising from the billowing sea of music is in reality nothing more than an enchanting *fata morgana*, visible at no other angle than that of our own eye . . . It is but something that we have half unconsciously imputed to music; nothing that really exists in music.

> William Foster Apthorp (1848–1913)
> *By the Ways About Music and Musicians*, 1898

The exaltation of the mind derived from things eternal bursting forth in sound.

> St. Thomas Aquinas (1225–74)

To some people music is like food; to others like medicine; to others like a fan.

> *The Arabian Nights' Entertainments*, c. 1450

There's only two ways to sum up music: either it's good or it's bad. If it's good you don't mess about it; you just enjoy it.

> Louis Armstrong (1900–71)

What I like about music is its ability to be convincing, to carry an argument through successfully to the finish, though the terms of the argument remain unknown quantities.

> John Ashbery (1927–   )
> Quoted in the New York *Times Magazine*,
> May 23, 1976

(Music) can be made anywhere, is invisible, and does not smell.

> W. H. Auden (1907–73)
> *In Praise of Limestone*, 1951

(Music is) An agreeable harmony for the honor of God and the permissible delights of the soul.

> Johann Sebastian Bach (1685–1750)

There are many things in music which must be imagined without being heard. It is the intelligent hearers who are endowed with that imagination whom we should endeavor to please especially.

> Carl Philipp Emanuel Bach (1714–88)

Music appeals to the heart, whereas writing is addressed to the intellect; it communicates ideas directly, like perfume.

> Honoré de Balzac (1799–1850)
> *Massimila Doni*, 1839

I cannot conceive of music that expresses absolutely nothing.

> Béla Bartók (1881–1945)

The search for a critical vocabulary in which we may speak of music by strict denotation is quite absurd: not even the conventional notes and signs of a score can precisely denote the sounds that we hear.

> Jacques Barzun (1907–   )
> *Pleasures of Music*, 1951

Music, not being made up of objects nor referring to objects, is intangible and ineffable; it can only be, as it were, inhaled by the spirit: the rest is silence.

> Jacques Barzun
> *Pleasures of Music*, 1951

. . . music is for delight; it is intended and designed for sentient beings that have hopes and purposes and emotions. Music does not tell about these movements of the human spirit, but it somehow transfixes them, elaborates them, and gives them enduring form and self-renewing vigor.

> Jacques Barzun
> Introduction to *The New Music*,
> by Joan Peyser, 1971

The more we know of music and the more we live with it, the more elusive and mysterious it becomes, always changing, capable of a thousand indescribable moods, a strange and somewhat mystical power in our lives, a fascination, a challenge, a craft. A language, a house of cards . . . the echo from an invisible world.

> Leslie Bassett (1923–   )
> *Edition Peters Contemporary Music
> Catalogue*, 1975

Music is the electrical soil in which the spirit lives, thinks and invents.

> Ludwig van Beethoven (1770–1827)
> Letter to Bettina von Arnim

. . . music is a higher revelation than all . . . wisdom and philosophy.

> Ludwig van Beethoven
> Letter to Bettina von Arnim, 1810

Music, verily, is the mediator between intellectual and sensuous life . . . the one incorporeal entrance into the higher world of

knowledge which comprehends mankind but which mankind cannot comprehend.

> Ludwig van Beethoven
> Letter from Bettina von Arnim to
> Johann Wolfgang von Goethe,
> Vienna, May 28, 1810

The best music always results from ecstasies of logic.

> Alban Berg (1885–1935)
> Quoted by Donal Henahan in the
> New York *Times Magazine*, May 11, 1975

Music alone speaks at once to the imagination, the mind, the
heart and the *senses*; and it is the reaction of the senses on the
mind and heart, and *vice versa*, that produces the impressions felt
by those who are gifted with the necessary organization, but of
which *others* (the barbarians) can know nothing.

> Hector Berlioz (1803–69)
> *Memoires*, 1847

Music . . . can name the unnamable and communicate the
unknowable.

> Leonard Bernstein (1918–   )
> *The Unanswered Question*, 1976

Einstein said that "the most beautiful experience we can have
is the mysterious." Then why do so many of us try to explain the
beauty of music, thus apparently depriving it of its mystery?

> Leonard Bernstein
> *The Unanswered Question*, 1976

Music, of all the arts, stands in a special region, unlit by any
star but its own, and utterly without meaning . . . except its own,
a meaning in musical terms . . . not in terms of words . . .

> Leonard Bernstein
> *The Joy of Music*, 1959

Much of the effect of music, I am satisfied, is owing to the association of ideas. The air which constantly and irresistibly excites in the Swiss, when in a foreign land, the *maladie du pays* has, I am told, no intrinsic power of sound. And . . . Scotch reels, though brisk, make me melancholy, because I used to hear them in my early years . . . whereas the airs in "The Beggar's Opera," many of which are very soft, never fail to render me gay, because they are associated with the warm sensations and high spirits of London.

> James Boswell (1740–95)
> *Life of Samuel Johnson*, 1791

Music is the fourth great material want of our nature—first food, then raiment, then shelter, then music.

> Christian Nestell Bovee (1820–1904)

Impudent futility, to endeavor to translate music into color or poetry or any dimension but its own!

> Catherine Drinker Bowen (1897–1973)
> *Friends and Fiddlers*, 1934

Music is neither secular nor religious. It can at best suggest the beating of the pulse, the rhythm of the blood that accompanies a given order of ideas.

> Henry Noel Brailsford (1873–1958)
> *On Handel's Largo*

Almost the only thing music can represent unambiguously is the cuckoo—and that it can't differentiate from a cuckoo-clock.

> Brigid Brophy (1929–)
> *A Literary Person's Guide to Opera*, 1965

Music was born free, and to win freedom is its destiny.

> Ferruccio Busoni (1866–1924)

If this word "music" is sacred and reserved for eighteenth and nineteenth-century instruments, we can substitute a more meaningful term: organization of sound.

> John Cage (1912–)
> *The Future of Music: Credo*, 1937

> And this song is considered a perfect gem,
> And as to the meaning, it's what you please.
>> Charles Stuart Calverley (1831–84)
>> *Ballad, after William Morris, The Auld Wife*

Who is there that, in logical words, can express the effect music has on us? A kind of inarticulate unfathomable speech, which leads us to the edge of the Infinite and lets us for moments gaze into that.

> Thomas Carlyle (1795–1881)
> *On Heroes, Hero-Worship, and the Heroic in History,* 1801

Music is well said to be the speech of angels: in fact, nothing among the utterances allowed to man is felt to be so divine. It brings us near to the infinite.

>> Thomas Carlyle
>> *The Opera,* 1832

Music is prophecy of what life is to be; the rainbow of promise translated out of seeing into hearing.

>> Lydia M. Child (1802–80)

Nothing is more odious than music without hidden meaning.

>> Frédéric Chopin (1810–49)
>> Quoted by Maurice Ravel in *Le*
>> *Courrier Musical,* January 1910

Look out! Be on your guard because alone of all the arts, music moves all around you.

>> Jean Cocteau (1889–1963)
>> *Cock and Harlequin,* 1918

Enough of clouds, waves, aquariums, nymphs, and perfumes of the night. We need a music that is down to earth—an everyday music.

>> Jean Cocteau

The sense of musical delight, with the power of producing it, is a gift of the imagination.

>> Samuel Taylor Coleridge (1772–1834)

Good music never tires, nor sends me to sleep.

> Samuel Taylor Coleridge
> *Table Talk,* July 6, 1833

If the music doesn't say it, how can words say it *for* the music?

> John Coltrane (1926–67)
> To Nat Hentoff in *Jazz Is,* 1976

From the depth of sentiment comes the clarity of form and from the strength of the mood comes the spirituality of its atmosphere. This harmony of spirit springs forth from the soul and finds expression or blossoms forth in the form of music.

> Confucius (551–479 B.C.)

The whole problem can be stated quite simply by asking, "Is there a meaning to music?" My answer to that would be, "Yes." And "Can you state in so many words what the meaning is?" My answer to that would be, "No."

> Aaron Copland (1900–   )
> *What to Listen for in Music,* 1939

The use of music as a kind of ambrosia to titillate the aural senses while one's conscious mind is otherwise occupied is the abomination of every composer who takes his work seriously.

> Aaron Copland
> *The Pleasures of Music,* 1959

> Water and air He for the Tenor chose,
> Earth made the Base, the Treble Flame arose,
> To th' active Moon, a quick brisk stroke He gave,
> To Saturn's string a touch more soft and grave,
> The motions strait, and round, and swift, and slow
> And short and long, were mixt and woven so,
> Did in such artful Figures smoothly fall,
> As made this decent measur'd Dance of all.
> And this is Musick.

> > Abraham Cowley (1618–67)
> > *Davidies,* 1656

Music might be defined as a system of proportions in the service of a spiritual impulse.

> George Crumb (1929–   )
> *Edition Peters Contemporary Music
> Catalogue,* 1975

Music is the arithmetic of sounds as optics is the geometry of light.

> Claude Debussy (1862–1918)

Music is an outburst of the soul.

> Frederick Delius (1862–1934)

It is only that which cannot be expressed otherwise that is worth expressing in music.

> Frederick Delius
> *At the Crossroads,* September 1920

Music . . . gives us the very essence of the dropping down and the exalted rising, the surging and retracting, the acceleration and retardation, the tightening and loosening, the sudden thrust and the gradual insinuation of things.

> John Dewey (1859–1952)
> *Art as Experience,* 1934

When you hear music, after it's over, it's gone in the air. You can never capture it again.

> Eric Dolphy (1928–64)

Music is the eye of the ear.

> Thomas Draxe
> *Bibliotheca,* 1616

He had never heard such music as this, never dreamt such music was possible. He was conscious, while it lasted, that he saw deeper into the beauty, the sadness of things, the very heart of them, and their pathetic evanescence, as with a new inner eye—even into eternity itself, beyond the veil.

> George Du Maurier (1834–96)
> *Trilby,* 1894

Music is in the air—you simply take as much of it as you want.

> Attributed to Sir Edward Elgar (1857–1934)

Music is the poor man's Parnassus.

> Ralph Waldo Emerson (1803–82)
> "Poetry and Imagination," 1875

So is music an asylum. It takes us out of the actual and whispers to us dim secrets that startle our wonder as to who we are, and for what, whence and whereto. All the great interrogatories, like questioning angels, float in on its waves of sound.

> Ralph Waldo Emerson
> *Journals,* 1836–38

> And music pours on mortals
> Her magnificent disdain.

> Ralph Waldo Emerson
> *The Sphinx*

Music is nothing else but wild sounds civilized into time and tune.

> Thomas Fuller (1608–61)
> *The History of the Worthies of England,* 1662

Music is the most disagreeable and the most widely beloved of all noises.

> Théophile Gautier (1811–72)
> *Le Figaro,* October 20, 1863

Music is something innate and internal, which needs little nourishment from without, and no experience drawn from life.

> Johann Wolfgang von Goethe (1749–1832)
> February 14, 1831

In music the dignity of art seems to find supreme expression. There is no subject matter to be discounted. It is all form and significant content. It elevates and ennobles whatever it expresses.

> Johann Wolfgang von Goethe
> *Maxims and Reflections*

Now the rich stream of music winds along, deep, majestic, smooth and strong.

> Thomas Gray (1716–71)
> *The Progress of Poesy*, 1757

Music may be regarded as a thermometer that makes it possible to register the degree of sensibility of every people, according to the climate in which it lives.

> André Ernest Grétry (1741–1813)
> *Memoirs*, 1789

Music means itself.

> Eduard Hanslick (1825–1904)
> *The Beautiful in Music*, 1854

The other arts persuade us, but music takes us by surprise.

> Eduard Hanslick
> *The Beautiful in Music*, 1854

The sole contents of music are moving, sounding forms.

> Eduard Hanslick
> Quoted by A. R. Parsons in translator's
> preface to *Beethoven*, by Richard Wagner

What is music? The very existence of music is wonderful, I might even say miraculous. Its domain is between thought and phenomena. Like a twilight mediator, it hovers between spirit and matter, related to both, yet differing from each. It is spirit, but spirit subject to the measurement of time; it is matter, but matter that can dispense with space.

> Heinrich Heine (1797–1856)
> *Letters on the French Stage*, 1837

Nothing is more futile than theorizing about music.

> Heinrich Heine
> *Letters on the French Stage*, 1837

Music represents the inner feeling in the exterior air, and expresses what precedes, accompanies, or follows all verbal utterance.
Wilhelm Heinse (1746–1803)
Ardinghello und die glücklichen Inseln, 1787

You can't mess with people's heads, that's for sure. But that's what music's all about, messing with people's heads.
Jimi Hendrix (1942–70)

Music . . . is the outward and audible signification of inward and spiritual realities.
Philip Heseltine (1894–1930)
Forward to Sackbut, 1920

Music is meaningless noise unless it touches a receiving mind.
Paul Hindemith (1895–1963)
A Composer's World, 1961

Music was a thing of the soul; a rose-lipped shell that murmured of the external sea; a strange bird singing the songs of another shore.
Josiah Gilbert Holland (1819–81)
Plain Talks on Familiar Subjects, 1858

Music can be translated only by music. Just so far as it suggests worded thought, it falls short of its highest office.
Oliver Wendell Holmes (1809–94)
Over the Teacups, 1891

Music is the vapor of art. It is to poetry what reverie is to thought, what fluid is to liquid, what the ocean of clouds is to the ocean of waves.
Victor Hugo (1802–85)
Les Rayons et les ombres, 1840

Music is an order of mystic, sensuous mathematics . . . a sounding mirror, an aural mode of motion. . . .
James G. Huneker (1860–1921)
Chopin, 1900

Music remains the only art, the last sanctuary, wherein originality may reveal itself in the face of fools and not pierce their mental opacity.

> James G. Huneker
> *Iconoclasts,* 1905

Music is an ocean, but the repertory . . . is hardly even a lake; it is a pond.

> Aldous Huxley (1894–1963)
> Quoted in *Time,* December 23, 1957

After silence that which comes nearest to expressing the inexpressible is music.

> Aldous Huxley
> "Music at Night," 1931

(Music is) a method of employing the mind without the labour of thinking at all.

> Samuel Johnson (1709–84)
> Accoiding to James Boswell,
> *Journal of a Tour to the Hebrides,* 1786

A musician should employ the images of the sounds he would represent, and not the sounds themselves.

> Joseph Joubert (1754–1824)
> *Pensées, essais, maximes et*
> *correspondance,* 1842

Music soothes us, stirs us up; it puts noble feelings in us; it melts us to tears, we know not how:—it is a language by itself, just as perfect, in its way, as speech, as words; just as divine, just as blessed . . . Music has been called the speech of angels; I will go further, and call it the speech of God himself.

> Charles Kingsley (1819–75)

No man is complete without a feeling for music and an understanding of what it can do for him.

> Zoltán Kodály (1882–1967)
> Santa Barbara *News-Press,*
> August 1, 1966

Of all the arts, music is practiced most and thought about least.
>Henry Edward Krehbiel (1854–1923)
>*How to Listen to Music,* 1896

The power and the magic of music lie in its intangibility and its limitlessness. It suggests image, but leaves us free to choose them and to accommodate them to our pleasure.
>Wanda Landowska (1877–1959)
>*Landowska on Music,* 1964

Music is our myth of the inner life.
>Susanne Langer (1895–)
>*Philosophy in a New Key,* 1942

If descriptive music is a mistake, let it be: the mistake usually lies in the description only, not in the music . . .
>Sidney Lanier (1842–81)
>*The Physics of Music,* 1875

It is purely because music is so great that it yields aid and comfort to so many theories.
>Sidney Lanier
>*Music Is Infinite*

As music takes up the thread which language drops, so it is where Shakespeare ends that Beethoven begins.
>Sidney Lanier
>*From Bacon to Beethoven*

Music is a calculation which the soul makes unconsciously in secret.
>Gottfried Wilhelm von Leibnitz
>*The Monadology,* 1714

There is no other human activity that asks for such a harmonious cooperation of "intellect" and "soul" as artistic creation and especially, music.
>Ernest Lévy (1895–)
>Letter to Barnett Byman, February 18, 1945

> Hidden in a brief adagio
> There is a sermon on the transient hour;
> And lured from inner depths by sweep of bow
> May be a vision of the perfect flower,
> Immortal blossom of divine intent
> Whose humblest seed explains the firmament.
>> Elias Lieberman (1883–1969)

Music is the universal language of mankind.
> Henry Wadsworth Longfellow (1807–82)
> *Outre-Mer*

> Yea, music is the Prophet's art
> Among the gifts that God has sent,
> One of the most magnificent!
>> Henry Wadsworth Longfellow

Music . . . is a language, but a language of the intangible, a kind of soul-language.
> Edward MacDowell (1861–1908)
> *Critical and Historical Essays*, 1912

Music is a science that would have us laugh and sing and dance.
> Guillaume de Machaut (c. 1300–77)

What is best in music is not to be found in the notes.
> Gustav Mahler (1860–1911)

. . . Music is a manifestation of the highest energy . . . almost the definition of God.
> Thomas Mann (1875–1955)
> *Doctor Faustus*, 1948

We say of course that music "addresses itself to the ear"; but it does so only in a qualified way, only in so far, namely, as the hearing, like the other senses, is the deputy, the instrument, and the receiver of the mind. Perhaps . . . it was music's deepest wish not to be heard at all, nor even seen, nor yet felt; but only—if that were possible—in some Beyond, the other side of sense and sentiment, to be perceived and contemplated as pure mind, pure spirit.

Thomas Mann
Doctor Faustus, 1948

Music, the mosaic of the Air.

Andrew Marvell (1621–78)
Music's Empire

Music must be an evidence for living.

Toshiro Mayuzumi (1929–   )
*Edition Peters Contemporary Music
Catalogue*, 1975

Music is the fragrance of the universe . . .

Giuseppe Mazzini (1805–72)
Journal, 1836

Once I had a dream to live and love, and this dream became music. It touched all of the beautiful experiences I have searched for or known. Each sound was a color, and each color was a warm feeling, and my heart kept the tempo.

Les McCann (1935–   )
World Jazz Association Newsletter,
February 1976

Music is more than a combination of sounds. It is colors too. I see the different keys like a rainbow. The key of D is daffodil yellow, B Major is maroon, and B Flat is blue.

Marian McPartland (1920–   )

There is no such thing as music divorced from the listener. Music as such is unfulfilled until it has penetrated our ears.

Yehudi Menuhin (1916–   )
Theme and Variations, 1972

Music creates order out of chaos; for rhythm imposes continuity upon the disjointed, and harmony imposes compatibility upon the incongruous.

> Yehudi Menuhin
> *Theme and Variations*, 1972

Music can never be an abstraction, however thoughtful and objectless—for its object is the living man in time—nor can it be accidental, however improvised . . . because improvisation is not the expression of accident but rather of the accumulated yearnings, dreams and wisdom of our very soul.

> Yehudi Menuhin
> *Theme and Variations*, 1972

Music is the art of expressing sensations by modulated sounds.

> C. F. Michaelis (1770–1834)
> *Über den Geist der Tonkunst*, 1800

Music is a beautiful opiate, if you don't take it too seriously.

> Henry Miller (1891–   )
> *The Air-Conditioned Nightmare*, 1945

Only life suffered can transform a symphony from a collection of notes into a message of humanity.

> Dimitri Mitropoulos (1896–1960)
> February 19, 1954

. . . you must have a care that when your matter signifieth ascending, high heaven and such like, you make your musick ascend: and by the contrarie where your dittie speaks of descending, lowness, depth, hell and others such, you must make your musick descend. For it will bee thought a great absurditie to talke of heaven and point downward to the earth: so it will be counted great incongruity if a musician upon the words "he ascended to heaven" should cause his musick to descend.

> Thomas Morley (1557–?1603)
> A *Plaine and Easie Introduction to Practicall Musick*, 1597

Like everything else in nature, music is a *becoming*, and it becomes its full self when its sounds and laws are used by intelligent man for the production of harmony, and so made the vehicle of emotion and thought.

Theodore T. Munger (1830–1910)
The Appeal to Life

A man responds or fails to respond to certain music by virtue not only of what the music is, but of what he is . . .

Sir Ernest Newman (1868–1959)
A Musical Critic's Holiday, 1925

Music shows us the soul of things at first hand.

Sir Ernest Newman

. . . it always makes us doubt another man's sanity to find that he has read into a given page of music a series of images quite different from our own . . .

Sir Ernest Newman
New Witness, 1917

I am writing on silent paper, which has no power of harmony or discord, and I will cease from these descriptions of an art which cannot be described.

Beverley Nichols
Are They the Same at Home?, 1927

Music scatters the sparks of images.

Friedrich Nietzsche (1844–1900)
The Birth of Tragedy from the Spirit of Music, translated 1910

Beethoven's music is music about music.

Friedrich Nietzsche
Human All-too-Human, 1878

Music paints the sentiments and speech defines them.
>   Georges Noufflard
>   *Hector Berlioz et le movement de*
>   *l'art contemporain,* quoted by Sir
>   Ernest Newman in *A Study of Wagner,*
>   1899

The *Darian* moode is the bestower of wisedome, the causer of chastity. The *Phrygian* causeth wars, and enflameth fury. The *Eolian* doth appease the tempests of the minds, and when it hath appeased them, luls them asleepe. The *Lydian* doth sharpen the wit of the dull and doth make them that are burdened with earthly desires, to desire heavenly things . . .
>   Ornithoparcus
>   *Musicae Activae Micrologus,* 1516

Music is not a science any more than poetry is. It is a sublime instinct, like genius of all kinds.
>   Ouida (Marie Louise de la Ramée) (1839–1908)

Whistle softly, and as each loving muscle snuggles under, and each tiny cilia wiggles free, you will see—shimmering before you —the curves of x million perceptible changes in pitch, at least 127 varieties of female giggles and no less than 17 kinds of falsetto wails in each cubic foot of free vibrating air.
>   Harry Partch (1901–   )
>   *Rolling Stone,* April 11, 1974

All art constantly aspires towards the condition of music, because, in its ideal, consummate moments, the end is not distinct from the means, the form from the matter, the subject from the expression; and to it, therefore, to the condition of its perfect moments, all the arts may be supposed constantly to tend and aspire.
>   Walter Pater (1839–94)
>   *The School of Giorgione: The Renaissance,* 1873

Infinite is the sweet variety that the theorique of musicke exerciseth the mind with all, as the contemplation of proportion, of

Concords and Discords, diversity of Moods and Tones, infinite-ness of Invention, etc.

> Henry Peacham (1576?–?1643)
> *The Compleat Gentleman*, 1622

Musick is the thing of the world that I love most.

> Samuel Pepys (1633–1703)
> *Diary of Samuel Pepys*, July 30, 1666

The excellence of music is to be measured by pleasure. But the pleasure must not be that of chance persons; the fairest music is that which delights the best and best educated, and especially that which delights the one man who is pre-eminent in virtue and education.

> Plato (c. 428–c. 347 B.C.)
> *Laws*

The affairs of music ought, somehow, to terminate in the love of the beautiful.

> Plato
> *Republic*

It is in music, perhaps, that the soul most nearly attains the great end for which, when inspired by the poetic sentiment, it struggles—the creation of supernal beauty.

> Edgar Allan Poe (1809–49)
> *The Poetic Principle*, 1845

Music is the perfection of the soul, or idea, of Poetry. The *vagueness* of exultation aroused by a sweet air (which should strictly be indefinite and never too strongly suggestive) is precisely what we should aim at in poetry.

> Edgar Allan Poe
> Letter to James Russell Lowell,
> July 2, 1844

Indefinitiveness is an element of true music—I mean of true musical expression. Give to it any undue decision—imbue it with any very determinate tone—and you deprive it, at once, of its ethereal, its ideal, its intrinsic and essential character. You dispel its luxury of dream. You dissolve the atmosphere of the mystic upon which it floats. You exhaust it of its breath of faery.

> Edgar Allan Poe
> *Marginalia,* 1844–49

Music resembles poetry; in each
Are nameless graces which no methods teach,
And which a master-hand alone can reach.

> Alexander Pope (1688–1744)
> *Essay on Criticism,* 1711

Light quirks of music, broken and uneven, make the soul dance upon a jig to heaven.

> Alexander Pope
> *Moral Essays,* 1733

Beethoven's Fifth Symphony may be Fate—or Kate—knocking at the door. That is up to you.

> C. B. Rees
> "The Purpose of Music," *Penguin Music Magazine,* 1946

Music is the moonlight in the gloomy night of life.

> Jean Paul Richter (1763–1825)
> *Titan,* 1800–3

Thou speakest of things which all my endless life I have never found and never shall find.

> Jean Paul Richter

The soul of music slumbers in the shell
Till waked and kindled by the master's spell;
And feeling hearts, touch them but
    rightly, pour
A thousand melodies unheard before!

> Samuel Rogers (1763–1855)
> *Human Life*

Everything is music for the born musician. Everything that throbs, or moves, or stirs, or palpitates—sunlit summer days, nights when the wind howls, flickering light, the twinkling of the stars, storms, the song of birds, the buzzing of insects, the murmuring of trees, voices loved or loathed, familiar fireside sounds, a creaking door, blood moving in the veins in the silence of the night—everything that is is music; all that is needed is that it should be heard.

> Romain Rolland (1866–1944)
> *Jean-Christophe,* 1904–12

Do not let us say Music can . . . or Music cannot express such and such a thing. Let us say rather, if genius pleases, everything is possible.

> Romain Rolland

Music is the sole art which evokes nostalgia for the future.

> Ned Rorem (1923–   )
> *Edition Peters Contemporary*
> *Music Catalogue,* 1975

Music: all logic, no reason. Interpret music logically and reveal the impasse. The themes are people, the notes are people's actions.

> Ned Rorem
> *The Final Diary,* 1974

To see itself through, music must have idea or magic. The best has both. Music with neither dies young, though sometimes rich.

> Ned Rorem
> *Pure Contraption,* 1974

The sound of music—as opposed to rustling leaves or words of love—is sensual only secondarily. First it must make sense.

> Ned Rorem
> *Music from Inside Out,* 1967

Meditation more than analysis will take us toward the heart of music . . . .

> Ned Rorem
> *The Final Diary*, 1974

The hardest of all the arts to speak of is music, because music has no meaning to speak of.

> Ned Rorem
> *Music from Inside Out*, 1967

Music is too idealistic a thing to permit itself to be bound to concrete references. You cannot have a white horse in music.

> Paul Rosenfeld (1890–1946)
> October 1921

Music is a kind of harmonious language.

> Gioacchino Rossini (1792–1868)
> Quoted by Antonio Zanolini in
> *Biografia di Gioacchino Rossini*, 1875

The art of the musician consists in substituting for the unconscious image of an object that of the movements which its presence arouses in the heart of the beholder. Not only can it agitate the sea, animate the flames of fire, make the brooks flow, the rains fall, and swell the torrents; it can paint the horror of a desert, darken the walls of a subterranean prison, calm the tempest, render the air tranquil and serene and through the orchestra, diffuse a new freshness through the woods.

> Jean Jacques Rousseau (1712–78)
> *Essai sur l'origine des langues*, 1753

Music is the nearest at hand, the most orderly, the most delicate, and the most perfect, of all bodily pleasures; it is also the only one which is equally helpful to all the ages of man.

> John Ruskin (1819–1900)
> "Music in Greek Education"

It is a singular privilege of this art to give form to what is naturally inarticulate and to express those depths of human nature which speak no language current in this world.

> George Santayana (1863–1952)

There are relatively few people who are capable of understanding, purely musically, what music has to say. Such trained listeners have probably never been very numerous, but that does not prevent the artist from creating only for them. Great art pre-supposes the alert mind of the educated listener.

> Arnold Schoenberg (1874–1951)
> *Memories and Commentaries,* 1960

Music is only understood when one goes away singing it and only loved when one falls asleep with it in one's head, and finds it still there on waking up the next morning.

> Arnold Schoenberg
> *Why No Great American Music,* 1934

Music is a sort of dream architecture which passes in filmy clouds and disappears into nothingness.

> Percy A. Scholes (1877–1958)
> *The Listener's Guide to Music,* 1919

Music is the occult metaphysical exercise of a soul not knowing that it philosophizes.

> Arthur Schopenhauer (1788–1860)

Music is an art so great and surpassingly glorious, it acts mightily upon the innermost being of man. There it is understood so completely and profoundly as an entirely universal language, and even more distinct than the language of the perceptible world.

> Arthur Schopenhauer

Music never expresses the phenomenon, but only the inner nature, the in-itself of all phenomena, the will itself.

> Arthur Schopenhauer
> *The World as Will and Idea,* 1818

Music is an activity: it is something done, an experience lived through, with varying intensity, by composer, performer and listener alike.

> Roger Sessions (1896–　　)
> *The Musical Experience of Composer,
> Performer, and Listener*, 1950

Music is what unifies.

> Seu-ma-tsen (Chinese philosopher)
> Quoted by Igor Stravinsky, *The Poetics
> of Music*, 1947

After the symphonies of Beethoven it was certain that the poetry that lies too deep for words does not lie too deep for music, and that the vicissitudes of the soul, from the roughest fun to the loftiest aspiration, can make symphonies without the aid of dance tunes.

> George Bernard Shaw (1856–1950)
> *The Perfect Wagnerite*, 1898

Music is the lost chord that has strayed here from heaven.
> P. A. Sheehan
> *Under the Cedars and the Stars*, 1903

If I were to begin life again, I would devote it to music. It is the only cheap and unpunished rapture on earth.

> Sydney Smith (1771–1845)
> Letter to the Countess of Carlisle,
> August 1844

The entire pleasure of music consists in creating illusions, and common-sense rationality is the greatest enemy of musical appreciation.

> Stendhal (1783–1842)
> *Life of Rossini*, 1824

The only reality in music is the state of mind which it induces in the listener.

> Stendhal
> *Life of Rossini*, 1824

Music is not an acquired culture . . . it is an active part of natural life.

> Isaac Stern (1920–   )
> Quoted in *Celebrity Register*, 1973

There is no such thing as Abstract music; there is good music and bad music. If it is good, it means something; and then it is Programme Music.

> Richard Strauss (1864–1949)

In the pure state, music is free speculation.

> Igor Stravinsky (1882–1971)
> *The Poetics of Music*, 1947

I hold that music is given to us to create order.

> Igor Stravinsky

If, as is nearly always the case, music appears to express something, this is only an illusion and not a reality.

> Igor Stravinsky
> *Chronicles of My Life*, 1936

Music is not illusion, but revelation rather. Its triumphant power resides in the fact that it reveals to us beauties we find nowhere else, and that the apprehension of them is not transitory, but a perpetual reconcilement to life.

> Peter Ilyich Tchaikovsky (1840–93)

Oh, how difficult it is to make anyone see and feel in music what we see and feel ourselves!

> Peter Ilyich Tchaikovsky
> Letter to Nadezhda Filaretovna von Meck,
> March 28, 1878

Music is the crystallization of sound.

> Henry David Thoreau (1817–62)
> *Journal*, February 5, 1841

The truth is, that within limits, any music can be made to fit any situation.

> Ralph Vaughan Williams (1872–1958)
> *Film Music Notes*, 1944

Music is the inarticulate speech of the heart, which cannot be compressed into words, because it is infinite.

> Richard Wagner (1813–83)

What music expresses is eternal, infinite and ideal . . . in such infinitely varied phrases as belong uniquely to music and which are foreign and unknown to any other tongue.

> Richard Wagner
> *A Happy Evening*, 1840

Where the speech of man stops short, then the art of music begins.

> Richard Wagner
> *A Happy Evening*, 1840

Music should not be regarded as a sort of private letter in which a composer describes his feelings and experiences. But sometimes, as with Beethoven, experiences are completely dissolved in music, entirely transformed into music, so that they cease to exist as experiences and no remnant of them can interrupt our enjoyment of something that proceeds purely as music . . .

> Bruno Walter (1876–1962)
> *The Moral Powers of Music*, 1935

Music is natural law as related to the sense of hearing.

> Anton von Webern (1883–1945)
> *The Path to the New Music*, tr. 1963

All music is what awakes from you when you are reminded by the instruments.

> Walt Whitman (1819–92)
> *A Song for Occupations*

After playing Chopin, I feel as if I had been weeping over sins
that I had never committed, and mourning over tragedies that
were not my own. Music always seems to me to produce that
effect. It creates for one a past of which one has been ignorant
and fills one with a sense of sorrows that have been hidden from
one's tears.

Oscar Wilde (1854–1900)

Music is the corporealization of the intelligence that is in
sound.

Hoëne Wronsky (1778–1853)
Quoted by Edgar Varèse in a
lecture at Yale University, 1962

Part Two
CREATORS AND COMPONENTS

MELODY, HARMONY, AND RHYTHM

Melody is the golden thread running through the maze of tones by which the ear is guided and the heart reached.

Anonymous

Composers should write tunes the chauffeurs and errand boys can whistle.

Sir Thomas Beecham (1879–1961)
New York *Times*, March 9, 1961

Melody is a series of repeated rising and falling intervals, which are subdivided and given movement by rhythm; containing a latent harmony within itself and giving out a mood feeling; it can and does exist independently of accompanying parts as a form; in its performance the choice of pitch and of the instrument makes no difference to its essence.

Ferruccio Busoni (1866–1924)

The heart of a melody can never be put down on paper.

Pablo Casals (1876–1973)
Conversations with Casals, 1956

The melody is generally what the piece is about.

Aaron Copland (1900–   )

A tune is always the same tune, whether it is sung loudly or softly, by a child or a man; whether it is played on a flute or on a trombone.

Charles Darwin (1809–82)
The Expressions of the Emotions in Man and Animals, 1872

Harmony in music does not consist merely in the construction of concordant sounds, but in their mutual relations, their proper succession in what I should call their audible reflex.

Eugène Delacroix (1798–1863)

A melody is a vocal or instrumental imitation using the sounds of a scale invented by art or inspired by nature, as you prefer; it imitates either physical noises or the accents of passion.

Denis Diderot (1713–84)
Rameau's Nephew, 1762

Where there is harmony, there is no need of eloquence.

Robert Dow
Comments on Composers, c. 1581

"Fascinating Rhythm"

Ira Gershwin (1896–   )
Popular song title, 1924

"I Got Rhythm"

Ira Gershwin
Popular song title, 1930

The greatest beauties of melody and harmony become faults and imperfections when they are not in their proper place.

Christoph Willibald Gluck (1714–87)

I like to recognize the tune
I want to savvy what the band is playing
I keep saying, "Must you bury the tune?"
Lorenz Hart (1895–1943)
"I Like to Recognize the Tune," 1939,
popular song

Melody is the main thing; harmony is useful only to charm the ear.

Joseph Haydn (1732–1809)
Quoted by Wanda Landowska,
Landowska on Music, 1969

The fairest harmony springs from discord.
> Heraclitus (c. 540–c. 480 B.C.)
> Quoted by Aristotle, *Nicomachean Ethics*

While listening to Negro banjo players, I have pondered the mysterious law of rhythm which seems to be a universal law, since rhythm is coordinated movement, and movement is life, and life fills the universe.
> Henri Herz (1803–88)

Tonality is a natural force, like gravity.
> Paul Hindemith (1895–1963)

Rhythm is order, not the order that moves with cosmic precision, but that of humanity with all its mercurial emotions. Within us is a flexible human metronome—the heart. It is regulated by an educated taste.
> Josef Hofmann (1876–1957)
> Quoted by Abram Chasins, *Speaking of Pianists*, 1957

Melody alone never grows old.
> Vincent d'Indy (1851–1931)

Three things belong to composing, first of all melody; then again melody; then finally, for the third time, melody.
> Salomon Jadassohn (1831–1902)
> *Book of Instrumentation*, 1889

"All God's Chillun Got Rhythm"
> Gus Kahn
> Popular song title, 1937

Heard melodies are sweet, but those unheard are sweeter.
> John Keats (1795–1821)
> *Ode on a Grecian Urn*, c. 1819

Fair Melody! kind siren! I've no choice;
I must be thy sad servant evermore;
I cannot choose but kneel here and adore.
                              John Keats
                              Endymion, 1818

Do you know that our soul is composed of harmony?
                    Leonardo da Vinci (1452–1519)
                    Notebooks

The highest activities of consciousness have their origins in physical occurrences of the brain just as the loveliest melodies are not too sublime to be expressed by notes.
                    W. Somerset Maugham (1874–1965)
                    A Writer's Notebook, 1949

Melody is a form of remembrance . . . It must have a quality of inevitability in our ears.
                    Gian-Carlo Menotti (1911–   )
                    Time, May 1, 1950

My secret desire of enchanted gorgeousness in harmony has pushed me toward those swords of fire, those sudden stars, those flows of blue-orange lavas, those planets of turquoise, those violet shades, those garnets of long-haired arborescence, those wheelings of sounds and colors in a jumble of rainbows . . .
                    Olivier Messiaen (1908–   )
                    Discussing his *Quartet for the*
                         End of Time, The Technique of My
                         Musical Language, 1956

Rest springs from strife, and dissonant chords beget Divinist harmonies.
                    Sir Lewis Morris (1833–1907)
                    Songs of Two Worlds, 1872–75

Melody is the very essence of music. When I think of a good melodist I think of a fine race-horse. A contrapuntist is only a post-horse.

> Wolfgang Amadeus Mozart (1756–91)
> To Michael Kelly, 1786

If only the whole world could feel the power of harmony.

> Wolfgang Amadeus Mozart

The most perfect expression of the inner being of music is melody; it is to harmony and rhythm what the external side of the organism is to the internal.

> Sir Ernest Newman (1868–1959)
> *A Study of Wagner,* 1899

What man with music in his soul, beholding the harmony in the intelligible world, but must be moved by the harmony of sounds that are heard in the ear?

> Plotinus (205–70 A.D.)
> *Enneads*

Medicine, to produce health, must know disease; music, to produce harmony, must know discord.

> Plutarch (c. 46–120 A.D.)

All discord, harmony not understood.

> Alexander Pope (1688–1744)
> *An Essay on Man,* 1732

Delight must be the basis and aim of this art. Simple melody— clear rhythm!

> Gioacchino Rossini (1792–1868)
> Letter, June 21, 1868

What distinguishes dissonances from consonances is not a greater or lesser degree of beauty, but a greater or lesser degree of comprehensibility.

> Arnold Schoenberg (1874–1951)
> *Style and Idea,* 1951

We have learned to express the more delicate nuances of feeling by penetrating more deeply into the mysteries of harmony.

> Robert Schumann (1810–56)
> *Aphorisms,* c. 1833

The evolution of the harmonic idiom has resulted from the fact that musicians of all generations have sought new means of expression. Harmony is a constant stream of evolution, a constantly changing vocabulary and syntax.

> Roger Sessions (1896–   )

Take but degree away, untune that string, and hark, what discord follows!

> William Shakespeare (1564–1616)
> *Troilus and Cressida,* 1602

The technical history of modern harmony is a history of the growth of toleration by the human ear of chords that at first sounded discordant and senseless to the main body of contemporary professional musicians.

> George Bernard Shaw (1856–1950)
> "The Reminiscences of a Quinquogenarian,"
> An improvised speech, December 6, 1910

Discord oft in musick makes the sweeter lay.

> Edmund Spenser (1552–99)
> *The Faerie Queene,* 1590

Melody . . . belongs to the noblest gifts which an invisible godhead has made to humanity . . . The melodic idea, coming straight out of the ether, which suddenly overtakes me, which appears without any material stimulus or psychic emotion . . . emerges from the imagination, immediate unconscious, without benefit of the intelligence . . . is the greatest of divine gifts, not to be compared with any other.

> Richard Strauss (1864–1949)
> *Melodic Inspiration,* 1940

What survives every change of system is melody.

> Igor Stravinsky (1882–1971)
> *Poetics of Music*, 1947

I am beginning to think together with the general public that melody should keep its place at the summit of the hierarchy of all elements which constitute music.

> Igor Stravinsky
> *Poetics of Music*, 1947

Rhythm and motion, not the element of feeling, are the foundations of musical art.

> Igor Stravinsky

Rhythm is the life of space of time danced through.

> Cecil Taylor (1933–   )
> *The Village Voice*, April 28, 1975

If there is nothing new to be found in melody then we must seek novelty in harmony.

> Georg Philipp Telemann (1681–1767)
> Letter to Carl Heinrich Graun,
> 1751

It is often said that melody can be heard farther than noise, that the finest melody farther than the coarsest.

> Henry David Thoreau (1817–62)
> November 20, 1851

The language of tones belongs equally to all mankind and melody is the absolute language in which the musician speaks to every heart.

> Richard Wagner (1813–83)
> *Beethoven*, 1870

Perhaps in our joy in musical rhythm, there is expressed something of the primal joy of procreation . . . Rhythm is both measurable and immeasurable . . . akin to nature, and yet the sensitive

child of the muses . . . The domain of rhythm extends from the
spiritual to the carnal . . .

> Bruno Walter (1876–1962)
> *Of Music and Music-Making*, 1957

. . . anyone who assumes that there's an essential difference between consonance and dissonance is wrong, because the entire
realm of possible sounds is contained within the notes that nature
provides.

> Anton von Webern (1883–1945)

> There is no music in a rest,
>   But there is music's making;
> For melody is best expressed
>   By pause and re-awaking.

> Mary E. Wisewell
> *Rests*, 1872

COMPOSERS AND COMPOSITION

A fugue is a piece of music in which the voices come in one after another and the audience go out one after another.

Anonymous

By constantly learning about all forms of music throughout the world, from Eskimo throat music to newly discovered Baroque composers, I am always amazed at what a beautiful language music is.

David Amram (1930–)
Edition Peters Contemporary Music Catalogue, 1975

Whether the angels play only Bach praising God, I am not quite sure; I am sure however, that *en famille* they play Mozart.

Karl Barth (1886–1968)
Quoted in his obituary, New
York *Times*, December 11, 1968

Beethoven can write music, thank God—but he can do nothing else on earth.

Ludwig van Beethoven (1770–1827)
Letter to Ferdinand Ries, December 22, 1822

Only the flint of a man's mind can strike fire in music.

Ludwig van Beethoven
Letter to Bettina von Arnim, August 1812

The prevailing characteristics of my music are passionate expression, intense ardour, rhythmical animation, and unexpected turns. When I say passionate expression, I mean an expression determined on enforcing the inner meaning of its subject, even when that subject is the contrary of passion, and when the feeling to be expressed is gentle and tender, or even profoundly calm.

Hector Berlioz (1803–69)
Memoires, 1847

Bach is Bach, as God is God.

Hector Berlioz, 1841

Instrumentation is, in music, the exact equivalent of color in painting.

Hector Berlioz
A Travers chants, 1862

Only one man knew both how to compose quasi-improvised music, or at least what seems such. That is Chopin. Here is a charming personality, strange, unique, inimitable.

Georges Bizet (1838–75)

As a musician I tell you that if you were to suppress adultery, fanaticism, crime, evil, the supernatural, there would no longer be the means for writing one note.

Georges Bizet
Letter to Edmond Galabert and G.,
October 1866

Do, do things, act. Make a list of the music you love, then learn it by heart. And when you are writing music of your own, write it as you hear it inside and never strain to avoid the obvious. The person who does that is living outside life.

Nadia Boulanger
Life, July 21, 1958

It is not hard to compose, but it is wonderfully hard to let the superfluous notes fall under the table.

Johannes Brahms (1833–97)

The metronome has no value . . . for I myself have never believed that my blood and a mechanical instrument go well together.

> Johannes Brahms
> Letter to George Henschel, February 1880

Composing is like driving down a foggy road toward a house. Slowly you see more details of the house—the color of the slates and bricks, the shape of the windows. The notes are the bricks and mortar of the house.

> Sir Benjamin Britten (1913–76)

I believe in Bach, the Father, Beethoven, the Son, and Brahms, the Holy Ghost of music.

> Hans von Bülow (1830–94)

Notation, the writing out of compositions, is primarily an ingenious expedient for catching an inspiration, with the purpose of exploiting it later. But notation is to improvisation as the portrait to the living model. It is for the interpreter *to resolve the rigidity of the signs* into the primitive emotion . . .

> Ferruccio Busoni (1866–1924)
> *Sketch of a New Aesthetic of Music*, tr. 1911

Where is the apparatus that man could invent and set in motion which would allow harmony's million tongues to sound? Where is and where will ever be the techniques which will allow the thousand registers of the world-organ to play?

> Ferruccio Busoni

It is better to make a piece of music than to perform one, better to perform one than to listen to one, better to listen to one than to misuse it as a means of distraction, entertainment, or acquisition of "culture."

> John Cage (1912–   )
> *Silence*, 1961

There is an essential difference between making a piece of music and hearing one. A composer knows his work as a woods-

man knows a path he traced and retraced, while a listener is con-
fronted by the same work as one in the woods by a plant he has
never seen before.

> John Cage
> *Silence*, 1961

Composing's one thing, performing's another, listening's a
third. What can they have to do with one another?

> John Cage
> Quoted by Peter Yates, *Twentieth
> Century Music*, 1967

To strip human nature until its divine attributes are made clear,
to inform ordinary activities with spiritual fervour, to give wings
of eternity to that which is most ephemeral; to make divine things
human and human things divine; such is Bach, the greatest and
purest moment in music of all time.

> Pablo Casals (1876–1973)
> At the Prades Bach Festival, 1950

The written note is like a strait-jacket, whereas music, like life
itself, is constant movement, continuous spontaneity, free from
any restriction.

> Pablo Casals
> *Conversations with Casals*, 1956

In order to be a great composer, one needs an enormous
amount of knowledge, which . . . one does not acquire from listening only to other people's work, but even more from listening
to one's own.

> Frédéric Chopin (1810–49)
> In a letter to Joseph Elsner
> December 14, 1831

An artist should never lose sight of the thing as a whole. He
who puts too much into details will find that the thread which
holds the whole thing together will break.

> Frédéric Chopin
> Quoted by Ernst Bacon, *Notes on
> the Piano*, 1963

Bach is like an astronomer who, with the help of ciphers, finds the most wonderful stars . . . Beethoven embraced the universe with the power of his spirit . . . I do not climb so high. A long time ago I decided that my universe will be the soul and heart of man.

> Frédéric Chopin
> Letter to Delphine Potocka

Play Mozart in memory of me.

> Frédéric Chopin
> Last words, 1849

Good music resembles something. It resembles the composer.
> Jean Cocteau (1889–1963)
> *Cock and Harlequin,* 1918

I am more and more convinced that music, by its very nature, is something that cannot be poured into a tight and traditional form. It is made up of colors and rhythms.

> Claude Debussy (1862–1918)
> Letter to Jacques Durand,
> September 3, 1907

The music of the ancients was more moving than ours, not because they were more learned, but because they were less.

> René Descartes (1596–1650)
> Letter to Mersenne

Tchaikovsky thought of committing suicide for fear of being discovered as a homosexual, but today, if you are a composer and *not* homosexual, you might as well put a bullet through your head.

> Sergei Diaghilev (1872–1929)
> Quoted by Vernon Duke, *Listen Here!,* 1963

Too many people today are trying to justify the precision with which organized musical sound is produced rather than the energy with which it is manipulated.

> David Diamond (1915–   )
> Letter, January 12, 1939

Composers shouldn't think too much—it interferes with their plagiarism.

> Howard Dietz
> To Goddard Lieberson, November 1974

The greatest advantage that a writer can derive from music is, that it teaches most exquisitely the art of development.

> Benjamin Disraeli (1804–81)
> *Contarini Fleming*, 1832

. . . it cannot be emphasized too strongly that art, as such does not "pay" . . . at least, not in the beginning—and that the art that has to pay its own way is apt to become vitiated and cheap.

> Antonin Dvořák (1841–1904)
> *Music in America*, 1895

Intonation, i.e., the "melody" of speech, is the foundation of music.

> Sergei Eisenstein (1898–1948)
> *Notes of a Film Director*, 1946

I like to look on the composer's vocation as the old troubadours or bards did. In those days it was no disgrace for a man to be turned on to step in front of an army and inspire them with a song. I know that there are a lot of people who like to celebrate events with music; To these people I have given tunes. Is that wrong? Why should I write a fugue or something that won't appeal to anyone, when the people yearn for things which can stir them?

> Sir Edward Elgar (1857–1934)

We're not worried about writing for posterity. We just want it to sound good right now!

> Duke Ellington (1899–1974)

Roaming through the jungle, the jungle of "oohs" and "ahs," searching for a more agreeable noise, I live a life of primitivity with the mind of a child and an unquenchable thirst for sharps and flats. The more consonant, the more appetizing and delectable they are. Cacophony is hard to swallow. Living in a cave, I am almost a hermit, but there is a difference, for I have a mistress. Lovers have come and gone, but only my mistress stays. She is beautiful and gentle. She waits on me hand and foot. She is a swinger. She has grace. To hear her speak, you can't believe your ears. She is ten thousand years old. She is as modern as tomorrow, a brand new woman every day, and as endless as time mathematics. Living with her is a labyrinth of ramifications. I look forward to her every gesture.

Music is my mistress, and she plays second fiddle to no one.

> Duke Ellington
> *Music Is My Mistress*, 1973

Anyone who listens to a Beethoven quartet or symphony and can't hear soul is in trouble. Maybe they can hear the sound of blackness, but they're deaf to soul.

> Ralph Ellison (1914–)
> *Harper's Magazine*, March 1967

It will be generally admitted that Beethoven's Fifth Symphony is the most sublime noise that has ever penetrated into the ear of man.

> E. M. Forster (1879–1970)
> *Howards End*, 1910

Composing is like making love to the future.

> Lukas Foss (1922–)
> New York *Post*, October 18, 1975

The sonata was said by a German critic to be intended by the earliest writers to show in the first movement what they could do, in the second what they could feel, in the last how glad they were to have finished.

> Philip H. Goepp (1864–1936)
> *Symphonies and Their Meaning*, 1897

Beethoven and Liszt have contributed to the advent of long hair.

> Louis Moreau Gottschalk (1829–69)

The misuse of science is more dangerous in the case of music than in that of any other art. It is with music as with magic: you must endeavour to take advantage of it, though you are uncertain of the results that will appear.

> André Ernest Grétry (1741–1813)
> *Memoires, ou essai sur la musique*, 1789

I should be sorry, my lord, if I have only succeeded in entertaining them; I wished to make them better.

> George Frideric Handel (1685–1759)
> To Lord Kinnoull, after the first
> London performance of *Messiah*,
> March 23, 1743

An inward singing, and not an inward feeling, prompts a gifted person to compose a musical piece.

> Eduard Hanslick (1825–1904)
> *Vom Musikalisch-Schönen*, 1854

I tell you before God and on my word as an honest man that your son is the greatest composer I have ever heard of.

> Joseph Haydn (1732–1809)
> To Leopold Mozart, in Vienna,
> February 12, 1785

I write according to the thoughts I feel. When I think upon my God, my heart is so full of joy that the notes dance and leap from my pen; and since God has given me a cheerful heart, it will be pardoned me that I serve Him with a cheerful spirit.

> Joseph Haydn

The free arts and the beautiful science of composition will not tolerate technical chains. The mind and soul must be free.

> Joseph Haydn
> Letter to the Tonkünstlersocietät, 1779

There are only twelve tones. You must treat them carefully.

> Paul Hindemith (1895–1963)

Never compose anything unless the not composing of it becomes a positive nuisance to you.

> Gustav Holst (1874–1934)
> Letter to William Gillies Whittaker,
> 1921

The composer, as in old China, joins Heaven and Earth with threads of sounds.

> Alan Hovhaness (1911–)
> May 6, 1975

Wagner, thank the fates, is no hypocrite. He says out what he means, and he usually means something nasty.

> James Huneker (1860–1921)
> *Old Fogy*, 1913

Beethoven is not beautiful. He is dramatic, powerful, a maker of storms, a subduer of tempests; but his speech is the speech of a self-centered egotist. He is the father of all the modern melomaniacs, who looking into their own souls, write what they see therein —misery, corruption, slighting, selfishness and ugliness.

> James Huneker
> *Old Fogy*, 1913

With my prying nose I dipped into all composers, and found that the houses they erected were stable in the exact proportion that Bach was used in the foundation.

> James Huneker
> *Old Fogy*, 1913

To play Chopin, one must have acute sensibility, a versatility of mood, a perfect mechanism, the heart of a woman and the brain of a man.

> James Huneker

Whoever studies music, let his daily bread be Haydn. Beethoven indeed is admirable, he is incomparable, but he has not the same usefulness as Haydn: he is not a necessity . . . Haydn the

great musician, the first who created everything, discovered everything, taught everything to the rest!

> Jean Ingres (1780–1867)

Strauss remembers; Beethoven dreams.

> Charles Ives (1874–1954)
> *Essays before a Sonata,* 1920

I am in love with Mozart like a young girl. Immortal Mozart! I
owe you everything; it is thanks to you that I lost my reason, that
my soul was awestruck in the very depths of my being . . . I have
you to thank that I did not die without having loved.

> Sören Kierkegaard (1813–55)
> *Either/Or,* 1843

There is no feeling—human or cosmic—no depth, no height
the human spirit can reach that is not contained in Mozart's
music.

> Lili Kraus (1908–   )
> New York *Times,* August 1, 1976

Almost anyone can grasp the vulgarity of Liszt and the lack of
it in Mozart; it is more difficult to grasp the vulgar lapses in
Wagner and the lack of them in Berlioz.

> Louis Kronenberger (1904–   )
> *A Mania for Magnificence,* 1972

There can no more be a new Beethoven than there can be a
new Christopher Columbus.

> René Leonormand
> *Étude sur l'harmonie moderne,* 1913

Mine was the kind of piece in which nobody knew what was
going on—including the composer, the conductor and the critics.
Consequently I got pretty good notices.

> Oscar Levant (1906–72)
> *A Smattering of Ignorance,* 1940

In the history of music, it has frequently been the case that a richly creative composer has broken no new paths nor defied any set rules.

> Goddard Lieberson (1911–   )
> Album notes to *Frank Sinatra Conducts*
> *the Music of Alec Wilder*, c. 1956

To us musicians the work of Beethoven parallels the pillars of smoke and fire which led the Israelites through the desert, a pillar of smoke to lead us by day, and a pillar of fire to light the night, so that we may march ahead both day and night. His darkness and his light equally trace for us the road we must follow; both the one and the other are a perpetual commandment, an infallible revelation.

> Franz Liszt (1811–86)
> Letter to Wilhelm von Lenz, 1852

Music is never stationary; successive forms and styles are only like so many resting places—like tents pitched and taken down again on the road to the Ideal.

> Franz Liszt

I don't like my music, but what is my opinion against that of millions of others.

> Frederick Loewe (1904–   )

There are two things John and I always do when we're going to sit down and write a song. First of all we sit down. Then we think about writing a song.

> Paul McCartney (1942–   )

He who writes and composes without feeling spoils both his words and his music.

> Guillaume de Machaut (1300–77)

Only when I experience do I compose—only when I compose do I experience.

> Gustav Mahler (1860–1911)
> Letter to Arthur Seidl,
> February 17, 1897

Humanly I make every concession; artistically, none!
                                                              Gustav Mahler

If one wishes to make music, one should not paint or write poetry or desire to describe anything. But what one makes music out
of is still the whole—that is the feeling, thinking, breathing,
suffering human being.
                                                              Gustav Mahler
                                                              Letter to Bruno Walter, 1906

To write a symphony is, for me, to construct a world.
                                                              Gustav Mahler

A symphony must be like the world, it must embrace everything.
                                                              Gustav Mahler
                                                              To Jean Sibelius in Helsingfors, Finland, 1907

I don't choose what I compose. It chooses me.
                                                              Gustav Mahler

The composer's task is to copy nature . . . to stir the passions
at will . . . to express the living movements of the soul and the
cravings of the heart.
                                                              Friedrich W. Marpurg (1718–95)
                                                              Der Critische Musicus an der Spree, Volume I, 1750

The sonata form lies at the heart of all the greatest music in
the world, and no intelligent comprehension of that music is possible unless its plan and its possibilities are clearly understood.
                                                              H. L. Mencken (1880–1956)
                                                              "Huneker in Motley," *Smart Set,* July 1914

                    If the composer's tone is grave,
                        He puts us all to sleep;
                    If the composer's tone is gay,
                        He isn't one bit deep.

> No matter how he turns his phrase,
> Nobody's content;
> Therefore the composer must
> Follow his own bent.
>> Felix Mendelssohn (1809–47)
>> March 15, 1826

A composer is unable to hide anything—by his music you shall know him.
> Yehudi Menuhin (1916–   )
> *Theme and Variations,* 1972

The abundance of technical means allows the heart to expand freely.
> Olivier Messiaen (1908–   )

I have no esthetic rules, or philosophy, or theories. I love to write music. I always do it with pleasure, otherwise I just do not write it.
> Darius Milhaud (1892–1974)
> Quoted by Aaron Copland, *Darius Milhaud,* 1947

Life, wherever it is shown; truth, however bitter; speaking out boldly, frankly, point-blank to men—that is my aim . . . I am a realist in the highest sense—that is, my business is to portray the soul of man in all its profundity.
> Modest Moussorgsky (1839–81)

Keep your eyes on him; he'll make the world talk of him some day.
> Wolfgang Amadeus Mozart (1756–91)
> Letter to his father about Beethoven, 1787

If I have time, I shall rearrange some of my violin concertos and shorten them. In Germany, we rather like length, but after all it is better to be short and good.
> Wolfgang Amadeus Mozart
> *Letters,* 1778

His music used to be original. Now it is aboriginal.

> Sir Ernest Newman (1868–1959)
> On Stravinsky, *Musical Times*,
> London, July 1921

The good composer is slowly discovered; the bad composer is slowly found out.

> Attributed to Sir Ernest Newman

If I had the power I would insist on all oratorios being sung in the costume of the period—with a possible exception in the case of the *Creation*.

> Sir Ernest Newman
> New York *Post*, 1924

He was taking a quantity of strictly opposed rhythms and, by some magic counterpoint of his own, weaving them into a glittering mass which was at once as well ordered as a route march and as drunken as an orgy.

> Beverley Nichols (1899–   )
> On George Gershwin, *Are They the*
> *Same at Home?*, 1927

Is Wagner actually a man? Is he not rather a disease? Everything he touches falls ill: he has made music sick.

> Friedrich Nietzsche (1844–1900)
> *The Twilight of the Idols*, 1889

So far as genius can exist in a man who is merely virtuous, Haydn had it. He went as far as the limits that morality sets to intellect.

> Friedrich Nietzsche
> *All-Too-Human*, 1878

To produce music is also in a sense to produce children.

> Friedrich Nietzsche
> *The Will to Power*, 1888

We seem to be getting near the time when people will look with some astonishment at the selfishness of those composers who scorn the idea of pleasing or moving their listeners and are concerned only with the praise of a small clique, and their own inaccessible egos. Music will have to become conscious again of its possibilities and of the part it should play in society in order to survive.

> Max d'Ollone (1875–1959)
> *Le Langage musical*

> We are the music makers,
> And we are the dreamers of dreams,
> Wandering by lone sea-breakers,
> And setting by desolate streams;
> World-losers and world forsakers,
> On whom the pale moon gleams:
> Yet we are the movers and shakers
> Of the world forever, it seems.
>
> Arthur O'Shaughnessy (1844–81)
> *Ode*

Scientific music has no claim to intrinsic excellence—it is fit for scientific ears only. In its excess it is the triumph of the physical over the morale of music. The sentiment is overwhelmed by the sense.

> Edgar Allan Poe (1809–49)
> *The Rationale of Verse,* 1843

We must have recourse to the rules (of music) only when our genius and our ear seem to deny what we are seeking.

> Jean Philippe Rameau (1683–1764)
> *Le Nouveau système de musique théorique,*
> 1726

It is often by seeing and hearing musical works rather than by rules, that taste is formed.

> Jean Philippe Rameau
> *Le Nouveau système de musique théorique,*
> 1726

I'm told that Saint-Saëns has informed a delighted public that since the war began he has composed music for the stage, melodies, an elegy and a piece for the trombone. If he'd been making shell-cases instead it might have been all the better for music.

> Maurice Ravel (1875–1937)
> Letter to Jean Marnold, October 7, 1916

I think and feel in sounds.

> Maurice Ravel
> Quoted in Jules Renard's *Journal*, 1907

What terrible harm Wagner did by interspersing his pages of genius with harmonic and modulatory outrages.

> Nikolai Rimsky-Korsakov (1844–1908)
> Letter, 1901

The power of subtle orchestration is a secret impossible to transmit, and the composer who possesses this secret should value it highly, and never debase it to the level of a mere collection of formulae learned by heart.

> Nikolai Rimsky-Korsakov
> *Principles of Orchestration*, 1896–1908

Composition is notation of distortion of what composers think they've heard before. Masterpieces are marvelous misquotations.

> Ned Rorem (1923–   )
> *The Paris Diary of Ned Rorem*, 1966

If a composer could state in words what being a composer means, he would no longer need to be a composer.

> Ned Rorem
> *Critical Affairs*, 1970

A three-voice fugue . . . resembles a family of identical triplets in perfect agreement, or a madman talking to himself.

> Ned Rorem
> *Pure Contraption*, 1974

Beethoven is the greatest composer—but Mozart is the only one.

> Gioacchino Rossini (1792–1868)
> Quoted by Lewis Kronenberger,
> *Animal, Vegetable, Mineral,* 1972

Give me a laundry list and I'll set it to music.

> Gioacchino Rossini

Wagner is a composer who has beautiful moments but awful quarter hours.

> Gioacchino Rossini

What gives Sebastian Bach and Mozart a place apart is that these two great expressive composers never sacrificed form to expression. As high as their expression may soar, their musical form remains supreme and all-sufficient.

> Camille Saint-Saëns (1835–1921)
> Letter to Camille Bellaigue

The artist who does not feel satisfied with elegant lines, well-balanced colors and a beautiful succession of harmonies, does not understand art.

> Camille Saint-Saëns
> Quoted in "The French Passion for the
> Piano," New York *Times,* August 24,
> 1975

He who does not take a thorough pleasure in a simple chord progression, well constructed, beautiful in its arrangement, does not love music; he who does not prefer the first "Prelude" in the *Well-Tempered Clavier* played without nuances as the composer wrote it for the instrument, to the same prelude embellished with a passionate melody, does not love music; he who does not prefer a folk tune of a lovely character, or a Gregorian chant without any accompaniment to a series of dissonant and pretentious chords does not love music.

> Camille Saint-Saëns
> *École buissonnière,* 1913

M. Ravel refuses the Legion of Honor, but all his music accepts it.

Erik Satie (1866–1925)

The sonatas of Mozart are unique; they are too easy for children, and too difficult for artists.

Artur Schnabel (1882–1951)

In music there is no form without logic, there is no logic without unity.

Arnold Schoenberg (1874–1951)

The principal function of form is to advance our understanding. By producing comprehensibility, form produces beauty.

Arnold Schoenberg

The composer reveals the innermost being of the world and expresses the deepest wisdom in a language which his own reason does not understand; like a somnambulist, who tells things of which he has no clear knowledge in his waking state. This is the reason why, in a composer more than in any other artist, man and artist are quite separate and distinct.

Arthur Schopenhauer (1788–1860)
The World as Will and Idea, 1818

O Mozart, immortal Mozart, what countless images of a brighter and better world thou hast stamped upon our souls!

Franz Schubert (1797–1828)
Diary, June 13, 1816

Music owes as much to Bach as religion to its founder.

Robert Schumann (1810–56)

The first concept is always the best and most natural. The intellect can err, the sentiment—never.

Robert Schumann

In order to compose, all you need do is remember a tune that no one else has thought of.

Attributed to Robert Schumann

People compose for many reasons: to become immortal; because the pianoforte happens to be open; to become a millionaire; because of the praise of friends; because they have looked into a pair of beautiful eyes; or for no reason whatsoever.

Robert Schumann

Only when the form is quite clear to you will the spirit become clear to you.

Robert Schumann
House Rules and Maxims for Young Musicians, c. 1833

The conception itself is a musical image, and in bringing it to fuller realization, the composer is not pursuing a line of reasoning, but producing an object.

Roger Sessions (1896–   )
Questions About Music, 1970

How sour sweet music is, when time is broke and no proportion kept! So is it in the music of men's lives.

William Shakespeare (1564–1616)
Richard II, Act V, Scene V, Line 42, 1595

From Mozart I learnt to say important things in a conversational way.

George Bernard Shaw (1856–1950)
Conversation with Ferruccio Busoni, c. 1922

What Wagner meant by "true art" is the operation of the artist's instinct, which is just as blind as any other instinct. Mozart, asked for an explanation of his works, said frankly, "How do I know?"

George Bernard Shaw
The Perfect Wagnerite, 1898

To me it seems quite obvious that the real Brahms is nothing more than a sentimental voluptuary . . . He is the most wanton of composers . . . Only his wantonness is not vicious; it is that of a great baby . . . rather tiresomely addicted to dressing himself up as Handel or Beethoven and making a prolonged and intolerable noise.

George Bernard Shaw
The World, June 21, 1893

The world is full of great musicians who are no composers, and great composers who are no musicians.

George Bernard Shaw
Music in London, 1890–1894, 1931

The fact is, there are no rules, and there never were any rules, and there never will be any rules of musical composition except rules of thumb; and thumbs vary in length, like ears.

George Bernard Shaw
Music in London, 1890–1884, 1931

A creative artist works on his next composition because he is not satisfied with his previous one. When he loses a critical attitude towards his own work, he ceases to be an artist.

Dimitri Shostakovich (1906–75)
New York *Times*, October 25, 1959

The value of a man's work resides in the music itself, and not in how frequently it is played, how many honors its composer has won, or how much critical acclaim he has received.

Elie Siegmeister (1909–   )

There has been demonstration of the universal truth by fugue, and it may be that more wisdom is to be found in that than in the religions and religious books of all the world together.

Sacheverell Sitwell (1897–   )
Orpheus and His Lyre

Nothing can be more disgusting than an oratorio. How absurd, to see five hundred people fiddling like madmen about the Israelites in the Red Sea!

Sydney Smith (1771–1845)

What Mozart did, that is, composed up to his thirty-sixth year, the best copyist of today could not write down in the same amount of time.

> Franz Strauss (1864–1949)
> Quoted by his son, Richard Strauss, *Melodic Inspiration*, 1940

I cannot compose what they want from me, which would be to repeat myself. That is the way people write themselves out.

> Igor Stravinsky (1882–1971)
> Letter to Alexandre Benois, October 1913

Vivaldi is greatly over-rated—a dull fellow who would compose the same form so many times over.

> Igor Stravinsky

My music is best understood by children and animals.

> Igor Stravinsky
> *Sunday Observer*, October 8, 1961

A good composer does not imitate; he steals.

> Igor Stravinsky
> To Peter Yates, *Twentieth Century Music*, 1967

We have a duty towards music, namely to invent it.

> Igor Stravinsky
> *Poetics of Music*, 1947

It is not art that rains down upon us in the song of a bird; but the simplest modulation, correctly executed is already art.

> Igor Stravinsky
> *Poetics of Music*, 1947

The highest function of music is to express the musician's experience and his organization of it.

> J. W. N. Sullivan
> *Beethoven, His Spiritual Development*, 1927

I like to play Bach, because it is interesting to play a good fugue; but I do not regard him, in common with many others, as a great genius. Handel is only fourth-rate, he is not even interesting. I sympathize with Gluck in spite of his poor creative gift. I also like some things of Haydn. These four great masters have been surpassed by Mozart. They are rays which are extinguished by Mozart's sun.

> Peter Ilyich Tchaikovsky (1840–93)
> Excerpt from diary, 1886

I have played over the music of that scoundrel Brahms. What a giftless bastard!

> Peter Ilyich Tchaikovsky
> Diary, October 9, 1886

Such an astounding lack of talent was never before united to such pretentiousness.

> Peter Ilyich Tchaikovsky
> On Richard Strauss in a letter to
> Modeste Tchaikovsky, January 1888

How can one interpret those vague feelings which course through one during the composition of an instrumental work, without reference to a definite subject? It is a purely lyrical process. A sort of confession of the soul in music; an accumulation of material flowing forth again in notes just as the lyric poet pours himself out in verse. The difference is that music possesses much richer means of expression and it is a more subtle medium for translating the thousand shifting moments of the feelings of the soul.

> Peter Ilyich Tchaikovsky
> Letter to Nadezhda Filaretovna von Mech,
> March 1, 1878

Departed Bach! Long since thy splendid organ playing
Alone brought thee the noble cognomen, "The Great,"
And what thy pen had writ, the highest art displaying,
Did some with joy and some with envy contemplate.

> Georg Philipp Telemann (1681–1767)
> *Poem in Praise of Bach*, 1751

Music requires a man to give himself entirely to it, but the world does not wholly agree with this. It demands that one learn and attempt other things (as if the head of a note could hold many topics!). Therefore it will be necessary to yield to the world. What the crowd wants finally becomes law. But it is also pleasant to know something of many things, and even if it doesn't bring in anything, it doesn't eat one's bread either.

Georg Philipp Telemann

In transmitting Nature into harmony, he (Debussy) has made sonorous his own emotions.

Oscar Thompson (1887–1945)
Debussy, Man and Artist, 1937

A composer's first responsibility is, and always will be, to write music that will reach and move the hearts of his listeners in his own day.

Randall Thompson (1899–   )

There must be form—the outer shape dictated by a work's inner organic life. That form will present, in some aspect, a struggle between differing concepts. There must be a curve as inevitable as the trajectory of a shell.

Ernst Toch (1887–1964)

Form is the balance between tension and relaxation.

Ernst Toch

All forms are equally good for expressing our emotions; it is our emotions that are not equally sharp and profound.

Jean d'Udine
Le Courrier Musical, 1906

All the worst things happen in the best works, and the worst music appears to be streaked all through with the most luscious bits.

Bernard Van Dieren (1884–1936)
Down Among the Dead Men, 1935

To reveal a new world is the function of creation in all the arts, but the act of creation defies analysis. A composer knows about as little as anyone else about where the substance of his work comes from.

> Edgar Varèse (1885–1965)
> Lecture at Princeton University, 1959

I don't know whether I like it, but it is what I meant.
> Ralph Vaughan Williams (1872–1959)
> Referring to his London Symphony,
> quoted by Sir Adrian Boult in a
> broadcast, August 1, 1965

I realize now it is not as boring as I thought it was.
> Ralph Vaughan Williams
> Referring to his London Symphony,
> quoted by Sir Adrian Boult in a
> broadcast, August 1, 1965

Never, never will I write my memoirs! It is quite enough for the musical world to have put up with my music for such a long time! . . . I will never condemn it to read my prose . . .
> Giuseppe Verdi (1813–1901)
> Letter to the Director of the
> Deutsche Verlagsanstalt, Stuttgart,
> June 21, 1895

If I had my way, a young man beginning to compose would never think about being a melodist, harmonist, realist, idealist, musician of the future, or whatever other pedantic formulas the Devil may have invented. Melody and harmony should be simply the means in the hand of the artist to make music.
> Giuseppe Verdi
> Letter to Opprandino Arrivabene,
> July 17, 1875

The artist must yield himself to his own inspiration, and if he has a true talent, no one knows and feels better than he *what* suits him. I should compose with utter confidence a subject that set my blood going, even though it were condemned by all other artists as anti-musical.

> Giuseppe Verdi
> *Letters,* 1854

A truly creative musician is capable of producing, from his own imagination, melodies that are more authentic than folklore itself.

> Heitor Villa-Lobos (1887–1959)

Behold, the Briton does you justice, the Frenchman admires you, but only the German can love you. You are his own, a bright day in his life, a drop of his blood, a particle of his heart.

> Richard Wagner (1813–83)
> Funeral oration for Carl Maria von Weber

The unconscious is the womb of all musical creation; all master-pieces are born there.

> Alan Walker (1930–   )
> *An Anatomy of Musical Criticism,* 1968

The composer who gets his subject matter . . . at the piano is nearly always born poor or apt to yield his spirit to the common and low. For it is these hands, these damned piano fingers—having acquired from constant practising, a wilful independent mind of their own—become unconscious tyrants, the despots of creative power. They refuse to invent anything new,—yes, new is inconvenient to them. Secretly and roguishly—true mechanical workers —they mould into a whole, parts of small tone bits, long familiar to them, because they sound so nice and round to the deluded ear, and seem to indicate the direction, and these are favorably accepted and employed.

But how differently does he create whose inner ear is sole judge of both the invented and the approved matter. The spiritual ear, with marvelous ability, embraces and grasps the tone figures and it is a sacred secret inherent in music, and incomprehensible to the layman.

> Carl Maria von Weber (1786–1826)

Your ears will always lead you right, but you must know why.

> Anton von Webern (1883–1945)

I like Wagner's music better than anybody's. It's so loud that one can talk the whole time without other people hearing what one says.

Oscar Wilde (1854–1900)
The Picture of Dorian Gray, 1891

Music is the art in which form and matter are always one, the art whose subject cannot be separated from the method of its expression, the art which most completely realizes the artistic ideal, and is the condition to which all the other arts are constantly aspiring.

Oscar Wilde
The English Renaissance of Art, 1882

THE AVANT-GARDE

We live in an age of remarkable progress in which all the arts are being daily perfected. Mechanics especially is advancing fast and will soon bring you relief as regards performing upon your instruments.

> The French Minister of Fine Arts
> Address to the Faculty of the
> Conservatoire, January 3, 1896

If we look around in modern music we will find that we have a terrible deal of mind and astonishingly few ideas.

> August Wilhelm Ambros (1816–76)

In olden times the feeling for nobility was always maintained in the art of music, and all its elements skillfully retained the orderly beauty appropriate to them. Today, however, people take up music in a haphazard and irrational manner. *The* musicians of our day set as the goal of their art success with their audiences.

> Athenaeus (c. 200 A.D.)
> *The Deipnosophists*

Wee have also Sound-Houses wher wee practise and demonstrate all Sounds, and their Generation. Wee have Harmonies which you have not, of Quarter-Sounds, and less Slides of Sounds. Diverse Instruments of Musick likewise to you unknowne, some sweeter then any you have; Together with Bells and Rings that are dainty and sweet. Wee represent Small Sounds as Great and Deepe; Likewise Great Sounds, Extenuate and Sharp; Wee make diverse Tremblings and Warblings of Sounds, which in their

Originall are Entire. Wee represent and imitate all Articulate
Sounds and Letters, and the Voices and Notes of Beasts and
Birds. Wee have certaine Helps, which sett to the Eare doe fur-
ther the Hearing greatly. Wee have also diverse Strange and
Artificial Eccho's, Reflecting the Voice many times, and as it were
Tossing it; And some that give back the Voice Lowder then it
came, some Shriller, and some Deeper; Yea some rendring the
Voice, Differing in the Letters or Articulate Sound, from that
they receyve. Wee have also meanes to convey Sounds in Trunks
and Pipes, in strange Lines, and Distances.

Sir Francis Bacon (1561–1626)
The New Atlantis, 1627

I believe that there is little probability that the twelve-note
scale will ever produce anything more than morbid or entirely cer-
ebral growths. It might deal successfully with neuroses of various
kinds, but I cannot imagine it associated with any healthy and
happy concept such as young love or the coming of Spring.

Sir Arnold Bax (1883–1953)
Music and Letters, 1951

Music and composition, in their latest evolution have now incorporated other branches of art and science and the composer of
the future may well be a combination physicist-mathematician,
architect-electronic engineer-musician.

Irwin Bazelon (1922–   )
Knowing the Score, 1975

Music was chaste and modest so long as it was played on
simpler instruments, but since it has come to be played in a variety of manners and confusedly, it has lost the mode of gravity and
virtue and fallen almost to baseness.

Anicius Manlius Severinus Boethius
(c. 480–524)
The Consolation of Philosophy

We look for new sonorities, new intervals, new forms. Where it
will lead, I don't know. I don't want to know. It would be like
knowing the date of my death.

Pierre Boulez (1925–   )

I believe that the use of noise to make music will continue and increase until we reach a music produced through the aid of electrical instruments.

> John Cage (1912–)
> *The Future of Music: Credo*, 1937

The century of aeroplanes deserves its own music. As there are no precedents, I must create anew.

> Claude Debussy (1862–1918)

Why cause words to be sung by four or five voices so that they cannot be distinguished, when the Ancients aroused the strongest passions by means of a single voice supported by a lyre? We must renounce counterpoint and different kinds of instruments and return to primitive simplicity.

> Vincenzo Galilei (d. 1581)
> *Dialogo della musica antics e della moderna*, 1581

Music, in the best sense, does not require novelty; nay, the older it is, and the more we are accustomed to it, the greater its effect.

> Johann Wolfgang von Goethe (1749–1832)

I occasionally play works by contemporary composers and for two reasons. First, to discourage the composer from writing any more, and secondly to remind myself how much I appreciate Beethoven.

> Jascha Heifetz (1901–)
> *Life*, July 28, 1961

It is a tremendous achievement to create a piece of music that incites riot . . . to cause peaceful lovers of music to scream out their agony, to arouse angry emotions and to tempt men to retire to the back of the theater and perform tympani concertos on each other's faces.

> William J. Henderson
> Review of Edgar Varèse's *Hyperprism*
> New York *Herald Tribune*, March 11, 1923

There are no new sounds, only new ideas.
> Bernard Hermann (1911–76)
> Quoted by Tony Thomas, *Music for the
> Movies,* 1973

At present, what plays the most important part in composition is the use of rhythmical shock in contrast to voluptuous melody. At the present rate we shall have by the end of this century an elementary, barbarous music which will combine elemental melody with brutally scanned rhythm. This will admirably suit the deformed ear of the music-lover of the year 2000!
> Arthur Honegger (1892–1955)

Music was originally discreet, seemly, simple, masculine, and of good morals. Have not the moderns rendered it lascivious beyond measure?
> Jacob of Liège, c. 1425

We have had an entire century of broad and stout, thick and violent, burning and sticky melodies. If modern melody is short of breath, a little asthmatic, and is not meant for powerful lungs, again, so much the better!
> Wanda Landowska (1877–1959)
> *Why Does Modern Music Lack Melody?,* 1913

It may well be . . . that the apotheosis of the machine age will demand a subtler tool than the tempered scale, capable of setting down arrangements of sounds hitherto neglected or unheard.
> Le Corbusier (Charles Édouard Jeanneret)
> (1887–1965)

The synthesizer world opens the door to musical infinity.
> John McLaughlin (1942–   )
> *Time,* February 22, 1975

Modern music is as dangerous as cocaine.
> Pietro Mascagni (1863–1945)
> Interview in Berlin, December 1927

The one unmistakable emotion that much of this modern music arouses is a hot longing for form, clarity, coherence, a tune . . . One yearns unspeakably for a composer who gives out his pair of honest themes, and then develops them with both ears open, and then recapitulates them unashamed, and then hangs a brisk coda to them, and then shuts up.

H. L. Mencken (1880–1956)
"Huneker in Motley," *Smart Set,* July 1914

There is not a single case in musical history of a composer being a century ahead of his time: the greatest composers have all been perfectly comprehensible to the average instructed music-lover of their day.

Sir Ernest Newman (1868–1959)
A *Musical Critic's Holiday,* 1925

All my concerts had no sounds in them: they were completely silent . . . people had to make their own music in their minds.

Yoko Ono (1933–)
Interview with Jonathan Cott,
Rolling Stone, 1968

The introduction of novel fashions in music is a thing to beware of as endangering the whole fabric of society, whose most important conventions are unsettled by any revolution in that quarter.

Plato (c. 428–c. 347 B.C.)
Republic

What we know as modern music is the noise made by deluded speculators picking through the slagpile.

Henry Pleasants (1910–)
The Agony of Modern Music, 1955

Both history and criticism have overlooked the one fact about the contemporary composer that is of any real importance to the understanding of modern music: he is obsolete.

Henry Pleasants
The Agony of Modern Music, 1955

Music has definitely reached and passed the greatest degree of dissonance and of complexity that it is practicable for it to attain . . . To achieve a more simple and melodic expression, is the inevitable direction for the musical art of the future.

Sergei Prokofiev (1891–1953)

Where is music going? Nowhere now. Eventually though, it will follow as it has in the past, wherever a great monster leads it.

Ned Rorem (1923–   )
Music and People, 1968

The current state of music presents a variety of solutions in search of a problem, the problem being to find somebody left to listen.

Ned Rorem
Music from Inside Out, 1967

This musical evolution is paralleled by the multiplication of machines which collaborate with man on every front. Not only in the roaring atmosphere of major cities, but in the country too, which was until yesterday normally silent, the machine today has created such a variety and rivalry of noises that pure sound, in its exiguity and monotony, no longer arouses any feeling.

Luigi Russolo (1855–1947)
1913

Music is now so foolish that I am amazed. Everything that is wrong is permitted, and no attention is paid to what the old generation wrote as composition.

Samuel Scheidt (1587–1654)

Part Three
EXPONENTS

CONDUCTORS AND CONDUCTING

You know why conductors live so long? Because we perspire so much.

> Sir John Barbirolli (1899–1970)

We do not expect you to follow us all the time, but if you would have the goodness to keep in touch with us occasionally . . .

> Sir Thomas Beecham (1879–1961)
> To an errant musician, quoted
> by Harold C. Schonberg, *The
> Great Conductors*, 1967

Musicians take all the liberties they can.

> Ludwig van Beethoven (1770–1827)
> Letter to Bettina von Arnim, August 1812

When I am with composers, I say I am a conductor. When I am with conductors, I say I am a composer.

> Leonard Bernstein (1918–   )
> *The World in Vogue*, 1963

You must have the score in your head, not your head in the score.

> Hans von Bülow (1830–94)
> To Richard Strauss, quoted by
> Harold C. Schonberg, *The Great
> Conductors*, 1967

With a perfect orchestra you can do what you like . . . You can draw a sort of immense emotional throb out of the air merely by curving your hand. You can get brilliant waves of sound merely by a twist of the wrist. You can make sudden and absolute silence by a gesture. It is the most wonderful of all sensations that any man can conceive. It really oughtn't to be allowed.

> Eugene Goossens (1893–1962)
> Quoted by Beverley Nichols,
> *Are They the Same at Home?*, 1927

The conductor has the advantage of not seeing the audience.

> André Kostelanetz (1901–   )

The basic parts of music, the fundamental phrasing and rhythm which affect every aspect of the sound—these must come from conscious, planned, firm authority . . . Sloppiness is not necessarily synonymous with warmth any more than intellectualism is synonymous with coldness.

> Erich Leinsdorf (1912–   )
> Quoted in *Show*, November 1963

He uses music as an accompaniment to his conducting.

> Oscar Levant (1906–72)
> (about Leonard Bernstein)
> *The Memoirs of an Amnesiac*, 1965

A conductor should reconcile himself to the realization that regardless of his approach or temperament the eventual result is the same—the orchestra will hate him.

> Oscar Levant
> *A Smattering of Ignorance*, 1940

Show me an orchestra that likes its conductor and I'll show you a lousy orchestra.

> Goddard Lieberson (1911–77)
> Quoted by Hubert Kupferberg,
> *Those Fabulous Philadelphians*, 1969

Written music is like handcuffs; and so is the pendulum in white-tie-and-tails up in the conductor's stand. Symphony means slavery in any jazzman's dictionary . . . One-hundred-men-with-a-fuehrer, a musical battalion hypnotized by a director's baton—that's no kind of a set-up for a man's inspired soul to shake loose and jump out of his instrument in a flood of carefree, truth-speaking, right-from-the-heart music.

> Mezz Mezzrow (1899–1972) and Bernard Wolfe (1915–)
> *Really the Blues,* 1946

I never use a score when conducting my orchestra . . . Does a lion tamer enter a cage with a book on how to tame a lion?

> Dimitri Mitropoulos (1896–1960)
> January 22, 1951

There are a million things in music I know nothing about. I just want to narrow down that figure.

> André Previn
> *As You Remember Them,*
> Time-Life Records, 1972

Oh! to be a conductor, to weld a hundred men into one singing giant, to build up the most gorgeous arabesques of sound, to wave a hand and make the clamoring strings sink to a mutter, to wave again, and hear the brass crashing out in triumph, to throw up a finger, then another and another, and to know that with every one the orchestra would bound forward into a still more ecstatic surge and sweep, to fling oneself forward, and for a moment or so keep everything still, frozen, in the hollow of one's hand, and then to set them all singing and soaring in one final sweep, with the cymbals clashing at every flicker of one's eyelid, to sound the grand Amen.

> J. B. Priestley (1894–)
> Quoted by Harold C. Schonberg,
> *The Great Conductors,* 1967

The hardest thing in the world is to start an orchestra, and the next hardest, to stop it.

> Hans Richter (1843–1916)
> Quoted by Beverley Nichols,
> *Are They the Same at Home?*, 1927

You are there, and I am here. But where is Beethoven?

> Artur Schnabel (1882–1951)
> To a conductor during a
> rehearsal of a Beethoven
> concerto

Orchestras only need to be sworn at, and a German is consequently at an advantage with them, as English profanity, except in America, has not gone beyond a limited technology of perdition.

> George Bernard Shaw (1856–1950)
> Quoted by Harold C. Schonberg,
> *The Great Conductors*, 1967

See to their desks Apollo's sons repair
Swift rides the rosin o'er the horse's hair!
In unison their various tones to tune,
Murmurs the oboe, growls the hoarse bassoon;
In soft vibration sighs the whispering lute,
Tang goes the harpsichord, too-too the flute,
Brays the loud trumpet, squeaks the fiddle sharp,
Winds the French-horn, and twangs the tingling harp;
Till, like great Jove, the leader figuring in,
Attunes to order the chaotic din.

> Horace and James Smith (1779–1849
> and 1775–1839)
> *Rejected Addresses*

On matters of intonation and technicalities I am more than a martinet—I am a martinetissimo.

> Leopold Stokowski (1882–1977)

You conductors who are so proud of your power! When a new man faces the orchestra—from the way he walks up the steps to the podium and opens his score—before he even picks up his baton—we know whether he is the master or we.

> Franz Strauss (1822–1905)
> A noted horn player, father of
> Richard Strauss

Conductors must give unmistakable and suggestive signals to the orchestra—not choreography to the audience.

> George Szell (1897–1970)
> *Newsweek,* January 28, 1963

I love music more than my own convenience. Actually I love it more than myself—but it is vastly more loveable than I.

> George Szell
> *Newsweek,* January 28, 1963

After I die, I shall return to earth as the doorkeeper of a bordello and I won't let a one of you in.

> Arturo Toscanini (1867–1957)
> To his orchestra during a
> difficult rehearsal

God tells me how the music should sound, but *you* stand in the way!

> Arturo Toscanini
> To a trumpet player, quoted in
> the New York *Times,* April 11, 1954

They are for *prima donnas* or corpses, I am neither.

> Arturo Toscanini
> Refusing a floral tribute after
> a performance

Assassins!

> Arturo Toscanini
> To his orchestra after an
> unsatisfactory performance

In Europe, when a rich woman has an affair with a conductor, they have a baby. In America, she endows an orchestra for him.

> Edgar Varèse (1885–1965)
> Quoted by Herman G. Weinberg,
> *Saint Cinema*, 1970

By concentrating on precision, one arrives at technique, but by concentrating on technique one does not arrive at precision.

> Bruno Walter (1876–1962)

INSTRUMENTS AND INSTRUMENTALISTS

When the people heard the sound of the trumpet, and the people shouted with a great shout, that the wall fell down flat, so that the people went up into the city.

> Old Testament
> Joshua

I was in the Spirit on the Lord's day, and heard behind me a great voice, as of a trumpet.

> New Testament
> Revelation of St. John the Divine

Poetry expresses the idea; song regulates the sounds; dance enlivens the attitudes; these three have their principal in man's heart, and it is only later that musical instruments lend their help.

> "Yo Ki" (Memorial of Music in
> *Li Chi*, Record of Rites),
> Chinese manuscript, c. 500 B.C.

Gladden thine heart, *drum thine drum*, and *pipe thine pipe*.
> *Arabian Nights' Entertainments*, c. 1450

Don't play it too fast, and not too slow—just half-fast.
> Louis Armstrong (1900–71)
> Network television show in the 1950s

There are today so many good musicians that it is becoming increasingly hard to find a great artist.

> Ernst Bacon (1898–)
> *Notes on the Piano*, 1963

That noise or sound which musicians make while they are tuning their instruments, is nothing pleasant to hear, but yet is a cause why the music is sweeter afterwards.

> Francis Bacon (1561–1626)
> *The Advancement of*
> *Learning,* 1605

When I scream with my horn, it's because the music needs screaming.

> Gato Barbieri (1934–   )
> Jazz tenor saxophonist, 1973

A musicianer just has to learn for himself, just by playing and listening . . . There ain't no one can write down the feeling you have to have. That's from inside yourself. The music has to let you be . . . you got to stay free inside it.

> Sidney Bechet (1897–1959)
> Quoted by Nat Hentoff, *The Jazz*
> *Life,* 1961

The plain fact is that music *per se* means nothing; it is sheer sound, and the interpreter can do no more with it than his own capacities, mental and spiritual, will allow, and the same applies to the listener.

> Sir Thomas Beecham (1879–1961)
> *A Mingled Chime,* 1944

Of producing artists, the composer is almost the only one . . . who depends upon a multitude of intermediate agents, either intelligent or stupid, devoted or hostile, active or inert, capable—from first to last—of contributing to the brilliancy of his work, or of disfiguring it, misrepresenting it, and even destroying it completely.

Hector Berlioz (1803–69)
Traité de l'instrumentation et d'orchestration moderns, 1856

The quality of tone of the trumpet is noble and brilliant; it comports with warlike ideas, with cries of fury, and of vengeance, as with songs of triumph; it lends itself to the expression of all energetic, lofty and grand sentiments, and to the majority of tragic accents.

Hector Berlioz

Accordion, n. An instrument in harmony with the sentiments of an assassin.

Ambrose Bierce (1842–?1914)
The Devil's Dictionary, 1911

From the vantage point of my 58 years—from learning and growing and investigating and searching—I have found only *one* absolute in music, and that is that there is no absolute. Everything in music is relative. Everything in music must be sifted through one's musical mind and personality. That's what music-making is all about.

Jorge Bolet (1914–   )

But God has a few of us whom
   he whispers in the ear;
The rest may reason and welcome:
   'tis we musicians know.

Robert Browning (1812–89)
Abt Vogler

If you couldn't blow a man down with your horn, at least you could use it to hit him alongside the head.

Mutt Carey (1892–1948)
Quoted in *Hear Me Talkin' to Ya,*
Edited by Nat Shapiro and Nat Hentoff, 1955

The cello is like a beautiful woman who has not grown older, but younger with time, more slender, more supple, more graceful.

Pablo Casals (1876–1973)
Time, April 29, 1957

The artist is responsible for the music he performs. He must experience it and create it again. It is necessary to insist that the greatest respect he can pay to the music consists of giving it life. That is the first commandment.

> Pablo Casals
> Quoted by J. Ma. Corredor,
> *Conversations with Casals*, 1956

The greatest respect an artist can pay to music is to give it life.
> Pablo Casals
> Quoted by Ernst Bacon, *Notes on*
> *the Piano*, 1963

We can never exhaust the multiplicity of nuances and subtleties which make the charm of music . . . How can we expect to produce a vital performance if we don't re-create the work every time? Every year the leaves of the trees reappear with the Spring, but they are different every time.

> Pablo Casals
> *Conversations with Casals*, 1956

I am a man first, an artist second. As a man, my first obligation is to the welfare of my fellow men. My contribution to world peace may be small. But at least I will have given all I can to an idea I hold sacred.

> Pablo Casals
> *Time*, November 5, 1973

The real splendor of music is a human splendor—the joy of realization—and its sole criterion the quality of disciplined expressivity.

> Abram Chasins (1903–)
> *Music at the Crossroads*, 1972

If I play an F in a tune called Peace, I don't think it should sound the same as an F that is supposed to express sadness.
> Ornette Coleman (1930–)

Bells, the poor man's only music.
> Samuel Taylor Coleridge (1772–1834)
> *Frost at Midnight*

The genius of interpretation is oblivion of oneself.
> Emile Jaques-Dalcroze (1865–1950)
> Quoted by Wanda Landowska,
> *Landowska on Music*, 1964

The attraction of the virtuoso for the public is very like that of the circus for the crowd. There is always the hope that something dangerous will happen.
> Claude Debussy (1862–1918)
> *Monsieur Croche, anti-dilettante*, 1927

The tuba is certainly the most intestinal of instruments, the very lower bowel of music.
> Peter De Vries (1910–   )
> *The Glory of the Hummingbird*, 1974

> The trumpet shall be heard on high,
> The dead shall live, the living die,
> And Music shall untune the sky!
>> John Dryden (1631–1700)
>> *A Song for St. Cecilia's Day*, 1687

My band is my instrument.
> Duke Ellington (1899–1974)
> *The New Yorker*, July 1944

There are only 1500 musicians of world class on this planet, and they must be handled with care and respect.
> Ernest Fleischmann (1924–   )
> New York *Times Magazine*,
> April 11, 1976

Where Drums speak out, Laws hold their tongues.
> Thomas Fuller (1608–61)

The noisy drum hath nothing in it, but mere air.
> Thomas Fuller

"Strike Up the Band!"

>Ira Gershwin (1896–   )
>Popular song title, 1927

>Strike the concertina's melancholy string!
>Blow the spirit-stirring harp like anything!
>Let the piano's martial blast
>Rouse the Echoes of the Past . . .
>>Sir William Schwenck Gilbert (1836–1911)
>>*Story of Prince Agib*, 1869

Voices, instruments, and all possible sounds—even silence itself —must tend toward one goal, which is expression . . .

>Christoph Willibald Gluck (1714–87)
>Letter to M. de la Harpe, *Journal de Paris*, October 12, 1777

Those who painfully and with bleeding feet have scaled the crags of mastery over musical instruments have yet their loss in this,—that the wild joy of strumming has become a vanished sense.

>Kenneth Grahame (1859–1932)
>*The Golden Age*, 1895

I think I know the reason why music, more than any other art, is subject to the changes of which it is accused: it depends all the time on those who perform it.

>André Ernest Grétry (1741–1813)
>*Memoires*, 1789

An interpretation of music based on the feelings cannot be acceptable either to art or science.

>Eduard Hanslick (1825–1904)
>*The Beautiful in Music*, 1854

The piece of music is worked out by the composer, but it is the performance which we enjoy. Thus the active and emotional principle in music occurs in the act of reproduction, which draws the electric spark from a mysterious source and directs it toward the heart of the listener.

Eduard Hanslick
The Beautiful in Music, 1854

The fundamental evil in music is the necessity of reproduction of its artistic creations by performance.

Ferdinand Hiller (1811–85)

People who make music together cannot be enemies, at least not while the music lasts.

Paul Hindemith (1895–1963)

How, then, would the perfect musician exercise his art? He would take his horse (answered a Chinese musician) and ride to a mountain far away from houses and men. There he would play his instrument and sing for his own enlightenment.

Paul Hindemith
A Composer's World, 1952

I blow through here;
The music goes 'round and around . . .
And it comes up here.
"Red" Hodgson
"The Music Goes 'Round and Around,"
Popular song, 1935

You think they are crusaders, sent
From some infernal clime,
To pluck the eyes of Sentiment
And dock the tail of Rhyme,
To crack the voice of melody
And break the legs of time.
Oliver Wendell Holmes (1809–94)
The Music Grinders

Bells are music's laughter.
Thomas Hood (1799–1845)
Miss Kilmansegg: Her Marriage, 1827

Technique is to be able to lay open the basic sense of a great work of art, to make it clear.

> Eugene Istomin (1925–   )
> Quoted by Robert Jacobson,
> *Reverberations*, 1974

I am very pleased with your project on the harmonica, and the prospect of your succeeding in the application of keys to it. It will be the greatest present which has been made to the musical world this century, not excepting the pianoforte.

> Thomas Jefferson (1743–1826)
> Letter to Francis Hopkinson, 1786

Bells, the music nighest bordering upon heaven.

> Charles Lamb (1775–1834)
> *Essays of Elia*, 1821

The tragedy in the interpretation of music of the past lies in the fact that it is confined to concert halls, congresses of musicology, or conservatory classes . . . Music needs air, sunlight, and liberty to be alive. It is only then that it will impart to us surprising secrets.

> Wanda Landowska (1877–1959)
> *Landowska on Music*, 1964

The timbre of the trombone is in its nature majestic and imposing. It is sufficiently powerful to dominate a whole orchestra and produces an impression of superhuman power . . . it can become terrible . . . or mournful and full of dismay; or it may have the serenity of the organ . . . It is a superb instrument of lofty dramatic power, which should be reserved for great occasions.

> Albert Lavignac (1846–1916)

> This world is a difficult world, indeed,
>   And people are hard to suit,
> And the man who plays on the violin
>   Is a bore to the man with the flute.

> Walter Learned (1847–1915)
> *Consolation*

The banjos rattled, and the tambourines Jing-jing-jingled in the hands of Queens!

> Vachel Lindsay (1879–1931)
> *General William Booth Enters Heaven*, 1913

You cannot imagine how it spoils one to have been a child prodigy.

> Franz Liszt (1811–86)

The trombones are too sacred for frequent use.

> Felix Mendelssohn (1809–47)

The price of freedom for all musicians, both composers and interpreters, is tremendous control, discipline and patience; but perhaps not only for musicians. Do we not all find freedom to improvise, in all art, in all life, along the guiding lines of discipline?

> Yehudi Menuhin (1916–   )
> *Theme and Variations*, 1972

The task for the performer consists in establishing an equilibrium between the composition and his own conscience.

> Yehudi Menuhin
> Quoted by J. Ma. Corredor,
> *Conversations with Casals*, 1956

To play great music, you must keep your eyes on a distant star.

> Yehudi Menuhin
> *Reader's Digest*, December 1953

An organist an accomplished man! . . . Well, I suppose it is possible, but it rather upsets one's notions, does it not?

> George Meredith (1828–1909)
> *Sandra Belloni*, 1864

> Then, crowned again, their golden harps they
>   took,
> Harps ever tuned, that glittering by their side
> Like quivers hung; and with preamble sweet
> Of charming symphony they introduce

Their sacred song, and waken raptures high;
No voice exempt, no voice but well could join
Melodious part; such concord is in heaven.

John Milton (1608–74)
Paradise Lost, 1667

The harp that once thro' Tara's halls
The soul of music shed,
Now hangs as mute on Tara's walls
As if that soul were fled.
Thomas Moore (1779–1852)
The Harp That Once Through Tara's Halls, 1808

The organ, to my eyes and ears, is the king of instruments.
Wolfgang Amadeus Mozart (1756–91)
Letter to his father, October 17, 1777

The music of the zither, the flute and the lyre enervates the mind.

Ovid (43 B.C.–18 A.D.)
Remedia Amoris

We shall never become musicians unless we understand the ideals of temperance, fortitude, liberality and magnificence.
Plato (c. 428–c. 347 B.C.)
Republic

Intellect and musical talent constitute a precarious partnership. Music is not an art of the intellect, and its greatest practitioners, while intelligent, as a rule, have rarely been intellectuals.
Henry Pleasants (1910–   )
Serious Music—and All That Jazz, 1969

You can chase a Beethoven symphony all your life and never catch up.

André Previn (1929–   )

Seated one day at the organ,
I was weary and ill at ease,

And my fingers wandered idly
Over the noisy keys.
                    Adelaide Anne Procter (1825–64)
                    A Lost Chord, 1858

Many excellent writers, very many painters and most musicians
are so tedious on any subject but their own.
                                    Arthur Rimbaud (1854–91)

The performer may have a responsibility toward the composer,
but the composer has none toward the performer beyond the prac-
tical one of making his music performable on some terms.
                                    Ned Rorem (1923–   )
                                    The Final Diary, 1974

Music lasts by itself and cares not who composed it; nor can
music recall the thousand anonymous fingers and mouths which
tamper with it, beautifully or badly.
                                    Ned Rorem
                                    Music from Inside Out, 1967

It isn't evil that's ruining the earth, but mediocrity. The crime
is not that Nero played while Rome burned, but that he played
badly.
                                    Ned Rorem
                                    The Final Diary, 1974

Would to heaven that a race of freaks could arise in the race of
artists, with one finger too many on each hand; then the dance of
virtuosity would be at an end.
                                    Robert Schumann (1810–56)
                                    Aphorisms, c. 1833

Lose no opportunity of practicing on the organ; there is no instrument which takes a swifter revenge on anything unclear or
sloppy in composition and playing.
                                    Robert Schumann
                                    Aphorisms, c. 1833

If we climb from that region of technique to the more spiritual sphere of interpretation, what anguish we experience in trying to find the soul of a composition behind the inert notation, and how many scruples and repentings we have before we dare to discover what does *not* lie hidden in the paper!

> Andrés Segovia (1893–)
> Letter to Bernard Gavoty,
> December 20, 1954

'Tis no matter how it be in tune, so it make noise enough.
> William Shakespeare (1564–1616)
> *As You Like It,* 1599–1600

Now, divine air! Now is his soul ravished! Is it not strange that sheeps' guts should hale souls out of men's bodies?
> William Shakespeare
> *Much Ado About Nothing,* 1598–99

For Orpheus' lute was strung with poets' sinews, whose golden touch could soften steel and stones, make tigers tame and huge leviathens forsake unsounded deeps to dance on sands.
> William Shakespeare
> *The Two Gentlemen of Verona,* 1594–95

My own friends are those who give good performances. My enemies are those who in any way debase music.
> George Bernard Shaw (1856–1950)

Unperformed music is like a cake in the oven—not fully baked.
> Isaac Stern (1920–)
> Quoted in *ASCAP Today,* Winter 1975

> Think NOTHING
> Wait until it is absolutely still within you
> When you have attained this
> Begin to play
> As soon as you start to think stop

And try to retain
The state of NON-THINKING
Then continue playing.
> Karlheinz Stockhausen (1928–   )
> Instructions to performers of the
> composition *Es*, reported in the New
> York *Times*, December 30, 1973

Music should be transmitted and not interpreted, because interpretation reveals the personality of the interpreter rather than that of the author, and who can guarantee that such an executant will reflect the author's vision without distortion.
> Igor Stravinsky (1882–1971)
> *Chronicles of My Life*, 1936

Blow, bugle, blow; set the wild
echoes flying
Blow, bugle; answer, echoes,
dying, dying, dying.
> Alfred, Lord Tennyson (1809–92)
> *The Princess*, 1947

Instruments sound sweetest when they be touched softest.
> John Tyly
> *Euphues and His England*, 1580

The composer is the only one of the creators today who is denied direct contact with the public. When his work is done, he is thrust aside and the interpreter enters, not to try to understand the work but impertinently to judge it . . .
> Edgar Varèse (1885–1965)
> *Manifesto of the International
> Composers Guild*, 1921

It takes perhaps a thousand poor musicians to produce one virtuoso.
> Ralph Vaughan Williams (1872–1958)
> New York *Times Magazine*,
> December 5, 1954

Today music is only the art of performing difficult things, but what is merely difficult ceases to please in the long run.

Voltaire (1694–1778)
Candide, 1759

O silver trumpets, be you lifted up,
And cry to the great race that is to come!
Long-throated swans upon the waves of time
Sing loudly, for beyond the wall of the world
That race may hear our music and awake.

William Butler Yeats (1865–1939)

PIANOS AND PIANISTS

He who plays the piano keeps sane.

Italian proverb

Old piano players never die, they simply fake away.

Anonymous

The piano need bow to no singer. In emulating song it may surpass song itself, just as Prometheus surpassed the gods in striving for godhood.

Ernst Bacon (1898–   )
Notes on the Piano, 1963

. . . the piano is the social instrument par excellence. It is drawing-room furniture, a sign of bourgeois prosperity, the most massive of the devices by which the young are tortured in the name of education and the grown-up in the name of entertainment. It is a rallying point for the convivial when letting off spirituous fumes through song, and for the amorous conducting a romance . . . At the same time, too, the piano is the individualist's instrument for nursing the illusion that he is a host in himself . . .

Jacques Barzun (1907–   )
Preface to Men, Women and Pianos,
by Arthur Loesser, 1954

The sound of a harpsichord: Two skeletons copulating on a galvanised tin roof.

Sir Thomas Beecham (1879–1961)

The great pianists have nothing to show save technique and affectation.

Ludwig van Beethoven (1779–1827)
To Marie Pachler-Koschak, 1817

"I Love a Piano"

Irving Berlin (1888–   )
Popular song title, 1915

When I consider the appalling platitudes to which the piano has given birth, I give grateful thanks to the good fortune that forced me to compose freely and in silence, and delivered me from the tyranny of the fingers, so dangerous to thought . . .

Hector Berlioz (1803–69)

For instrumental composers the piano is a veritable guillotine that severs the head of nobleman and churl with the same impartial indifference.

Hector Berlioz

Piano, n. A parlor utensil for subduing the impenitent visitor. It is operated by depressing the keys of the machine and the spirits of the audience.

Ambrose Bierce (1842–?1914)
The Devil's Dictionary, 1911

Bach is the foundation of piano playing, Liszt the summit. The two make Beethoven possible.

Ferruccio Busoni (1866–1924)
Rules for Practicing the Piano, 1898

Respect the pianoforte! It gives a single man command over something complete: in its ability to go from very soft to very loud in one and the same register it excels all other instruments. The trumpet can blare, but not sigh; the flute is contrary; the pianoforte can do both. Its range embraces the highest and lowest practicable notes. Respect the pianoforte!

Ferruccio Busoni

They laughed when I sat down at the piano. But when I started to play!

> John Caples (1900–   )
> Advertisement for U. S. School
> of Music, 1925

If the devil some good night should take his hammer and smite in slivers all and every piano of our European world, so that in broad Europe there was not one piano left soundable, would the harm be great? Would not, on the contrary, the relief be considerable? For once that you hear any real music from a piano, do you not five hundred times hear mere artistic somersaults, distorted jingling, and the hapless pretense of music?

> Thomas Carlyle (1795–1881)

It's a pity to shoot the pianist when the piano is out of tune.
> René Coty (1882–1962), President of France
> Quoted in *Time*, January 4, 1957

'Tis wonderful how soon a piano gets into a log-hut on the frontier.

> Ralph Waldo Emerson (1803–82)
> "Civilization," 1870

All I know is, for every note, there is another note that melts it. I just hear a sound coming into my head and hope to catch it with my hands.

> Erroll Garner (1921–77)

(Bernard Shaw) persisted in regarding the fortissimos of Paderewski . . . as brutal contests between the piano and the pianist to settle the question of the survival of the fittest.

> Archibald Henderson (1877–1963)
> *George Bernard Shaw: Man of the Century,* 1956

Don't be ashamed if you can't play the piano; be proud of it.
> E. W. Howe
> *Country Town Sayings,* 1911

A pianoforte is a harp in a box.

> Leigh Hunt (1784–1859)
> *The Seer*, 1840

I never practice; I always play.

> Wanda Landowska (1877–1959)
> *Time*, December 1, 1952

My whole trick is to keep the tune well out in front. If I play Tchaikovsky I play his melodies and skip his spiritual struggles. Naturally I condense. I have to know just how many notes my audiences will stand for. If there's time left over I fill in with a lot of runs up and down the keyboard.

> Liberace (1919–   )
> Quoted in *The Popular Arts*, edited
>   by Stuart Hall and Paddy Whannel, 1964

Many persons still wear vests, read books, write their own Christmas greetings, go to the theater, shave with straight razors, and play the piano.

> Arthur Loesser (1894–1969)
> *Men, Women and Pianos*, 1954

There was a gentleman who rendered a selection at the piano, very marvelous music that made me want to play the piano very, very much. The only trouble was that this gentleman had long, bushy hair, and because the piano was known in our circle as an instrument for a lady, this confirmed me in my idea that if I played piano I would be misunderstood.

> Ferdinand "Jelly Roll" Morton
> Quoted in *Hear Me Talkin' to Ya*,
>   edited by Nat Shapiro and Nat Hentoff, 1955

If I don't practice for one day, I know it; if I don't practice for two days, the critics know it; if I don't practice for three days, the audience knows it.

> Ignacy Paderewski (1860–1941)

Piano playing is more difficult than statesmanship. It is harder to wake emotions in ivory keys than it is in human beings.

Ignacy Paderewski

. . . And when he jams with the bass and guitar they holler "Aw, Beat me daddy, eight to the bar."

"Beat Me Daddy, Eight to the Bar,"
Popular song by Don Raye, Hughie Prince,
and Eleanor Sheehy, 1940

The piano bard, the piano rhapsodist, the piano mind, the piano soul is Chopin. Tragic, romantic, lyric, heroic, dramatic, fantastic, soulful, sweet, dreamy, brilliant, grand, simple: all possible expressions are found in his compositions, and all are sung by him upon his instrument.

Anton Rubinstein (1829–94)

I cannot tell you how much I love to play for people . . . sometimes when I sit down to practice and there is no one else in the room I have to stifle my impulse to ring for the elevator man and offer him money to come in and hear me.

Arthur Rubinstein (1887–   )
Holiday, May 1963

Please don't tell Mr. Hurok, but I love playing the piano so much, I would do it for nothing.

Arthur Rubinstein
"Rubinstein Speaking," New York
Times Magazine, January 26, 1964

Have I a secret about playing the piano? It is a very simple one. I sit down on the piano-stool and make myself comfortable—and I always make sure that the lid over the keyboard is open before I start to play.

Artur Schnabel (1882–1951)

The notes I handle no better than many pianists. But the pauses between the notes—ah, that is where the art resides!

Artur Schnabel
Chicago *Daily News*, June 11, 1958

The most difficult things written by one perfectly versed in the difficulties of the keyboard are far easier to play than the easiest things conceived by an amateur.

> Robert Schumann (1810–56)

The pianoforte is the most important of all musical instruments: its invention was to music what the invention of printing was to poetry.

> George Bernard Shaw (1856–1950)
> "The Religion of the Pianoforte,"
> *The Fortnightly Review*, February 1894

The indefatigable pursuit of an unattainable perfection, even though it consists in nothing more than in the pounding of an old piano, is what alone gives a meaning to our life on this unavailing star.

> Logan Pearsall Smith (1865–1946)
> *Afterthoughts*, 1931

He (Rachmaninoff) was the only pianist I have ever seen who did not grimace. That is a great deal.

> Igor Stravinsky (1882–1971)
> *Conversations with Igor Stravinsky*,
> by Robert Craft, 1958

I need to touch music as well as to think it, which is why I have always lived next to a piano.

> Igor Stravinsky
> Quoted in *ASCAP Today*, Winter 1975

Ladies and gentlemen, I play the piano, but God is in the house tonight.

> Thomas "Fats" Waller (1904–43)
> To a nightclub audience when informed
>   that virtuoso jazz pianist Art Tatum
>   was present in the audience

Over the piano was printed a notice: "Please do not shoot the pianist. He is doing his best."

Oscar Wilde (1854–1900)
Impressions of America, 1883

Her ivory hands on the ivory keys
    Strayed in fitful fantasy,
Like the silver gleam when the poplar trees
    Rustle their pale leaves listlessly
    Or the drifting foam of restless sea
When the waves show their teeth in the
    flying breeze.

Oscar Wilde
In the Gold Room. A Harmony

VIOLINS AND/OR FIDDLES

There were three roaring fiddlers
Came lately out of France,
That light and nimbly can
Teach maidens how to dance.

Anonymous, c. 1575

He could fiddle all the bugs off a sweet-potato vine.

Stephen Vincent Benét (1898–1943)
The Mountain Whippoorwill, 1923

Fiddle, n. An instrument to tickle human ears by friction of a horse's tail on the entrails of a cat.

Ambrose Bierce (1842–?1914)
The Devil's Dictionary, 1911

A fiddle is not a fiddle until it touches a human shoulder, until it is tucked warmly under a human chin.

Catherine Drinker Bowen (1897–1973)
Friends and Fiddlers, 1934

From this did Paganini comb the fierce Electric sparks, or to tenuity Pull forth the inmost wailing of the wire—No cat-gut could swoon out so much soul.

Robert Browning (1812–89)
Red Cotton Night-Cap Country, 1873

There's many a good tune played on an old fiddle.

Samuel Butler (1835–1902)
The Way of All Flesh, 1903

. . . what can be more strange, than that the rubbing of a little Hair and Cat-gut together, shou'd make such a mighty alteration in a Man that sits at a distance?

> Jeremy Collier (1650–1726)
> *An Essay on Musick,* 1702

In came a fiddler—and tuned like fifty stomach-aches.

> Charles Dickens (1812–70)
> *A Christmas Carol,* 1843

'Tis God gives skill,
But not without men's hands:
He could not make Antonio Stradivari's violins
Without Antonio.

> George Eliot (1819–80)
> *Poems: Stradivarius*

A fiddler on the roof,
A most unlikely sight.
It might not mean a thing,
But then again it might.

> Sheldon Harnick (1924–   )
> "Fiddler on the Roof," song, 1964

In the house of a fiddler, all fiddle.

> George Herbert (1593–1633)
> *Outlandish Proverbs,* 1640

Perhaps it was because Nero played the fiddle, they burned Rome.

> Oliver Herford (1863–1935)

Had I learned to fiddle, I should have done nothing else.

> Samuel Johnson (1709–84)

There is nothing, I think, in which the power of art is shown so much as in playing the fiddle . . . Any man will forge a bar of iron, if you give him a hammer; not so well as a smith, but tolerably. A man will saw a piece of wood, and make a box, though a clumsy one; but give him a fiddle and a fiddle-stick, and he can do nothing.

> Samuel Johnson
> Quoted by James Boswell, *The Life of*
> *Samuel Johnson,* 1791

It is fiddling while Rome is burning.

> Charles Kingsley (1819–75)
> *Westward Ho!,* 1855

> A squeak's heard in the orchestra,
> As the leader draws across
> The intestines of the agile cat
> The tail of the noble hoss.
>
> George T. Lanigan (1845–86)
> *The Amateur Orlando,* 1875

The viola is a philosopher, sad, helpful; always ready to come to the aid of others, but reluctant to call attention to himself.

> Albert Lavignac (1846–1916)

Everybody is talking of Paganini and his violin. The man seems to be a miracle. The newspapers say that long streamy flakes of music fall from his string, interspersed with luminous points of sound which ascend the air and appear like stars. This eloquence is quite beyond me.

> Thomas Babington Macaulay (1800–59)
> Letter to his sister, May 25, 1831

Man's peculiar privilege is walking erect on two feet and thereby being forced to stretch his hands upwards to heaven. This conquering of gravity, space and height, as well as of horizon, is essential in violin playing.

> Yehudi Menuhin (1916–   )
> *Theme and Variations,* 1972

Very well, I can wait.

> Attributed to Arnold Schoenberg (1874–1951)
> when told that his violin concerto
> required a soloist with six fingers

Fiddlers, dogs and flies come to feasts uncalled.
Scottish Proverbs, 1649

God hath given to some men wisdom and understanding, and to others the art of playing the fiddle.
Robert Southey (1774–1843)
The Doctor, 1812

. . . when a man is not disposed to hear musick, there is not a more disagreeable Sound in Harmony than that of a violin.
Sir Richard Steele (1672–1729)
The Tatler, April 1, 1710

Violins are the lively, forward importunate wits that distinguish themselves by the flourishes of imagination, sharpness of repartee, glances of satire and bear away the upper part in every consort.
Richard Steele
The Tatler, April 1, 1710

He was a fiddler, and consequently a rogue.
Jonathan Swift (1667–1745)
Letter to Stella, July 25, 1711

Fiddler's fare: meat, drink, and money.
John Taylor (1580–1653)
Wandering to See the Wonders of the West,
1649

A violin should be played with love, or not at all.
Joseph Wechsberg (1907–   )
The First Time Around, 1970

The tongues of violins!
(I think, O tongues, ye tell this heart,
    that cannot tell itself;
This brooding, yearning heart, that
    cannot tell itself.)
Walt Whitman (1819–92)
Proud Music of the Storm, 1870

For the good are always the merry,
Save by an evil chance,
And the merry love the fiddle,
And the merry love to dance:
                    William Butler Yeats (1865–1939)
                    The Fiddler of Dooney, 1899

WOODWINDS

A tutor who tooted a flute
Tried to teach two young tutors to toot;
Said the two to the tutor:
Is it harder to toot, or
To tutor two tutors to toot?

Anonymous

Tom, Tom, the piper's son,
He learned to play when he was young,
But all the tune that he could play
Was "Over the hills and far away."

Nursery rhyme, c. 1650

Jack Whaley had a cow,
    And he had naught to feed her;
He took a pipe and played a tune,
    And bid the cow consider.

Anonymous
Jack Whaley, c. 1725

The oboe is an ill wind that nobody blows good.

Anonymous

What is worse than a flute? Two flutes.

Anonymous

And the people piped with pipes, and rejoiced with great joy, so that the earth rent with the sound of them.

> Old Testament
> I Kings

The flute is not an instrument with a good moral effect. It is too exciting.

> Aristotle (384–322 B.C.)
> *Politics*

Did you ever hear Pete Go "Tweet, tweet, tweet on his piccolo?"

> Phil Baxter (1896–1972)
> "Piccolo Pete," 1929,
> Popular song

The saxophone is the embodied spirit of beer.
> Attributed to Arnold Bennett (1867–1931)

Clarionet, n. An instrument of torture operated by a person with cotton in his ears. There are two instruments that are worse than a clarionet—two clarionets.

> Ambrose Bierce (1842–?1914)
> *The Devil's Dictionary*, 1911

Flute, n. A variously perforated hollow stick intended for the punishment of sin, the minister of retribution being commonly a young man with straw-colored eyes and lean hair.

> Ambrose Bierce
> *The Enlarged Devil's Dictionary*

> The soft complaining flute
> In dying notes, discovers
> The woes of hopeless lovers.
> > John Dryden (1631–1700)
> > *A Song for St. Cecilia's Day*, 1687

Blowing is not playing the flute, you must make use of your fingers.

> Johann Wolfgang von Goethe (1749–1832)

> Anon they move
> In perfect phalanx to the Dorian mood
> of flutes and soft recorders.
>
> > John Milton (1608–74)
> > *Paradise Lost*

Alcibiades refused to learn the flute, as a sordid thing, and not becoming a free citizen; saying that to play on the lute or the harp does not in any way disfigure a man's body or face, but one is hardly to be known by the most intimate friends when playing on the flute.

> Plutarch (c. 46–120 A.D.)
> *Lives*

The sound of the flute will cure epilepsy, and a sciatic gout.

> Theophrastus (c. 370–c. 287 B.C.)

GUITARS

Yes, we three were so happy, my wife, my guitar and me.
                              Big Bill Broonzy (1893–1958)

A guitar has moonlight in it.

                    James M. Cain (1892–   )
                    Serenade, 1937

            My guitar, I sing of thee;
            'Tis with thee that I decoy
            And ensnare enchantingly
            The ladies I enjoy.
                         Pierre de Ronsard (1524–85)

A chattel with a soul—a personal possession often owning its
possessor—being quaint and quiet, dedicated to the dulcet rather
than the diapason—
A portable companion always ready to go where you go—a
small friend weighing less than a fresh born infant—to be shared
with few or many—just two of you in sweet meditation.
                    Carl Sandburg (1878–1967)
                    The Guitar (for Andrés Segovia)

Electric guitars are an abomination, whoever heard of an electric violin? An electric cello? Or for that matter an electric singer?
                    Andrés Segovia (1893–   )
                    On The Beatles, quoted in *The
                    Beatles, Words Without Music*, 1968

The turning point in the history of western civilization was reached with the invention of the electric guitar.

Leni Sinclair
Quoted by John Sinclair,
Guitar Army, 1972

CONCERTS

It is not unjust to define amateur concerts by saying that the music performed at them seems to have been composed to make those who render it happy and drive those who listen to despair.

Adolphe Adam (1803–56)
Souvenirs d'un musicien

Concerts in England have no future; I have no future; nobody has any future.

Sir Thomas Beecham (1879–1961), 1926

All festivals are bunk . . . Festivals are for the purpose of attracting trade to the town. What that has to do with music I don't know.

Sir Thomas Beecham
Quoted in *Jazz Journal*, October 1956

The concert season of the year 1837 is not worth mentioning. Equally dull was the opera season . . .

Rev. John Edmund Cox
*Musical Recollections of the Last
Half-Century*, 1872

The music-hall singer attends a series of masses
and fugues and 'ops'
By Bach, interwoven
With Spohr and Beethoven
At classical Monday Pops.

Sir William Schwenck Gilbert (1836–1911)
The Mikado, 1885

Last year, more Americans went to symphonies than to baseball games. This may be viewed as an alarming statistic, but I think that both baseball and the country will survive.

> President John F. Kennedy (1917–63)
> At a White House concert,
> August 16, 1962

Even before the music begins there is that bored look on people's faces. A polite form of self-imposed torture, the concert.

> Henry Miller (1891–   )
> *Tropic of Cancer*, 1934

To the social-minded, a definition for Concert is: that which surrounds an intermission.

> Ned Rorem (1923–   )
> *The Final Diary*, 1974

A concert is like a bullfight—the moment of truth.

> Arthur Rubinstein (1887–   )
> Quoted by Robert Jacobson,
> *Reverberations*, 1974

The worst feeling in the world is to go back into an empty hall after the audience has left. You see the work lights and the bare stage, and you can't believe there was so much happening in there just a few minutes ago. I can never be left alone after a concert, I need someone to help me come down.

> Melanie Safka (1948–   )
> *Rolling Stone*, April 1, 1971

Applause is a receipt, not a bill.

> Artur Schnabel (1882–1951)
> Explaining his refusal to play encores,
> quoted by Irving Kolodin, *The Musical
> Life*, 1958

If nobody wants to go to your concert, nothing will stop them.

> Isaac Stern (1920–   )

THE MUSIC TRADE

These three take crooked ways: carts, boats, and musicians.
Hindu proverb

No song, no supper.

Latin proverb

Whose bread I eat, his song I sing.

Latin proverb

> Little Tommy Tucker
> Sings for his supper;
> What shall we give him?
> White bread and butter.
> Anonymous
> *Tommy Thumb's Pretty Song Book*, c. 1744

He must be a poor sort of man, for otherwise he would not be so good a piper.
Attributed to Antisthenes (c. 455–c. 360 B.C.)

For I consider music as a very innocent diversion, and perfectly compatible with the profession of a clergyman.
Jane Austen (1775–1817)
Pride and Prejudice, 1813

Competition is for horses, not artists.
Béla Bartók (1881–1945)
Saturday Review, August 25, 1962

This is the only country in the world where musicians are not expected to live. Of course, composers and musicians have always starved and, as this is a sentimental country, we think the tradition should be continued.

Sir Thomas Beecham (1879–1961)

There should be a single Art Exchange in the world, to which the artist would simply send his works and be given in return as much as he needs. As it is, one has to be half a merchant on top of everything else, and how badly one goes about it!

Ludwig van Beethoven (1770–1827)
Letter to Franz Anton Hoffmeister,
January 15, 1801

The human brain is not a saleable commodity . . .

Ludwig van Beethoven
From the draft of a plan for a
complete edition of his works,
Vienna, 1822

It is the best of all trades, to make songs, and the second best to sing them.

Hilaire Belloc (1870–1953)

Opera has no business making money.

Sir Rudolf Bing (1920–   )
New York *Times*, November 15, 1959

Ah, music! What a beautiful art! But what a wretched profession!

Georges Bizet (1838–75),
August 3, 1867

I want to know a butcher paints,
A baker rhymes for his pursuit,
Candlestick-maker much acquaints
His soul with song, or haply mute,
Blows out his brains upon the flute.

Robert Browning (1812–89)
Saul

Have little care that life is brief,
And less that art is long.
Success is in the silences
Though fame is in the song.

Bliss Carman (1861–1929)
Songs from Vagabondia

A line of demarcation between the Musical Art and that other
and more worldly pursuit known as the Musical Business . . . is
difficult to trace.

Paul S. Carpenter (1894–1949)
Music, an Art and a Business, 1950

Music is a calling rather than a profession.

Abram Chasins (1903–)
Music at the Crossroads, 1972

You won't do any business if you haven't got a band;
The folks expect a street parade and uniforms so grand.

George M. Cohan (1878–1942)
"You Won't Do Any Business,"
Popular song, 1902

Music is the only noise for which one is obliged to pay.

Attributed to Alexandre Dumas (1824–95)

. . . it cannot be emphasized too strongly that art, as such does
not "pay" . . . at least, not in the beginning—and that the art that
has to pay its own way is apt to become vitiated and cheap.

Antonin Dvořák (1841–1904)
Music in America, 1895

I ask not for wages, I only seek room in the garden of song.

Arthur Wentworth Hamilton Eaton (1859–1937)
The Garden of Song

A musical profit can put you way ahead of a financial loss.

Edward Kennedy "Duke" Ellington (1899–1974)
Quoted in *The Village Voice,*
August 23, 1976

. . . when it came to dollars, everyone got uptight. Probably the biggest bringdown in my life—it's so hypocritical—was being in a pop group and finding out just how much it was like everything it was supposed to be against.

> Mama Cass Elliot (1941–74)
> Quoted by Ellen Sander in *Trips,* 1973

Give the piper a penny to play, and two pence to leave off.

> Thomas Fuller (1608–61)

> Sing for your supper
> And you'll get breakfast
> Songbirds always eat,
> If their song is sweet to hear.
>> Lorenz Hart (1895–1943)
>> "Sing for Your Supper," 1938
>> Popular song

Romanticism, and sorrow, and greed—they can all be put into music. I can definitely recognize greed. I know when a man is playing for money.

> Coleman Hawkins (1904–   )
> Quoted by Stanley Dance, *The World of Swing,* 1974

The singing man keeps his shop in his throat.

> George Herbert (1593–1633)
> *Jacula Prudentum,* 1640

The collapse of music is obvious . . . The profession of composer discloses the singularity . . . of a person who troubles himself to produce something for which there are no consumers . . . The contemporary composer is a gate-crasher trying to push his way into a company to which he has not been invited.

> Arthur Honegger (1892–1955)
> *Je suis compositeur,* 1951

What you said hurt me very much. I cried all the way to the bank.

> Liberace (1919–)
> In response to critics after a
> concert in New York, June 1954

I have learned from experience that it is easier to make a business man out of a musician than a musician out of a business man.

> Goddard Lieberson (1911–)

With recording, the music of the world becomes available at any moment—just like an encyclopedia. We begin to develop a vast tribal encyclopedia of musics. Music becomes plural. You cannot speak of it any longer in the singular, or refer to it as the international language. We know from recordings that the old pet cliché of the 19th century—music the universal language—just isn't so.

> Marshal McLuhan (1911–)

If you're in jazz and more than ten people like you, you're labeled commercial.

> Herbie Mann (1930–)
> Quoted by Henry Pleasants,
> *Serious Music—and All That Jazz!*, 1969

I want to tell the mothers and fathers of our great country never to permit their children to become professional musicians, because if they do, they are going into a starvation business.

> James C. Petrillo (1892–), former President
> of the American Federation of Musicians,
> on *Person to Person*, CBS-TV,
> October 16, 1953

If I was a good trumpet player I wouldn't be here. I got desperate. I hadda look for a job. I went in the union business.

> James C. Petrillo, former President
> of the American Federation of Musicians,
> New York *Times*, June 14, 1956

The truth is that every great composer, without exception, has been appreciated, admired, applauded, and loved in his own time. Even those who died miserably, died famous.

> Henry Pleasants (1910–   )
> *The Agony of Modern Music*, 1955

A man does not rise to eminence in the world who is merely a good singer and dancer.

> Jean Jacques Rousseau (1712–78)
> *Confessions*, 1781–88

Music with her silver sound, because musicians have no gold for sounding.

> William Shakespeare (1564–1616)
> *Romeo and Juliet*, 1594

I have occasionally, remarked that the only entirely creditable incident in English history is the sending of £100 to Beethoven on his deathbed by the London Philharmonic Society; and it is the only one that historians never mention.

> George Bernard Shaw (1856–1950)
> Letter to *The Times*, London,
> December 20, 1932

The professional musician, as such, can have no special social status whatever, because he may be anything, from an ex-drummer boy to an artist and philosopher of world-wide reputation.

> George Bernard Shaw
> *The World*, January 11, 1893

Plenty corrupts the melody that made thee famous once, when young.

> Alfred, Lord Tennyson (1809–92)
> *The Blackbird*

Every composer's music reflects in its subject-matter and in its style the source of the money the composer is living on while writing the music.

> Virgil Thomson (1896–   )
> *The State of Music*, 1939

George Szell. (Photo courtesy of Columbia Records, Inc.)

Igor Stravinsky. (Photo courtesy of Columbia Records, Inc.)

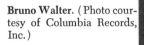

Bruno Walter. (Photo courtesy of Columbia Records, Inc.)

Pablo Casals. (Photo courtesy of Columbia Records, Inc.)

Mel Brooks. (Photo courtesy Pictures Corp.)

Leonard Bernstein. (Photo courtesy of Columbia Records, Inc.)

Sir Thomas Beecham.
(Photo courtesy of Columbia Records, Inc.)

Duke Ellington. (Photo courtesy of Columbia Records, Inc.)

Oscar Levant. (Photo courtesy of Columbia Records, Inc.)

Virgil Thomson. (Photo by Milburn McCarty Associates.)

Miles Davis. (Photo courtesy of Columbia Records, Inc.)

Louis Armstrong. (Photo by Studios Lafe.)

Noel Coward. (Photo courtesy of Columbia Records, Inc.)

Part Four
PROPONENTS AND OPPONENTS

CRITICS AND CRITICISM

How seldom do we meet with a proper amount of sympathy, knowledge, honesty and courage in a critic . . . It is sad indeed for the world of music that criticism, in many respects so useful, should often be the occupation of persons in no way endowed with these qualities.

Carl Philipp Emanuel Bach
Autobiography, 1773

A critic is a bundle of biases held loosely together by a sense of taste.

Whitney Balliett (1926–   )
Dinosaurs in the Morning, 1962

. . . Drooling, driveling, doleful, depressing, dropsical drips.

Sir Thomas Beecham (1879–1961)
On critics, May 21, 1955

Poor devils! Where do they come from? At what age are they sent to the slaughter house? What is done with their bones? Where do such animals pasture in the daytime? Do they have females, and young? How many of them handled the brush before being reduced to the broom?

Hector Berlioz (1803–69)
Les Grotesques de la musique, 1859

A piece of music is an art work, and to try to judge it by "instinct" in four seconds has about as much validity as trying to evaluate the worth of a woman by the size of her bust.

> Elmer Bernstein (1922–   )
> *Film Music Notebook,* Winter 1974–75

Critics can't even make music by rubbing their back legs together.

> Mel Brooks (1927–   )
> Interview in the New York *Times,*
> March 30, 1975

Who does that Frog think he is to come over here and try to tell us how to play? We don't go over there and tell them how to jump on a grape.

> Eddie Condon (1904–73)
> The Dixieland jazz guitarist's
>   reaction to criticism by French
>   jazz authority Hugues Panassié

Only paper flowers are afraid of the rain. We are not afraid of the noble rain of criticism because with it will flourish the magnificent garden of music.

> Konstantin Dankevich (1905–   )
> New York *Times,* November 19, 1959

You know, the critics never change; I'm still getting the same notices I used to get as a child. They tell me I play very well for my age . . .

> Mischa Elman (1891–1967)
> Quoted by Anthony Hopkins,
> *Music All Around Me,* 1967

For the most part jazz criticism has been conducted by those whose passionate love of the music was never quite passionate enough for them to learn the rudiments of jazz making.

> Benny Green (1927–   )
> Notes for Art Tatum record album, 1974

What criticism requires is not the knowledge of the composer, the doer, the insider, but instead the perception, judgement and taste of the non-doer, the outsider, the listener—which is to say, the professional listener, the critic.

> B. H. Haggin (1900–)
> *A Decade of Music*, 1973

The only true criticism of music is the playing thereof.

> James Huneker (1860–1921)
> *Bedouins*, 1920

There are three worlds of music—the composer's, the performer's and the critic's.

> Erich Leinsdorf (1912–)

Keep on good terms with the critics! Visit the gentlemen now and then! Consider that you cannot behave with the "dignity of man" in a kennel, but that you have only to take care that the watchdogs leave you alone.

> Gustav Mahler (1860–1911)
> Letter to Bruno Walter, 1897

It is a common grievance of the musical critic that he generally has to do his work with one eye on the clock. Perhaps that is just as well, after all; it may keep him from the too fond vanity of fixing both eyes on eternity.

> Sir Ernest Newman (1868–1959)
> *New Witness*, 1916–18

I am sitting in the smallest room in the house. I have your review in front of me. Soon it will be behind me.

> Max Reger (1873–1916)
> To a music critic, quoted by
> Eliot Fremont-Smith, *New York* magazine,
> July 8, 1974

One can criticize only the music one knows well.

> Arthur Rubinstein (1887–)
> Quoted by Robert Jacobson,
> *Reverberations*, 1974

Last year I gave several lectures on "Intelligence and the Appreciation of Music among Animals." Today I am going to speak to you about "Intelligence and the Appreciation of Music among Critics." The subject is very similar.

Erik Satie (1866–1925)

The true critic . . . is the man who becomes your personal enemy on the sole provocation of a bad performance, and will only be appeased by good performances.

George Bernard Shaw (1856–1950)
Music in London, 1890–94

Some day I must write a supplement to Schumann's "Advice to Young Musicians." The title will be "Advice to Old Musicians"; and the first precept will run, "Don't be in a hurry to contradict G.B.S., as he never commits himself on a musical subject until he knows at least six times as much about it as you do." But then, I hate saying conceited things, however true they may be . . .

George Bernard Shaw
Music in London, 1890–94

Pay no attention to what the critics say; no statue has ever been put up to a critic.

Attributed to Jean Sibelius (1865–1957)

I had another dream the other day about music critics. They were small and rodent-like with padlocked ears, as if they had stepped out of a painting by Goya.

Igor Stravinsky (1882–1971)
Evening Standard, London, England,
October 29, 1969

I have read your lousy review of Margaret's concert. I've come to the conclusion that you are an "eight ulcer man on four ulcer pay" . . . Some day I hope to meet you. When that happens you'll need a new nose, a lot of beefsteak for black eyes, and perhaps a supporter below.

> President Harry S. Truman (1884–1972)
> In response to the Washington *Post*
>   critic Paul Hume's review of a concert
>   by Margaret Truman,
>   *Time*, December 18, 1950

You cannot have critics with standards; you can only have *music* with standards which critics may observe.

> Alan Walker (1930–   )
> *An Anatomy of Musical Criticism*, 1968

Criticism is the rationalization of intuitive musical experience.
> Alan Walker
> *An Anatomy of Musical Criticism*, 1968

I seriously advise all sensitive composers to die at the age of thirty-seven. I know I've gone through the first halcyon period, and am just about ripe for my critical damnation.

> Sir William Walton (1902–   ), 1939

MUSICAL MISANTHROPY

If any person or persons . . . commonly called Fidlers or Minstrels shall be taken playing, fidling, or making music, in any Inn,
Alehouse, or Tavern . . . or shall be taken intreating any person
. . . to hear them play . . . that every such person shall be ad-
judged rogues, vagabonds, and sturdy beggars . . . and be
punished as such.

Act of Parliament, England, 1642

He is verye often drunke and by means there of he hathe by
unorderlye playing on the organs putt the quire out of time and
disordered them.

From the records of Lincoln Cathedral
regarding Thomas Kingston, organist
from 1599 to 1616

You ask my opinion about taking the young Salzburg musician
into your service. I do not know where you can place him, since I
feel that you do not require a composer, or other useless people
. . . It gives one's service a bad name when such types run around
like beggars; besides, he has a large family.

Letter from Archduke Ferdinand's
mother upon learning of his interest
in Mozart, 1771

A song now and then is very desireable as it is a relief to conversation; but half a dozen consecutively, even from St. Cecilia in
person, would become a bore.

"A Lady of Rank"
Hints on Etiquette, London, 1834

He knew music was Good, but it didn't sound right.

> George Ade (1866–1944)
> *Fables in Slang,* 1900

Music is now the primary weapon used to make the perverse seem glamorous, exciting and appealing. Music is used to ridicule religion, morality, patriotism, and productivity—while glorifying drugs, destruction, revolution and sexual promiscuity.

> Gary Allen
> *That Music—The Age of Rock: 2,*
> Edited by Jonathan Eisen, 1970

The more beautiful music is, the less it is relished by the ignorant.

> Honoré de Balzac (1799–1850)
> *Ursule Mirouet,* 1841

I love Wagner, but the music I prefer is that of a cat hung up by its tail outside a window and trying to stick to the panes of glass with its claws.

> Charles Baudelaire (1821–67)

Jam sessions, jitterbugs and cannibalistic rhythmic orgies are wooing our youth along the primrose path to Hell!

> The Most Reverend Francis J. L. Beckman (1875–1948)
> An address to the National Council of
>   Catholic Women, Biloxi, Mississippi,
> October 25, 1938

. . . "I don't," she added, "know anything about music, really. But I know what I like."

> Max Beerbohm (1872–1956)
> *Zuleika Dobson,* 1911

A Musitian is his own Syren that turns himself into a beast with musick of his own making. His perpetual study to raise passion has utterly debased his reason; and musick is wont to set false

values upon things, the constant use of it has render'd him a
stranger to all true ones.

> Samuel Butler (1612–80)
> *Characters: A Musitian, 17th Century,* 1759

To know whether you are enjoying a piece of music or not you
must see whether you find yourself looking at advertisements of
Pears' soap at the end of the libretto.

> Samuel Butler (1835–1902)

In fact he had no singing education, an ignorant, noteless, timeless, tuneless fellow.

> George Gordon, Lord Byron (1788–1824)
> *Don Juan,* 1819–24

Music has charms to soothe a savage breast—but not the unmusical one.

> Alexander Chase
> *Perspectives,* 1966

A taste of sculpture and painting is in my mind as becoming as
a taste of fiddling and piping is unbecoming a man of fashion.
The former is connected with history and poetry, the latter, with
nothing that I know of but bad company.

> Lord Chesterfield (1694–1773)
> To his son, June 22, 1749

A *great* fondness for music is a mark of great weakness, great
vacuity of mind: not of hardness of heart; not of vice; not of
downright folly; but of a want of capacity, or inclination, for sober
thought.

> William Cobbett (1763–1835)
> *Advice to Young Men and (Incidentally)*
> *to Young Women, in the Middle and*
> *Higher Ranks of Life,* 1829

The ear disapproves but tolerates certain musical pieces;
transfer them into the domain of our nose, and we will be forced
to flee.

> Jean Cocteau (1889–1963)

An ear for music is a very different thing from a taste for music. I have no ear whatever; I could not sing an air to save my life; but I have the intensest delight in music, and can detect good from bad.

> Samuel Taylor Coleridge (1772–1834)
> *Table Talk,* July 6, 1833

Nor cold, nor stern, my soul! Yet I detest
  These scented rooms, where to a gaudy throng,
Heaves the proud harlot her distended breast
  In intricacies of laborious song.

> Samuel Taylor Coleridge
> *Lines Composed in a Concert-Room,* 1799

Music is almost as dangerous as gunpowder; and it maybe requires looking after no less than the press, or the mint. 'Tis possible a public regulation might not be amiss.

> Jeremy Collier (1650–1726)
> A *Short View of the Immorality and*
> *Profaneness of the English State,* 1698

The lewd trebles squeak nothing but bawdy, and the basses roar blasphemy.

> William Congreve (1670–1729)
> *The Way of the World,* 1700

Composers tend to assume that everyone loves music. Surprisingly enough, everyone doesn't.

> Aaron Copland (1900–)
> New York *Times Magazine,* February
> 16, 1964

A musician, the most skillful can only divert himself and a few others.

> William Cowper (1731–1800)
> Letter to Lady Hesketh, January 16, 1786

Music, to a nice ear, is a hazardous amusement, as long attention to it is very fatiguing.

> William Cullen (1710–90)
> *First Lines of the Practice of Physic*, 1774

When a lady in the audience once complained that she didn't understand what Miles Davis was playing, he responded with one of the sage statements on the art. "It took me twenty years study and practice to work up to what I wanted to play in this performance. How can she expect to listen five minutes and understand it?"

> Miles Davis (1926–)
> Quoted by Duke Ellington, *Music Is My Mistress*, 1973

A certain skillful action of his fingers as he hummed some bars and beat time on the seat beside him seemed to denote the musician; and the extraordinary satisfaction he derived from humming something very slow and long, which had no recognizable tune, seemed to denote that he was a scientific one.

> Charles Dickens (1812–70)
> *Dombey and Son*, 1846

I hate music—especially when it's played.

> Jimmy Durante (1893–)

Music sweeps by me like a messenger carrying a message that is not for me.

> George Eliot (1819–80)
> *The Spanish Gypsy*, 1868

Music was invented to deceive and delude mankind.

> Ephorus (4th century B.C.)
> Preface to the *History*

The worst kind of music is that which is insipid to the ear. Even that which has an aggressively vulgar flavour is preferable to it.

And when the former cloaks itself either in cheap morality or in cheap sentiment, it reaches the pinnacle of bad taste.

> Edwin Evans (1874–1945)
> *The Margin of Music*

Now on some hollow tree the owl, shrill chorister of the night, hoots forth some notes which might charm the ears of some modern connoisseurs in music.

> Henry Fielding (1707–54)
> *Tom Jones*, 1749

. . . Beverly Stills, who can sing everything from Verdi ballads to Strauss operations.

> President Gerald R. Ford (1913–   )
> Introducing opera singer Beverly Sills
> at the White House, 1975

Music might tame and civilize wild beasts, but 'tis evident it never yet could tame and civilize musicians.

> John Gay (1685–1732)
> *Polly*, 1729

. . . Bestial cries are heard: neighing horses, the squeal of a brass pig, crying jackasses, amorous quacks of a monstrous toad . . . This excruciating medley of brutal sounds is subordinated to a barely perceptible rhythm. Listening to this screaming music for a minute or two, one conjures up an orchestra of madmen, sexual maniacs, led by a man-stallion beating time with an enormous phallos.

> Maxim Gorky (1868–1936)
> On listening to an American dance band

I only know two tunes; one of them is "Yankee Doodle" and the other isn't.

> President Ulysses S. Grant (1822–85)

He might have been a great composer if he had not been such a perfect gentleman.

>Cecil Gray (1895–1951)
>*A Survey of Contemporary Music*, 1924

I like most music unless it's wrong.

>Coleman Hawkins (1904–69)
>Quoted by Stanley Dance, *The World of Swing*, 1974

What is the voice of song, when the world lacks the ear of taste?

>Nathaniel Hawthorne (1804–64)
>*The Snow-Image and Other Twice-Told Tales*, 1851

Song: the licensed medium for bawling in public things too silly or sacred to be uttered in ordinary speech.

>Oliver Herford (1863–1935)

Those who have no ear for music must be very careful how they speak about that mysterious world of thrilling vibrations which are idle noises to them.

>Oliver Wendell Holmes (1809–94)
>*Pages from an Old Volume of Life*, 1883

The public doesn't want new music; the main thing that it demands of a composer is that he be dead.

>Arthur Honegger (1892–1955)

Classic music is the kind we keep thinking will turn into a tune.

>Frank McKinney, "Kin" Hubbard (1868–1930)

Of all the noises, I think music the least disagreeable.

>Samuel Johnson (1709–84)
>*Morning Chronicle*, August 16, 1816

It (music) excites in my mind no ideas, and hinders me from contemplating my own.

>Samuel Johnson

'Tis the common disease of all your musicians, that they know no mean to be entreated either to begin or to end.

> Ben Jonson (1572–1637)
> *The Poetaster*, 1601

In the judgment of Reason music has less worth than any other of the beautiful arts.

> Immanuel Kant (1724–1804)
> *Critique of Judgment*, 1790

Musicians have the reputation of being not overly bright. This happens to be only too fatally true in the case of singers.

> Alexander King (1900–65)
> *Rich Man, Poor Man*, 1965

A carpenter's hammer, in a warm summer noon, will fret me into more than midsummer madness. But those unconnected, unset sounds are nothing to the measured malice of music.

> Charles Lamb (1775–1834)
> "A Chapter on Ears," *Essays of Elia*, 1821

I think that sentimentally, I am disposed to harmony. But *organically*, I am incapable of a tune. I have been practicing "God Save the King" all my life, whistling and humming of it over to myself in solitary corners; and am not yet arrived, they tell me, within many quavers of it.

> Charles Lamb
> "A Chapter on Ears," *Essays of Elia*, 1820–25

O Music! How it grieves me that imprudence, intemperance, gluttony, should open their channels into thy sacred stream.

> Walter Savage Landor (1820–64)
> *Pericles and Aspasia*, 1836

> Man was never meant to sing:
> And all his mimic organs e'er expressed
> Was but an imitative howl at best.
>
> John Langhorne (1735–79)
> *The Country Justice*, c. 1766

Music has two ills, the one mortal the other wasting; the mortal is ever allied with the instant which follows that of the music's utterance, the wasting lies in its repetition, making it seem contemptible and mean.

Leonardo da Vinci (1452–1519)
Notebooks

Leonard Bernstein has been disclosing musical secrets that have been known for over four hundred years.

Oscar Levant (1906–72)
The Memoirs of an Amnesiac, 1965

This is not music—believe me! I have always flattered myself I know something about music—but this is chaos. This is demagogy, blasphemy, insanity, madness! It is a perfumed fog, shot through with lightning! It is the end of all honesty in art.

Thomas Mann (1875–1955)
A character in *Buddenbrooks*, 1901,
discussing Richard Wagner's *Tristan and Isolde*

There are only two kinds of music; German music and bad music.

H. L. Mencken (1880–1956)

What strange impulse is it which induces otherwise trustful people to say they like music when they do not, and thus expose themselves to hours of boredom?

Agnes Repplier (1858–1950)
Under Dispute, 1924

The lack of expression is perhaps the greatest enormity of all. I should prefer music to say something other than it should, rather than it should say nothing at all.

Jean Jacques Rousseau (1712–78)
Dictionary of Music, 1767

Of bestial howling, and entirely frantic vomiting up of damned souls through their still carnal throats, I have heard more than, please God, I will ever endure the hearing of again, in one of His summers.

> John Ruskin (1819–1900)
> On Italian singing

Beethoven always sounds to me like the upsetting of bags of nails, with here and there an also dropped hammer.

> John Ruskin
> Letter to John Brown, February 6, 1881

Whether in music or in personal appearance, ugliness, is, no doubt, an acquired taste, like the taste for tobacco, and similar nauseous appetites.

> C. K. Salaman (1814–1901)
> *On Music Criticism*, 1875

Music is essentially useless, as life is.

> George Santayana (1863–1952)
> *The Life of Reason*, 1905–6

How irksome is this music to my heart! When such strings jar, what hope of harmony?

> William Shakespeare (1564–1616)
> *Henry VI*, Part 2, 1590

I am never merry when I hear sweet music.

> William Shakespeare
> *The Merchant of Venice*, 1596

Let a short Act of Parliament be passed, placing all street musicians outside the protection of the law, so that any citizen may assail them with stones, sticks, knives, pistols, or bombs without incurring any penalties—except, of course, in the case of the instrument itself being injured; for Heaven forbid that I should advocate any disregard of the sacredness of property . . .

> George Bernard Shaw (1856–1950)
> *Morning Leader*, November 27, 1893

Hell is full of musical amateurs: music is the brandy of the damned.

> George Bernard Shaw
> *Man and Superman,* 1903

To the average Briton the fugue is still an acute phase of a disease of dulness which occasionally breaks out in drawing rooms, and is known there as classical music.

> George Bernard Shaw
> "Fugue out of Fashion," *Magazine of Music,* November 1885

I *hate* performers who debase great works of art: I long for their annihilation: if my criticisms were flaming thunderbolts, no prudent Life or Fire Insurance Company would entertain a proposal from any singer within my range, or from the lessee of any opera-house or concert-room within my circuit.

> George Bernard Shaw
> May 30, 1894

. . . I realize with a gasp . . . that this progressively more belligerent caterwauling can sell anything—concerts, records, movies. And I feel as if our entire society were ready to flush itself down in something even worse than a collective death wish—a collective will to live in ugliness and self-debasement.

> John Simon (1925–   ) from a review of
> *A Star Is Born* in *New York* magazine,
> January 10, 1977

It takes approximately twenty years to make an artistic curiosity out of a modernistic monstrosity, and another twenty years to elevate it to a masterpiece.

> Nicolas Slonimsky (1894–   )
> *The Lexicon of Musical Invective,* 1953

Those things that act through the ears are said to make a noise, discord, or harmony, and this last has caused men to lose their heads to such a degree that they have believed God himself is delighted with it.

> Benedict (Baruch) Spinoza (1632–77)
> *Ethics*, 1677

Do you remember when everyone began analysing Beatle songs? I don't think I understood what some of them were supposed to be about.

> Ringo Starr (1940–   ), 1969

The French are the wittiest, the most charming and (up to the present, at all events) the least musical race on earth.

> Stendhal (1783–1842)
> *Life of Rossini*, 1824

Today we hear so much musical sound all the time, in trains, in airplanes, in restaurants, that we are becoming deadened to it. Our sensitivity to music is in danger of being lost, just as we are becoming insensitive to the stupid brutality we see so much on television or in motion pictures. Still, we are able to turn off television, or walk out of a bad motion picture or poor concert. You can't walk out of an airplane.

> Leopold Stokowski (1882–1977)

Dear Mr. Edison,
For myself, I can only say that I am astonished and somewhat terrified at the result of this evening's experiment. Astonished at the wonderful form you have developed and terrified at the thought that so much hideous and bad music will be put on records forever.

> Sir Arthur Sullivan (1842–1900)
> On a "phonogram" to Thomas Alva Edison, 1888

I shall hate sweet music my whole life long.

> Algernon Charles Swinburne (1837–1909)
> *The Triumph of Time*

An "orchestra" in radio circles is any ensemble comprising more than three players, while a "symphony" program is one that includes Liszt's "Liebestraum."

> Deems Taylor (1885–1966)
> *Radio—A Brief for the Defence*

I never learned how to tune a harp, or play upon a lute; but I know how to raise a small and inconsiderable city to glory and greatness.

> Themistocles (?527–?460 B.C.)
> From Plutarch's *Parallel Lives*

Nobody is ever patently right about music.

> Virgil Thomson (1896–   )
> Quoted in *Pleasures of Music*,
> Edited by Jacques Barzun, 1951

We often feel sad in the presence of music without words; and often more than that in the presence of music without music.

> Mark Twain (1835–1910)

The harmony of a concert, to which you listen with delight, must have on certain classes of minute animals the effect of terrible thunder; perhaps it kills them.

> Voltaire (1694–1778)
> *Philosophical Dictionary*, 1764

I can't sing. As a singist I am not a success. I am saddest when I sing. So are those who hear me. They are sadder even than I am.

> Artemus Ward (Charles Farrar Browne)
> (1834–67)

Sweetest the strain when in the song the singer has been lost.

> Elizabeth Stuart Phelps Ward (1844–1911)
> *The Poet and the Poem*

> Listed into the cause of sin,
> Why should a good be evil?
> Music, alas! too long has been

Pressed to obey the Devil.
Drunken, or lewd, or light, the lay
Flower to the soul's undoing;
Widened and strewed with flowers the way
Down to eternal ruin.

Charles Wesley (1707–88)
The True Use of Music, 1749

If one hears bad music it is one's duty to drown it by one's conversation.

Oscar Wilde (1854–1900)
The Picture of Dorian Gray, 1891

Musical people are so absurdly unreasonable. They always want one to be perfectly dumb at the very moment when one is longing to be absolutely deaf.

Oscar Wilde
An Ideal Husband, 1895

If one plays good music people don't listen, and if one plays bad music people don't talk.

Oscar Wilde
The Importance of Being Earnest, 1895

Most people wouldn't know music if it came up and bit them on the ass.

Frank Zappa (1940–   )

Good music isn't nearly as bad as it sounds.

Harry Zelzer

Part Five
LIFT EVERY VOICE

WORDS AND/WITH/FOR/TO MUSIC

Pour not out words where there is a musician.
> Old Testament Apocrypha
> *Ecclesiasticus*

Speech is a sound in which song is locked.
> Anonymous

Verses are children of the lyre; they should be sung and not read.
> French proverb

How can chaste Minds delight in the Languishments of wanton Poetry, made yet more languishing by the Graces of Music?
> *The Ladies Library, Written by*
> *a Lady*, published by Richard Steele, 1732

Nothing is well capable of being well set to music that is not nonsense.
> Joseph Addison (1672–1719)
> *Spectator*

For music any words are good enough.
> Aristophanes (c. 450–388 B.C.)
> *Birds*, translation by J. R. Planché, 1846

A verbal art like poetry is reflective; it stops to think. Music is immediate; it goes on to become.

> W. H. Auden (1907–73)
> Quoted by Aaron Copland, *Music
> and Imagination*, 1952

Singing is speech made musical, while dancing is the body made poetic.

> Ernst Bacon (1898–)
> *Notes on the Piano*, 1963

Modern music, a language a thousand times richer than the language of words, is to speech what thought is to utterance; it arouses sensations and ideas in their primitive form, in that part of us where sensations and ideas have their birth, but leaves them as they are in each of us. That power over our inmost being is one of the grandest facts in music.

> Honoré de Balzac (1799–1850)
> *Massimilla Doni*, 1839

That which is not worth saying is sung.

> Pierre Augustin Caron de Beaumarchais (1732–99)
> *The Barber of Seville*, 1775

English is a terrible language for vocalising. Try singing "love" or "death." But ah!—*Liebe, Amore, tod!*

> Sir Thomas Beecham (1879–1961)

Lyrics should be heard, not seen.

> Jerry Bock (1928–)
> *Playwrights, Lyricists, Composers
> on Theater*, 1974

Songs used to have rhymes without reason. Now they have reason without rhymes.

> Sammy Cahn (1913–)
> Quoted in *ASCAP Today*, Winter 1975

Let a man try the uttermost to speak what he means, before singing is had recourse to.

> Thomas Carlyle (1795–1881)
> *Journal*, November 17, 1843

All speech, even the commonest speech, has something of song in it: not a parish in the world but has its parish-accent;—the rhythm or tune to which the people there sing what they have to say.

> Thomas Carlyle
> *Heroes and Hero Worship*, 1840

A poet always has too many words in his vocabulary, a painter too many colors in his palette, a musician too many notes on his keyboard.

> Jean Cocteau (1889–1963), 1918

> But he (his musical finesse was such,
> So nice his ear, so delicate his touch)
> Made poetry a mere mechanic art;
> And ev'ry warbler has his tune by heart.
> > William Cowper (1731–1800)
> > *Table Talk*, 1782

As poetry is the harmony of words, so music is that of notes!
> John Dryden (1631–1700)
> Dedication to Purcell's *Dioclesian*,
> 1690

A verse without music is a mill without water.
> Folquet of Marseilles (Middle Ages)

Nor is he a stranger to Poetry, which is musick in words; nor to Musick, which is poetry in sound.

> Thomas Fuller (1608–61)
> *The Holy State*, 1642

A libretto is work in verse that is handed over to a musician so that he may convert it into prose.

> Louis Gallet
> *Notes d'un librettiste*, 1891

Since most of the lyrics . . . were arrived at by fitting words to music already composed, any resemblance to actual poetry, living or dead, is highly improbable.

> Ira Gershwin (1896–   )
> *Lyrics on Several Occasions*, 1959

To be a lyricist, you've got to be a euphoric masochist.

> E. Y. "Yip" Harburg (1898–   )

Where words leave off, music begins.

> Heinrich Heine (1797–1856)
> Quoted by Peter Ilyich Tchaikovsky in
> a letter to Nadezhda Filaretovna
> von Meck, March 1, 1878

Sweet are the pleasures that to verse belong, and doubly sweet a brotherhood in song.

> John Keats (1795–1821)
> *Epistele to G. F. Mathew*

Music is a universal language. Where speech fails, then music begins. It is the natural medium for the expression of our emotions—the art that expresses in tones our feelings which are too strong and deep to be expressed in words.

> Charles W. Landon (1846–?)
> *The Study of Music in Public Schools*,
> 1886

Why "words for music" are almost invariably trash now, though the words of Elizabethan songs are better than any music, is a gloomy and difficult question.

> Andrew Lang (1844–1912)

Music is *not* a species of language, but language is a species of music.

Sidney Lanier (1842–81)
The Science of English Verse, 1880

Music and poetry together are a combination capable of realizing the most mystic conception. Through them the world, nature as a whole, is released from its profound silence and opens its lips in song.

Gustav Mahler (1860–1911)

Of every music it is true to say that the song begins where the word stops.

Jacques Maritain (1882–1973)
Creative Intuition in Art and Poetry, 1953

When I think of anything properly describable as a beautiful idea, it is always in the form of music. I have written and printed probably 10,000,000 words in English . . . but all the same I shall die an inarticulate man, for my best ideas beset me in a language I know only vaguely and speak only as a child.

H. L. Mencken (1880–1956)
Happy Days, 1940

Poetry that is all music is obviously relatively rare, for only a poet who is also a natural musician can write it, and natural musicians are much rarer in the world than poets.

H. L. Mencken
Smart Set, June 1920

. . . words seem to me so ambiguous, so vague, so easily misunderstandable in comparison with genuine music, which fills the soul with things a thousand times better than words.

Felix Mendelssohn (1809–47)

The thoughts which are expressed to me by music that I love are not too indefinite to be put into words, but on the contrary, too definite.

Felix Mendelssohn
Letter to Marc-André Souchay, 1842

. . . Verbalizations of emotions, particularly those evoked by music, are usually deceptive and misleading.

> Leonard B. Meyer (1918–   )
> *Emotion and Meaning in Music,* 1956

Let the word be the master of the melody, not the slave.

> Claudio Monteverdi (1567–1643)

> Music, oh how faint, how weak,
> Language fades before thy spell!
> Why should Feeling ever speak,
> When thou canst breathe her soul
> So well?
>
> > Thomas Moore (1779–1852)
> > *On Music*

Melody and speech belong together. I reject the idea of a pure music.

> Carl Orff (1895–   )

Music, when combined with a pleasurable idea, is poetry; music without the idea is simply music; the idea without the music is prose from its very definiteness.

> Edgar Allan Poe (1809–49)

Musick is the exaltation of poetry. Both of them may excell apart, but surely they are most excellent when they are joyn'd, because nothing is then wanting to either of their proportions; for thus they appear like wit and beauty in the same person.

> Henry Purcell (1659–95)
> *Preface to Dioclesian,* 1690

If music could be translated into human speech, it would no longer need to exist.

> Ned Rorem (1923–   )
> *Music from Inside Out,* 1967

Speech is man's most confused and egocentric expression; his most orderly and magnanimous utterance is song.

>Ned Rorem
>*The Final Diary*, 1974

Cheap music set to noble words exposes the cheapness of the music; beautiful and profound music set to insignificant words still communicates the beauty of the music.

>Artur Schnabel (1882–1951)
>*Music and the Line of Most Resistance,*
>1942

I can only speak of music in broken sentences.

>Robert Schumann (1810–56)
>Letter to Clara Wieck, April 13, 1838

Voltaire said that what was too silly to be said could be sung. Now you seem to think that what is too delicate to be said can be whistled.

>George Bernard Shaw (1856–1950)
>*Man and Superman,* 1903

It is only when a thought interpenetrated with intense feeling has to be expressed . . . that coherent words must come with the music.

>George Bernard Shaw
>*Music in London,* 1890–94

Verbal communication about music is impossible except among musicians.

>Virgil Thomson (1896–   )
>*The State of Music,* 1939

Poetry is the expression of earnest thought, singing is the prolonged utterance of that expression.

>Attributed to Chinese Emperor Ts'in
>(225–206 B.C.)

Having verse set to music is like looking at a painting through a stained-glass window.

> Paul Valéry (1871–1945)

Music must come first:
Chose for this an irregular rhythm,
More indefinite, more soluble in air,
With nothing clumsy or affected.
You must not at all
Chose your words without some contempt:
The finest song is a vague song
Where indecision joins precision.

> Paul Verlaine (1844–96)
> *The Art of Poetry,* 1884

Do not commit your poems to pages alone. Sing them, I pray you.

> Virgil (70–19 B.C.)
> *Aeneid*

Soft words, with nothing in them, make a song.
> Edmund Waller (1606–89)
> *To Mr. Creech,* c. 1635

If verbal language and its development has to be considered one of the most admirable achievements of the human spirit, then we must admire, in the creation of musical language, a prodigious feat of the human soul . . .

> Bruno Walter (1876–1962)
> *Of Music and Music-Making,* 1957

The highest poetry does not tend towards music, and the greatest music stands in no need of words.
> René Wellek (1903–   ) and Austin Warren (1899–   )
> *Theory of Literature,* 1956

Poetry is the true source of my music.

> Hugo Wolf (1860–1903)

A musician who would give me pleasure should not repeat a line, or put more than one note to a syllable. I am a poet not a musician, and dislike to have my words distorted or their animation destroyed, even though the musician claims to have expressed their meaning in a different medium.

William Butler Yeats (1865–1939)
A Note on the Setting of These
Poems to Music, 1922

Have not poetry and music emerged, as it seems, out of the sounds the enchanters made to help their imagination to enchant, to charm, to bind with a spell themselves and the passers-by?

William Butler Yeats

THE WINGS OF SONG

A well composed song or ballad strikes the mind, and softens
the feelings, and produces greater effect than a moral work, which
convinces our reason but does not warm our feelings or effect the
slightest alteration of our habits.

> Napoleon Bonaparte (1769–1821)

> To drop some golden orb of perfect song
> Into our deep, dear silence.
>> Elizabeth Barrett Browning (1806–61)
>> *Sonnets from the Portuguese*, 1850

Would you have your songs endure? Build on the human heart.
> Robert Browning (1812–89)
> *Sordello*, 1840

> Yet though I'm full of music
>   As choirs of singing birds,
> "I cannot sing the old songs"—
>   I do not know the words.
>> Robert Jones Burdette (1844–1914)
>> *Songs Without Words*

> I can not sing the old songs now!
>   It is not that I deem them low,
>   'Tis that I can't remember how
>   They go.
>> Charles Stuart Calverley (1831–84)
>> *Changed*

And this song is considered a perfect gem,
And as to the meaning, it's what you please.
> Charles Stuart Calverley
> *Ballad, after William Morris (The Auld Wife)*

And deep things are song. It seems somehow the very central essence of us, song; as if all the rest were but wrappings and hulls.
Thomas Carlyle (1795–1881)
On Heroes and Hero-Worship, and the Heroic in History, 1840

> There is an old French air,
> A little song of loneliness and grief—
> Simple as nature, sweet beyond compare—
> And sad—past all belief!
> > George Du Maurier (1834–96)
> > *Peter Ibbetson,* 1891

A song will outlive all sermons in the memory.
> Henry Giles (1809–82)

> I breathed a song into the air;
> That little song of beauty rare
> Is flying still, for all I know
> Around the world by radio.
> > Arthur Guiterman (1871–1943)
> > *Radiolatry*

You can't write a good song about a whore-house unless you been in one.
> Woody Guthrie (1912–67)
> Quoted in *Broadside,* 1, 1964

> From grief to great to banish
> Come songs, my lyric minions.
> > Heinrich Heine (1797–1856)
> > *Aus meinen grossen Schmerzen,*
> > translation by Louis Untermeyer

The question is whether a noble song is produced by nature or by art. I neither believe in mere labor being of avail without a rich vein of talent, nor in natural cleverness which is not educated.

> Horace (65–8 B.C.)
> *Ars Poetica*

By song the gods are pleased, and by song the deities below.

> Horace

Unlike poets, who frequently confess that they suffer frightful pangs, in partial compensation for which they allow themselves to feel superior, songwriters, reporters, and actors enjoy the superiority without any suffering whatever.

> Edward B. Marks (1865–1945)
> *They All Sang*, 1934

Song is man's sweetest joy.

> Musaeus (c. 900 B.C.)
> Quoted by Aristotle (384–322 B.C.)
> *Politics*

The most despairing songs are the most beautiful, and I know some immortal ones that are pure tears.

> Alfred de Musset (1810–57)

The song that we hear with our ears is only the song that is sung in our hearts.

> Ouida (Louise de la Ramée) (1839–1908)

Let kings and the triumphs of kings yield before songs.

> Ovid (43 B.C.–18 A.D.)
> *Amores*

Songs spring forth web-like from a mind at peace.

> Ovid
> *Tristia*

I would much rather have written the best song of a nation than its noblest epic.

> Edgar Allan Poe (1809–49)

The art of song had its origin in flattery.
> W. Winwood Reade (1838–75)
> *The Martyrdom of Man,* 1872

If unmelodious was the song, it was a hearty note and strong.
> Sir Walter Scott (1771–1832)
> *Marmion,* 1808

> For lo! the days are hastening on,
>   By prophet-bards foretold,
> When with the ever-circling years,
>   Comes round the age of gold;
> When Peace shall over all the earth
>   Its ancient splendors fling
> And the whole world send back the song
>   Which now *the angels sing.*
> > Edmund Hamilton Sears (1810–76)
> > *The Angels' Song*

I love a ballad but even too well; if it be doleful matter, merrily set down, or a very pleasant thing indeed, and sung lamentably.
> William Shakespeare (1564–1616)
> *The Winter's Tale,* 1610–11

> Now, good Cesario, but that piece of song,
> That old and antique song we heard last night;
> Methought it did relieve my passion much,
> More than light airs and recollected terms
> Of these most brisk and giddy-paced times:
> Come, but one verse.
> > William Shakespeare
> > *Twelfth Night,* 1599–1600

I can suck melancholy out of a song, as a weasel sucks eggs.
> William Shakespeare
> *As You Like It,* 1599–1600

> Our sincerest laughter
> With some pain is fraught;

Our sweetest songs are those
That tell of saddest thought.
                    Percy Bysshe Shelley (1792–1822)
                    To a Skylark, 1821

And this shall be for music when no one else
    is near,
The fine song for singing, the rare song to hear!
                    Robert Louis Stevenson (1850–94)
                    Romance (I Will Make You Brooches)

Is the sun yet cast out of heaven?
Is the song yet cast out of man?
Life that had song for its leaven
To quicken the blood that ran.
                    Algernon Charles Swinburne (1837–1909)
                    The Last Oracle

Of all of God's prerogatives, song is the fairest.
                    Theocritus (3rd century B.C.)
                    Idylls, c. 270 B.C.

Go, songs, for ended is our brief, sweet play;
    Go, children of swift joy and tardy sorrow:
And some are sung, and that was yesterday,
    And some unsung, and that may be tomorrow.
                    Francis Thompson (1859–1907)
                    Envoy

Nothing but songs is wanting here.

                    Virgil (70–19 B.C.)
                    Eclogues, 37 B.C.

Let me write the songs of a nashun and I don't care a cuss who
goes to the legislater.
                    Artemus Ward (Charles Farrar Browne) (1834–67)
                    In Washington, 1863

Slight not the songsmith.

> Sir William Watson (1858–1935)

> Lo, with the ancient
> Roots of man's nature,
> Twines the eternal
> Passion of song.

> Sir William Watson
> *England My Mother*

Melodrama, cleverness, contrivance, imitativeness, pretentiousness, aggressiveness, calculatedness, and shallowness may be elements which result in a hit song but never in a great song.

> Alec Wilder (1907–   )
> *American Popular Songs: The Great*
> *Innovators, 1900–1950,* 1972

> God guard me from the thoughts men think
> In the mind alone;
> He that sings a lasting song
> Thinks in the marrow-bone.

> William Butler Yeats (1865–1939)
> *A Prayer for Old Age,* 1935

SINGING AND SINGERS

There are three sexes: men, women and tenors.

Anonymous

A contralto is a low woman who sings.

Anonymous

Hark to the red-faced beeritone—Gargling, gorgling, gurgling.

Anonymous

There is no baseness in those who sing songs.

Gaelic proverb

Two people can sing together, but not speak together.

German proverb

Good singing is often wearisome.

French proverb, c. 1498

She was a town-and-country soprano of the kind often used for augmenting grief at a funeral.

George Ade (1866–1944)

Sing with your voices, and with your hearts, and with all your moral convictions, sing the new songs, not only with your tongue, but with your life.

St. Augustine (354–430)

To sing is to love and affirm, to fly and to soar, to coast into the hearts of the people who listen, to tell them that life is to live, that love is there, that nothing is a promise, but that beauty exists, and must be hunted for and found.

> Joan Baez (1941–)

Come sing now, sing; for I know ye sing well, I see ye have a singing face.

> Francis Beaumont (1584–1616) and
> John Fletcher (1579–1625)
> *The Wild Goose Chase,* 1621

Most of them sound like they live on seaweed.

> Sir Thomas Beecham (1879–1961)
> On sopranos, *Newsweek,* April 30, 1956

A singer able to sing so much as sixteen measures of good music in a natural, well-poised and sympathetic voice, without effort, without affectation, without tricks, without exaggeration, without hiatuses, without hiccupping, without barking, without baa-ing— such a singer is a rare, a very rare, an excessively rare bird.

> Hector Berlioz (1803–69)
> *A travers chants,* 1862

If she can strike a low G or F like a death-rattle and high F like the shriek of a little dog when you step on its tail, the house will resound with acclamations.

> Hector Berlioz
> *A travers chants,* 1862

He who finds himself gifted with a tunable Voice, and yet neglects to cultivate it, not only hides in the Earth a Talent of the highest value, but robs himself of that peculiar Pleasure, of which they only are conscious who exercise that Faculty.

> William Billings (1746–1800)
> Preface to *The New England*
> *Psalm Singer,* October 7, 1770

A tenor is not a man but a disease.

> Hans von Bülow (1830–94)
> Quoted by Harold C. Schonberg,
> *The Great Conductors,* 1967

There is not any Musicke of Instruments whatsoever, comparable to that which is made of the voyces of Men, where the voyces are good, and the same well sorted and ordered.

> William Byrd (1543–1623)
> *Reasons . . . To Persuade Everyone to
> Learn to Sing,* 1588

The tenor's voice is spoilt by affectation
    and for the bass, the beast can only bellow;
In fact, he had no singing education,
    an ignorant, noteless, timeless, tuneless fellow.

> George Gordon, Lord Byron (1788–1824)
> *Don Juan,* 1819–24

The prima-donna, though a little old,
    and haggard with a dissipated life,
And subject, when the house is thin, by cold,
    has some good notes.

> George Gordon, Lord Byron
> *Don Juan,* 1819–24

And her voice was the warble of a bird,
    So soft, so sweet, so delicately clear,
That finer, simpler music ne'er was heard;
    The sort of sound we echo with a tear,
Without knowing why—an overpowering tone,
    Whence Melody descends as from a throne.

> George Gordon, Lord Byron
> *Don Juan,* 1819–24

Let the singing singers
With vocal voices, most vociferous,

> In sweet vociferation, out-vociferise
> Ev'n sound itself.
>
> Henry Carey (1687–1743)
> *Chrononhotonthologos*, 1734

He that can charm a whole company by singing, and at the age of thirty, has no cause to regret so dangerous a gift, is a very extraordinary, and I may add, a very fortunate man.

> C. C. Colton (?1780–1832)
> *Lacon*, 1820

Her voice was precisely like a stringed instrument that one imagined to have fallen into disuse when the viola came along to replace it.

> Sir Noël Coward (1899–1973)
> Quoted by William Marchant,
> *The Privilege of His Company*, 1975

He who sings worse let him begin first.

> Desiderius Erasmus (?1466–1536)
> *Colloquia*, 1516

It seems simple to me, but for some people, I guess feelin' takes courage. When I sing, I'm saying: "Dig it, go on and try. Ain't nobody goin' make ya. Yeah, baby, dig me—dig me if you dare."

> Aretha Franklin (1942–   )

> Singin' in the rain . . .
>
> Arthur Freed (1894–   )
> "Singin' in the Rain,"
> Popular song title, 1929

The singing man keeps his shop in his throat.

> Thomas Fuller
> *Gnomologia*, 1732

> Let not the Ballad-Singer's shrilling Strain
> Amid the Swarm thy list'ning Ear detain:

Guard well thy Pocket; for these Syrens stand,
To aid the labours of the diving Hand.

> John Gay (1685–1732)
> *Trivia: or, The Art of Walking*
> *the Streets of London,* 1727

A wand'ring minstrel I,
A thing of shreds and patches,
of ballads, songs and snatches,
And dreamy lullaby!
My catalogue is long,
Through ev'ry passion ranging,
And to your humour's changing
I tune my supple song.

> Sir William Schwenck Gilbert (1836–1911)
> *The Mikado,* 1885

Let but thy voice engender with the string,
And angels will be borne, while thou dost sing.

> Robert Herrick (1591–1674)
> *Upon Her Voice*

Singing is near miraculous because it is the mastering of what is
otherwise a pure instrument of egotism: the human voice.

> Hugo von Hofmannsthal (1874–1929)

I would both sing thy praise and praise thy singing.

> Hugh Holland (d. 1633)
> *To Giles Farnaby*

A few can touch the magic string,
And noisy Fame is proud to win them:—
Alas for those that never sing,
But die with all their music in them!

> Oliver Wendell Holmes (1809–94)
> *The Voiceless*

She gave him the gift of sweet song.

> Homer (estimated between 12th and
> 9th centuries B.C.)
> *Odyssey*

All singers have this fault: if asked to sing among their friends they are never so inclined, if unasked they never leave off.

> Horace (68–5 B.C.)
> *Satires*, 35 B.C.

> If you hear a song that thrills you,
>   Sung by any child of song,
> Praise it. Do not let the singer
>   Wait deservèd praises long.
> Why should one who thrills your heart
>   Lack the joy you may impart?
>> Daniel Webster Hoyt (1845–1936)
>> *A Sermon in Rhyme*, 1878

Miss Truman is a unique American phenomenon with a pleasant voice of little size and fair quality . . . There are few moments during her recital when one can relax and feel confident that she will make her goal, which is the end of the song.

> Paul Hume (1915–   )
> Washington *Post*, December 18, 1950

The moment the human voice intrudes in an orchestral work, my dream-world of music vanishes, Mother Church is right in banishing from within the walls of her temples the female voice. The world, the flesh, and the devil lurk in the larynx of the soprano or alto, and her place is before the footlights, not as a vocal staircase to paradise.

> James Gibbons Huneker (1860–1921)
> *Ivory Apes and Peacocks*, 1915

She showed me the air and taught me how to fill it.

> Janis Joplin (1943–70)
> In tribute to Bessie Smith,
> Quoted by Chris Albertson, *Bessie*,
> 1972

Every modulated sound is not a song, and every voice that executes a beautiful air does not sing. Singing should enchant. But to produce this effect there must be a quality of sound and voice which is by no means common even with great singers.

Joseph Joubert (1754–1824)
Pensées, essais, maximes et correspondance, 1842

There is delight in singing, tho' none hear beside the singer.

Walter Savage Landor (1775–1864)
To Robert Browning

Singing . . . is as natural and common to all men as it is to speak high when they threaten in anger, or to speak low when they are dejected and ask for a pardon.

William Law (1686–1761)
A Serious Call to a Devout
and Holy Life, 1728

A vile beastly rottenheaded foolbegotten brazenthroated pernicious piggish screaming, tearing, roaring, perplexing, split-mecrackle crashmecriggle insane ass of a woman is practicing howling below-stairs with a brute of a singing master so horribly that my head is nearly off.

Edward Lear (1812–88)
Letter to Lady Strachey, January 24, 1859

As a singer, you're a great dancer.

Amy Leslie (1860–1939)
To George Primrose, *They All Sang*,
Quoted by Edward C. Marks, 1934

Singing is a noble art and a good exercise. It has nothing to do with worldly affairs, with the strife of the market place and the rivalries of the court. The singer fears no evil; he forgets all worry and is happy . . .

Martin Luther (1483–1546)
Table Talk, December 17, 1538

When in doubt, sing loud.

> Robert Merrill (1919–   )
> *The Saturday Evening Post*, October 26, 1957

. . . and likewise you shall be perfectly understood of the auditor what you sing, which is one of the highest degrees of praise which a musician in dittying can attain unto or wish for.

> Thomas Morley (c. 1557–1603)
> A *Plaine and Easie Introduction to Practicall Musicke*, 1597

My own objection to the prima donna is that, as a rule, she represents merely tone and technique without intelligence.

> Sir Ernest Newman (1868–1959)
> A *Musical Motley*, 1919

Choristers bellow the tenor, as it were oxen; bark a counterpart, as it were a kennel of dogs; roar out a treble, as it were a sort of bulls; and grunt out a bass, as it were a number of hogs.

> William Prynne (1600–69)
> *Histriomastix*, 1632

How much more finally rewarding for a composer to hear his songs sung by the Mindless Singer with a voice than by the Intelligent Artist without a voice.

> Ned Rorem (1923–   )
> *The Final Diary*, 1974

Bel canto is to opera what pole-vaulting is to ballet, the glorification of a performer's prowess and not a creator's imagination.

> Ned Rorem
> *The New Republic*, June 3, 1972

The good singer should be nothing but an able interpreter of the ideas of the master, the composer . . . In short, the composer and the poet are the only true creators.

> Gioacchino Rossini (1792–1868)
> Letter to Ferdinando Guidicini,
> February 12, 1851

I am convinced that people applaud a prima donna as they do the feats of the strong man at a fair. The sensations are painfully disagreeable, hard to endure, but one is so glad when it is all over that one cannot help rejoicing.

Jean Jacques Rousseau (1712–78)

It is quite possible to lead a virtuous and happy life without books, or ink; but not without wishing to sing, when we are happy; not without meeting with continual occasions when our song, if right, would be a kind service to others.

John Ruskin (1819–1900)

If you have any soul worth expressing, it will show itself in your singing.

John Ruskin
Sesame and Lilies, 1865

Tenors are usually short, stout men (except when they are Wagnerian tenors, in which case they are large, stout men) made up predominantly of lungs, rope-sized vocal chords, large frontal sinuses, thick necks, thick heads, tantrums and *amour propre* . . . It is certain that they are a race apart, a race that tends to operate reflexively rather than with due process of thought.

Harold C. Schonberg (1915–   )
Show, December 1961

Much is to be learned from singers male and female, But do not believe all they tell you.

Robert Schumann (1810–56)
Aphorisms, c. 1833

For my voice, I have lost it with halloing and singing of anthems.

William Shakespeare (1564–1616)
Henry IV, Part 2, 1597–98

Warble, child; make passionate my sense of hearing.

William Shakespeare
Love's Labour's Lost, 1594–95

She will sing the savageness out of a bear.

>William Shakespeare
>*Othello*, 1604

Come, sing me a bawdy song; make me merry.

>William Shakespeare
>*Henry IV*, Part 1, 1597–98

She sings like one immortal, and she dances as goddess—like to her admired lays.

>William Shakespeare
>*Pericles*, 1608–9

Actors and singers who have small voices should remember that the problem for them is to make themselves *heard*, and by no means to make themselves loud. Loudness is the worst defect of quality that any voice, large or small, can have.

>George Bernard Shaw (1856–1950)
>*Music in London*, 1890–94

Sing again, with your dear voice revealing
A tone
Of some world far from ours,
Where music and moonlight and feeling
Are one.

>Percy Bysshe Shelley (1792–1822)
>*To Jane: The Keen Stars Were Twinkling*

My spirit like a charmed bark doth swim
Upon the liquid waves of thy sweet singing.

>Percy Bysshe Shelley
>*Fragment: To One Singing*

When I'm performing I don't even think about whether I'm a girl or a boy or even what planet I'm from. My whole concept of performing is like screwing without touching.

>Patti Smith
>*Cash Box*, January 24, 1976

No instrument is satisfactory except in so far as it approximates to the sound of the human voice.

> Stendhal (1783–1842)
> *Life of Rossini*, 1824

Sweeter is your singing to the ear than honey to the lip.

> Theocritus (3rd century B.C.)
> *Idylls*, c. 270 B.C.

. . . The human voice is the oldest musical instrument and through the ages it remains what it was, unchanged; the most primitive and at the same time the most modern, because it is the most intimate form of human expression.

> Ralph Vaughan Williams (1872–1958)
> *National Music*, 1934

The Most High has a decided taste for vocal music, provided it be lugubrious and gloomy enough.

> Voltaire (1694–1778)
> *Philosophical Dictionary*, 1764

The oldest, truest, most beautiful organ of music, the origin to which alone our music owes its being, is the human voice.

> Richard Wagner (1813–83)
> *Opera and Drama*, 1851

A singer who is not able to recite his part according to the intention of the poet cannot possibly sing it according to the intention of the composer.

> Richard Wagner

Sweetest the strain when in the song the singer has been lost.

> Elizabeth Stuart Phelps Ward (1844–1911)
> *The Poet and the Poem*

Tenors are noble, pure and heroic and get the soprano, if she has not tragically expired before the final curtain. But baritones are born villains in opera. Always the heavy and never the hero . . .

> Leonard Warren (1911–60)
> New York *World-Telegram and Sun,*
> March 13, 1957

> Five-and-thirty black slaves,
>> Half-a-hundred white,
> All their duty but to sing
>> For their Queen's delight.
>>> Sir William Watson (1858–1935)
>>> *The Key-Board*

> For I will for no man's pleasure
> Change a syllable or measure;
> Pedants shall not tie my strains
> To our antique poets' veins;
> Being born as free as these,
> I will sing as I shall please.
>> George Wither (1588–1667)
>> *The Shepherd's Hunting,* 1615

OPERA AND OPERA SINGERS

There is nothing that has more startled our *English* Audience, than the *Italian Recitativo* at its first Entrance upon the Stage. People were wonderfully surprised to hear Generals singing the Word of Command, and Ladies delivering Messages in Musick. Our Countrymen could not forbear laughing when they heard a Lover chanting out a Billetdoux, and even the Superscription of a Letter set to a Tune . . .

> Joseph Addison (1672–1719)
> *Spectator*

I am ravished by opera, on condition that I have only a vague idea of what it is about. In this I wholly agree with Arnold Bennett, who maintained that opera was tolerable only when sung in a language he didn't understand.

> James Agate (1877–1947)
> *The Later Ego*, June 24, 1945

The opera is like a husband with a foreign title: expensive to support, hard to understand, and therefore a supreme social challenge.

> Cleveland Amory (1917–)
> On NBC Television, April 6, 1961

I do not mind what language an opera is sung in so long as it is a language I don't understand.

> Sir Edward Appleton (1892–1965)
> *The Observer*, London, August 28, 1955

No good opera plot can be sensible, for people do not sing when they are feeling sensible.

> W. H. Auden (1907–73)
> *Time*, December 29, 1961

Music in an opera should be like poetry—only another means of embellishing speech and one which must not be used to excess.

> Pierre Augustin Caron de Beaumarchais (1732–99)

If an opera cannot be played by an organ-grinder—as Puccini and Verdi's melodies were played—then that opera is not going to achieve immortality.

> Sir Thomas Beecham (1879–1961)
> May 21, 1955

Opera, n. A play representing life in another world, whose inhabitants have no speech but song, no motions but gestures and no postures but attitudes. All acting is simulation, and the word *simulation* is from *simia*, an ape; but in opera the actor takes for his model *Simia audibilis* (or *Pithecanthropos stentor*)—the ape that howls.

> Ambrose Bierce (1842–?1914)
> *The Devil's Dictionary*, 1911

The actor apes a man—at least in shape;
The opera performer apes an ape.

> Ambrose Bierce
> *The Devil's Dictionary*, 1911

A good opera will never be written. Music does not know how to narrate.

> Nicolas Boileau (1636–1711)
> Letter to Racine

In opera, as in decorative art, details and minutiae are out of place. Bold outlines only are necessary; all should be clear and straight forward . . . The voices should occupy the first place, the orchestra the second.

> Alexander Borodin (1833–87)
> Letter to Madame Ivanova Karmalina,
> June 10, 1876

The absurdity of opera lies in the fact that rational elements are used and three-dimensional reality is aimed at while at the same time everything is neutralized by the music.

> Bertholt Brecht (1898–1956)
> "The Modern Theatre Is the Epic
> Theatre," 1930

If an inhabitant of another planet should visit the earth, he would receive, on the whole, a truer notion of human life by attending an Italian opera than he would by reading Emerson's volumes. He would learn from the Italian opera that there were two sexes . . .

> John Jay Chapman (1862–1933)
> *Emerson, and Other Essays,* 1898

As for operas, they are essentially too absurd and extravagant to mention; I look upon them as a magic scene contrived to please the eyes and the ears at the expense of the understanding.

> Lord Chesterfield (1694–1773)
> Letter to his son, January 23, 1752

People are wrong when they say that the opera isn't what it used to be. It is what it used to be. That's what's wrong with it.

> Sir Noël Coward (1899–1973)
> *Design for Living,* 1933

Nobody really sings in an opera—they just make loud noises.

> Amelita Galli-Curci (1889–1963)

Opera is when a guy gets stabbed in the back and instead of bleeding, he sings.

> Ed Gardner (1905–63)
> *Duffy's Tavern* (radio show)

I endeavored to reduce music to its proper function, that of seconding poetry by enforcing the expression of the sentiment, and the interest of the situations, without interrupting the action, or weakening it by superfluous ornament.

> Christoph Willibald Gluck (1714–87)
> Preface to *Alceste*, 1767

Acting is very, very important in opera. But, of course, it is just as well if you also have a voice.

> Tito Gobbi (1915–)

The Opera is the most artificial of all things . . . It does not subsist as an imitation of nature, but in contempt of it; and, instead of seconding, its object is to pervert and sophisticate all our natural impressions of things.

. . . At the theater, we see and hear what has been said, thought and done by various people else where; at the Opera we see and hear what was never said, thought or done anywhere but at the Opera.

> William Hazlitt (1778–1830)
> *The Opera*

Opera is like an oyster; it must be swallowed whole or not at all.

> Spike Hughes (1908–) and Barbara McFadyean
> *Nights at the Opera*, 1948

Opera: an exotic and irrational entertainment.
> Samuel Johnson (1709–84)
> *Dictionary of the English Language*, 1755

The Greeks created superb tragedies in which some parts were sung; the French write poor ones, the whole of which is sung.
> Pier Jacopo Martelli (1665–1727)
> *Della tragedia antica e moderna*, 1715

Opera in English is, in the main, just about as sensible as baseball in Italian.

> H. L. Mencken (1880–1956)

The opera . . . is to music what a bawdy house is to a cathedral.

> H. L. Mencken
> Letter to Isaac Goldberg, May 6, 1925

Any subject is good for opera if the composer feels it so intently he must sing it out.

> Gian-Carlo Menotti (1911–   )
> *Time*, May 1, 1950

I think the music of an opera, like its poetry, is nothing more than a new artistic way of embellishing words, and one that should not be used to excess.

> Honoré Gabriel Riquetti, Count de Mirabeau (1749–91)

Going to the Opera, like getting drunk, is a sin that carries its own punishment with it, and that a very serious one.

> Hannah More (1745–1833)
> Letter to her sister, 1775

I should say that in an opera the poetry must be the obedient daughter of music . . . All the more will an opera succeed when the plot is well worked out, the words expressly written for the music and not twisted around for some miserable rhyme . . . Verse is no doubt indispensable to music, but rhyme, for the sake of rhyme—is a curse.

> Wolfgang Amadeus Mozart (1756–91)
> Letter to his father, October 13, 1781

Parsifal is the kind of opera that starts at 6 o'clock. After it has been going three hours you look at your watch and it says 6.20.

> David Randolph (1914–   )
> Quoted in *The American Treasury*,
> Edited by Clifton Fadiman, 1955

I shall say nothing here about this celebrated establishment (the Opera), unless it be that of all the Academies of the kingdom and the world it is assuredly that which makes the most noise.

> Jean Jacques Rousseau (1712–78)
> *Dictionnaire de musique*, 1768

Of all the affected, sapless, soulless, beginningless, endless, topless, bottomless, topsiturviest, scrannel-pipiest, tongs and boniest doggrel of sounds I ever endured the deadliest of, that eternity of nothing was the deadliest.

> John Ruskin (1819–1900)
> *On Die Meistersinger*, June 30, 1882

If you wish to know what an OPERA is, I shall tell you that it is a fantastical work of Poetry and of Music, in which the Poet and the Musician, equally embarrassed the one with the other, take great pains to turn out an evil work.

> Charles de Saint-Denis de Saint-Évremond (?1616–1703)
> Letter to George Villiers, Duke of Buckingham, 1678

Opera is free from any servile imitation of nature. By the power of music it attunes the soul to a beautiful receptiveness.

> Friedrich von Schiller (1759–1805)
> Letter to Johann Wolfgang von Goethe

If you will only take the precaution to go in long enough after it commences and to come out long before it is over, you will not find it wearisome.

> George Bernard Shaw (1856–1950)
> On Gounod's *La Rédemption*, 1882

Opera must not be a musical production in which one sings for the sake of singing, where everything moves along according to the beat . . . where the baton is of principal importance. Opera must be lifted to the realm of drama where one forgets the external workings of the machinery.

> Bedřich Smetana (1824–84)

We went to Mannheim and attended a shivaree—otherwise an opera—the one called "Lohengrin." The banging and slamming and booming and crashing were something beyond belief.

Mark Twain (1835–1910)
A Tramp Abroad, 1880

The present opera was "Parsifal" . . . The first act of the three occupied two hours, and I enjoyed that in spite of the singing.

Mark Twain
At the Shrine of St. Wagner

One goes to see a tragedy to be moved, to the opera one goes either for want of any other interest or to facilitate digestion.

Voltaire (1694–1778)

The Opéra is nothing but a public gathering place, where we assemble on certain days without precisely knowing why.

Voltaire
Letter to Cideville, 1732

Part Six
THE UNIVERSAL ART

THE MEDICINE OF A TROUBLED MIND

As vinegar upon nitre, so is he that singeth songs to a heavy heart.

> Old Testament
> Proverbs

And it came to pass, when the evil spirit from God was upon Saul, that David took the harp and played with his hand: so Saul was refreshed and was well, and the evil spirit departed from him.

> Old Testament
> I Samuel

We have to sing, you see, here in the darkness
All men have to sing—poor broken things,
We have to sing here in the darkness in the roaring flood.

> Sherwood Anderson (1876–1941)
> *Song of Industrial America*

Rugged the breast that music cannot tame.

> John Codrington Bampfylde (1754–96)
> *Sonnet,* 1778

Is there a heart that music cannot melt? Alas! how is that rugged heart forlorn.

> James Beattie (1735–1803)
> *The Minstrel,* 1771–74

In the germ, when the first trace of life begins to stir, music is the nurse of the soul; it murmurs in the ear, and the child sleeps;

the tones are companions of his dreams—they are the world in which he lives.

Antoine Bettini (1396–1487)

Music hath charms to sooth a savage beast.

James Bramston (?1694–1744)
The Man of Taste, 1733

Who hears music, feels his solitude peopled at once.

Robert Browning (1812–89)
Balaustion's Adventure, 1871

Among the instrumentalities of love and peace, surely there can be no sweeter, softer, more effective voice than that of gentle peace breathing music.

Elihu Burritt (1810–79)

Many men are melancholy by hearing music, but it is a pleasing melancholy that it causeth; and therefore, to such as are discontent, in woe, fear, sorrow, or dejected, it is a most present remedy.

Robert Burton (1577–1640)
The Anatomy of Melancholy, 1621

Music doth extenuate fears, furies, appeaseth cruelty, abateth heaviness, and to such as are wakeful it causeth quiet rest; it cures all irksomeness and heaviness of soul.

Cassiodorus (c. 485–c.585)

Where there is music, there can't be mischief.

Miguel de Cervantes Saavedra (1547–1616)
Don Quixote, 1605–15

Though the entertainments of music are very engaging; though they make a great discovery of the soul; and show it capable of strange diversities of Pleasure: yet to have our passion lie at the mercy of a little minstrelsy; to be fiddled out of our reason and sobriety; to have our courage depend upon a drum, or our devotions upon an organ, is a sign we are not as great as we might be.

Jeremy Collier (1650–1726)
"An Essay of Musick," 1702

Music hath charms to soothe a savage breast,
To soften rocks, or bend a knotted oak.
>>> William Congreve (1670–1729)
>>> *The Mourning Bride,* 1697

Music alone with sudden charms can build the wand'ring sense,
and calm the troubled mind.
>>> William Congreve
>>> *Hymn to Harmony*

Play, orchestra play,
Play something light and sweet and gay,
For we must have music
We must have music
To drive our fears away.
>>> Sir Noël Coward (1899–1973)
>>> "Play, Orchestra Play," popular song,
>>> 1935

People, if you hear me hummin' on this song
    both night and day—
I'm just a poor boy in trouble, trying
    to drive my blues away.
>>> Walter Davis
>>> "Worried Man Blues," 1932

Music charms every living thing if it follows its true nature.
>>> Robert Dow
>>> *Comments on Composers,* c. 1581

I went darkling, and whistling to keep myself from being afraid.
>>> John Dryden (1631–1700)
>>> *Amphitryon,* 1690

Where griping griefs the heart would wound
And doleful dumps the mind oppress,

There music with her silver sound
With speed is wont to send redress.
"A Song to the Lute in Music,"
Attributed to Richard Edwards (?1523–66)
Paradyse of Daynty Devises, 1576
(Quoted in Shakespeare's *Romeo and
Juliet*), 1594–95

Is it any weakness, pray, to be wrought on by exquisite music? to feel its wondrous harmonies searching the subtlest windings of your soul, the delicate fibres of life where no memory can penetrate, and binding together your whole being, past and present, in one unspeakable vibration; melting you in one moment with all the tenderness, all the love, that has been scattered through the toilsome years, concentrating in one emotion of heroic courage or resignation all the hard-learned lessons of self-renouncing sympathy, blending your present joy with past sorrow, and your present sorrow with all your past joy?

George Eliot (1819–80)

There is no feeling, perhaps, except the extremes of fear and grief, that does not find relief in music—that does not make a man sing or play the better.

George Eliot
The Mill on the Floss, 1860

Musick is said to be the rejoysing
of the hart:
Musicke comforteth the mynde,
and feareth the enimie.
John Florio (?1553–1625)
First Fruites, 1578

And if there come the singers and the dancers—buy of their gifts also. For they too are gatherers of fruit and frankincense, and that which they bring, though fashioned of dreams, is raiment and food for your soul.

Kahlil Gibran (1883–1931)
The Prophet, 1923

Music is a friend of labor; it lightens the task by refreshing nerves and spirit.

> William Green (1873–1952)
> Former President, American Federation
> of Labor

And I thought of the chord in the heart of man,
    that lies untouched so long,
From whence, though the summer days of
    joy, there comes no sound of song;
Till the wild black night of trouble descends
    and the hurricane sweeps the strings,
And out of the wail of passionate pain the
    perfect music rings.

> Horace George Groser
> *Legend of the Rhine*, c. 1885

Music is the medicine of a troubled mind.

> Walter Haddon (1516–72)
> *Lucubrationes Poemata:* Musica, 1567

Whenever I feel afraid
I hold my head erect
And whistle a happy tune
So no one will suspect I'm afraid.

> Oscar Hammerstein II (1895–1960)
> "I Whistle a Happy Tune,"
> Popular song, 1951

No friend like music when the last word's spoken
    And every pleading is a plea in vain;
No friend like music when the heart is broken,
    To mend its wings and give it flight again.

> Daniel Whitehead Hicky (1902–)
> *No Friend Like Music*

Take a music-bath once or twice a week for a few seasons, and you will find that it is to the soul what the water-bath is to the body.

>   Oliver Wendell Holmes (1809–94)
>   *Over the Teacups,* 1891

If you can sing a song that would make people forget their troubles . . . I'll give you a medal.

>   President Herbert Hoover (1874–1964)
>   Said to popular singer Rudy Vallee,
>   Quoted by Arthur M. Schlesinger, Jr.,
>   *The Crisis of the Old Order,* 1957

Black care shall be lessened by sweet song.

>   Horace (65–8 B.C.)
>   *Odes,* 24 B.C.

Who among us has not sought peace in a song?

>   Victor Hugo (1802–85)
>   *Les Rayons et les ombres,* 1840

Music furnishes a delightful recreation for the hours of respite from the cares of the day, and lasts us through life.

>   President Thomas Jefferson (1743–1826)

>   And the night shall be filled with music,
>   And the cares, that infest the day,
>   Shall fold their tents, like the Arabs,
>   And as silently steal away.
>   Henry Wadsworth Longfellow (1807–82)
>   *The Day Is Done*

Music is the art of the prophets, the only art that can calm the agitations of the soul; it is one of the most magnificent and delightful presents God has given us.

>   Martin Luther (1483–1546)

Every troublesome and laborious occupation useth musicke for solace and recreation; hence it is that manual labourers and mechanical artificers of all sorts keepe such a chaunting and singing in their shoppes—the tailor on his bulk, the shoemaker at his last, the mason at his wall, the ship boy at this oar, and the tinker at his pan.

> Thomas Mace (c. 1620–1710)

The sweetness and delightfulness of music has a natural power to lessify melancholy passions.

> Increase Mather (1639–1723)
> *Remarkable Providences*, 1684

And ever, against eating cares,
Lap me in soft Lydian airs,
Married to immortal verse,
Such as the meeting soul may pierce
In notes, with many a winding bout
Of linked sweetness long drawn out,
With wanton heed, and giddy cunning,
The melting voice through mazes running,
Untwisting all the chains that tie
The hidden soul of harmony.

> John Milton (1608–74)
> *L'Allegro*, 1632–33

How valuable a thing music is, and how useful for checking the mad impulses of the mind . . .

> Richard Mulcaster (?1530–1611)
> *For the Music of Thomas Tallis and*
> *William Byrd*, 1575

Music's the cordial of a troubled breast,
The softest remedy that grief can find;
The gentle spell that charms our care to rest
And calms the ruffled passions of the mind.
Music does all our joys refine,
And gives the relish to our wine.

> John Oldham (1653–83)
> *An Ode on St. Cecilia's Day*

Music has charms alone for peaceful minds.

> Alexander Pope (1688–1744)
> *Sappho to Phaon*, 1712

Music can soften pain to ease.

> Alexander Pope
> *Ode on St. Cecilia's Day*, 1713

Music, like balm, eases grief's smarting wound.

> Samuel Pordage (1633–?91)
> *The Siege of Babylon*, 1678

Music's force can tame the furious beast; can make the wolf or foaming boar restrain His rage; the lion drop his crested mane attentive to the song.

> Matthew Prior (1664–1721)
> *Solomon on the Vanity of the World*, 1718

> When things go wrong,
> A man ain't got a friend
> Without a song.
>> William (Billy) Rose (1899–1966) and
>> Edward Eliscu (1902–   )
>> "Without a Song," popular song, 1929

> In sweet music is such art,
> Killing care and grief of heart
> Fall asleep, or hearing die.
>> William Shakespeare (1564–1616)
>> *Henry VIII*, 1612

Naught so stockish, hard and full of rage,
But music for the time doth change his nature.
> William Shakespeare
> *The Merchant of Venice*, 1596–97

Where should the music be? i' the air or the earth? . . . This music crept by me upon the waters, allaying both their fury and my passion with its sweet air.

> William Shakespeare
> *The Tempest,* 1611–12

Sounds and sweet airs, that give delight
        and hurt not.
Sometimes a thousand twangling instruments
Will hum about mine ears, and sometime voices
That, if I then had waked after long sleep,
Will make me sleep again; and then, in dreaming,
The clouds methought would open and show riches
Ready to drop upon me, that when I waked,
I cried to dream again.

> William Shakespeare
> *The Tempest,* 1611–12

Without music we shall surely perish of drink, morphia, and all sorts of artificial exaggerations of the cruder delights of the senses.

> George Bernard Shaw (1856–1950)
> "The Religion of the Pianoforte," 1894

And music lifted up the listening spirit until it walked, exempt from mortal care, Godlike, o'er the clear billows of sweet sound.

> Percy Bysshe Shelley (1792–1822)
> *Prometheus Unbound,* 1819

A lamentable tune is the sweetest music to a woeful mind.

> Sir Philip Sidney (1554–86)
> *Arcadia,* 1590

A certain music, never known before, here lulled the pensive, melancholy mind.

> James Thomson (1700–48)
> *The Castle of Indolence,* 1748

When I hear music, I fear no danger. I am invulnerable. I see no foe. I am related to the earliest times, and to the latest.

Henry David Thoreau (1817–62)
Journals, January 13, 1857

I want to say something comforting in the way that music is comforting . . . In the end we shall have had enough of cynicism and scepticism and humbug and we shall want to live more musically.

Vincent van Gogh (1853–90)
Letters

Let us sing on our journey as far as we go; the way will be less tedious.

Virgil (70–19 B.C.)
Eclogues, 37 B.C.

Music has indeed nothing to do with the common seriousness of life; its character, on the contrary, is a sublime and grief-assuaging radiance . . . Though it smiles on us, it never makes us laugh . . .

Richard Wagner (1813–83)
On Poetry and Composition, 1879

Soft is the music that would charm forever.

William Wordsworth (1770–1850)
Not Love, Not War

When trouble troubles you,
Sing, baby, sing!
Do like the birdies do,
Sing, baby, sing!

Jack Yellen (1892–   )
"Sing, Baby, Sing," popular song, 1936

EMOTIONS, VAPORS, AND DISPOSITIONS

On certain natures, sound loud and meaningless has an exciting, almost an intoxicating effect, like crude colors and strong perfumes, the sight of flesh or the sadic pleasure in blood . . .

> From an article on jazz in
> the New Orleans *Times-Picayune*, 1918

> Music can noble hints impart
> Engender fury, kindle love;
> With unsuspected eloquence can move,
> And Manage all the man with secret art.
> Joseph Addison (1672–1719)

Why do rhythms and melodies, which are mere sounds, resem-
ble dispositions, while tastes do not, nor yet colors or smells?

> Aristotle (384–322 B.C.)

Music has its origins and its roots in the world of sentiment and
sensation. Musically melodious sounds are a sealed book to the intellect, which only describes and analyzes sensations . . .

> Amadeus Autodidaktus
> *Aphorismen über Musik*, 1847

The force of sound in alarming the passions is prodigious . . .
and thus, by the musician's art, we are by turns elated with joy, or
sunk in pleasing sorrow, roused to courage or quelled by grateful
terrors, melted into pity, tenderness and love, or transported to
the regions of bliss, in an ecstacy of divine praise.

> Charles Avison (?1710–70)
> *An Essay on Musical Expression*, 1752

It appears to me that it is the special province of music to move the heart.

Carl Philipp Emanuel Bach (1714–88)

Generally, music feedeth the disposition of spirit which it findeth.

Francis Bacon (1561–1626)

Music alone has the power to make us penetrate into ourselves; the other arts offer us only eccentric pleasures.

Honoré de Balzac (1799–1850)
Gambara, 1837

From the heart, may it go to the heart.

Ludwig van Beethoven (1770–1827)
Inscription on the manuscript score of
Missa Solemnis, Opus 123, 1824

Music is the art of expressing sentiments and passions through the medium of sound.

Fermo Bellini
Manuale di musica, 1853

Tone and sound are subordinate to ideas. Ideas are subordinate to feelings and passions.

Hector Berlioz (1803–69)
A travers chants, 1862

For music (which is earnest of a heaven,
Seeing we know emotions strange by it,
Not else to be revealed,) is like a voice,
A low voice calling fancy, as a friend,
To the green woods in the gay summer time.

Robert Browning (1812–89)
Pauline, 1833

Chords that vibrate sweetest pleasure thrill the deepest notes of woe.

Robert Burns (1759–96)
Sensibility How Charming

Truly fertile Music, the only kind that will ever move us . . . will be a Music conducive to Dream, which banishes all reason and all analysis.

> Albert Camus (1913–60)
> "Essay on Music," 1932

> When music, heavenly maid, was young,
> While yet in early Greece she sung,
> The Passions oft, to hear her shell,
> Thronged around her magic cell.
>> William Collins (1721–59)
>> *The Passions,* 1747

Music produces a kind of pleasure which human nature cannot do without.

> Confucius (c. 551–479 B.C.)
> *The Book of Rites,* c. 500 B.C.

> There is in souls a sympathy with sounds,
> And, as the mind is pitched the ear is pleased
> With melting airs, or martial, brisk, or grave.
> Some chord in unison with what we hear
> Is touched within us, and the heart replies.
>> William Cowper (1731–1800)
>> *The Winter Walk at Noon*

Music should sound, not screech; Music should cry, not howl; Music should weep, not bawl; Music should implore, not whine.
> Maud Cuney-Hare
> *Negro Musicians and Their Music,* 1936

Music arouses in us various emotions, but not the more terrible ones of horror, fear, rage, etc. It awakens rather the gentler feelings of tenderness and love, which readily passes into devotion . . . it likewise stirs up in us the sense of triumph and the glorious ardor for war.

> Charles Darwin (1809–82)
> *The Descent of Man,* 1871

The music I desire must be supple enough to adapt itself to the lyrical effusions of the soul and the fantasy of dreams.

Claude Debussy (1862–1918)

The object of music is sound. Its purpose is to give pleasure and excite various passions in us.

René Descartes (1596–1650)

What passion cannot music raise and quell!

John Dryden (1631–1700)
Song for St. Cecilia's Day, 1687

. . . be it laughter or tears, feverish passion or religious ecstasy, nothing, in the category of human feelings, is a stranger to music.

Paul Dukas (1865–1935)

No other art tells us such forgotten secrets about ourselves . . . It is in the mightiest of all instincts, the primitive sex traditions of the race before man was, that music is rooted.

Havelock Ellis (1859–1939)

O Music
In your depths we deposit our hearts and souls.
Thou hast taught us to see with our ears
And hear with our hearts.

Kahlil Gibran (1883–1931)

To music's pipe the passions dance.

Matthew Green (1696–1737)
The Spleen, 1737

To picture, or rather to rouse the passions is the chief and final aim of music.

Wilhelm Heinse (1746–1803)
Musikal Dialoge, 1805

The mellow touch of music most doth wound
The soul when it doth rather sigh, then sound.

Robert Herrick (1591–1674)
Hesperides, 1648

Begin to charme, and as thou stroak'st mine eares
With thy enchantment, melt me into tears.
Then let thy active hand scu'd o're thy Lyre:
And make my spirits frantick with the fire.
That done, sink down into a silv'rie straine;
And make me smooth as Balme and Oile againe.

Robert Herrick
To Musick

The reactions music evokes are not feelings, but they are the images, memories of feelings.

Paul Hindemith (1895–1963)
A Composer's World, 1952

Is not music the mysterious language of a distant realm of spirits, whose lovely sounds re-echo in our soul and awaken a higher, because more intensive life? All the passions, arrayed in shining and resplendent armor, vie with each other, and ultimately merge in an indescribable longing that fills our breasts. This is the heavenly effect of instrumental music.

Ernst Theodor Amadeus Hoffmann (1776–1822)
The Poet and the Composer, 1816

Music opens to man an unknown region, a world that has nothing in common with the world that surrounds him, a world in which he leaves behind all ordinary feelings to surrender himself to an inexpressible longing.

Ernst Theodor Amadeus Hoffmann

Music is an order of mystic, sensuous mathematics. A sounding mirror, an aural mode of motion, it addresses itself on the formal side to the intellect, in its content of expression it appeals to the emotions.

James Huneker (1860–1921)
Chopin: The Man and His Music, 1900

The imagination that responds to music is personal and associative and logical, tinged with affect, tinged with bodily rhythm, tinged with dream, but *concerned* with a wealth of formulations for its wealth of wordless knowledge, its whole knowledge of emotional and organic experience, of vital impulse, balance, conflict, the ways of living and dying and feeling.

>   Susanne K. Langer (1895–   )
>   *Philosophy in a New Key*, 1942

>   There's no passion in the human soul,
>   But finds its food in music.

>   George Lillo (1693–1739)
>   *Fatal Curiosity*, 1736

What rapturous flights of sound! What thrilling, pathetic chimes! What wild, joyous revelry of passion! What an expression of agony and woe! All the feelings of suffering and rejoicing humanity sympathized with and finding a voice in those tones.

>   Henry Wadsworth Longfellow (1807–82)
>   *Hyperion*, 1839

It is a glistening music we seek, giving to the aural sense voluptuously refined pleasures. At the same time, this music should be able to express noble sentiments.

>   Olivier Messiaen (1908–   )

Nevertheless, the passions, whether violent or not, should never be so expressed as to reach the point of causing disgust; and music, even in situations of the greatest horror, *should never be painful to the ear but should flatter and charm it, and thereby always remain music.*

>   Wolfgang Amadeus Mozart (1756–91)

Music hath two ends, first to please the sense, and that is done by the pure Dulcor of Harmony . . . and secondly to move ye affections or excite passion. And that is done by measures of time joyned with the former. And it must be granted that pure Impuls artificially acted and continued, hath great power to excite men to act but not to think . . . The melody is only to add to the diversion.

>   Roger North (1653–1734)
>   *The Musicall Gramarian*, 1728

There are certain pleasures which only fill the outward senses, and there are others also which pertain only to the mind or reason; but music is a delectation so put in the midst that both by the sweetness of the sounds it moveth the senses, and by the artificiousness of the number and proportions it delighteth reason itself.

> John Northbrooke (1568–79)
> *Against Dicing*, 1577

The half of music, I have heard men say, is to have grieved.

> Stephen Phillips (1864–1915)
> *Marpessa*, 1897

Music is born of feeling to appeal to feeling. It is created out of emotion to move the emotions. It is the product of human experience even if it transcends experience by crystallizing feeling.

> Julius Portnoy (1910–   )
> *The Philosopher and Music*, 1954

Music, I feel, must be emotional first and intellectual second.

> Maurice Ravel (1875–1937)

Music promotes an acute sensibility more powerful than passion itself. Music is a danger, but a blessing for those who can accept it.

> Odilon Redon (1840–1916)

Music, in and by itself, should generate a flow of pure emotion without the least tinge of extraneous rationalization.

> Max Reger (1873–1916)
> Letter to Adalbert Lindner, June 6, 1891

It (music) makes the dumb speak, and plucks from the animal heart potentialities of expression which might render it perhaps, even more than human.

> George Santayana (1862–1952)
> *Reason in Art*, 1905

Music stands quite alone. It is cut off from all the other arts
. . . It does not express a particular and definite joy, sorrow, anguish, horror, delight or mood of peace, but joy, sorrow, anguish,
horror, delight, peace of mind *themselves*, in the abstract, in their
essential nature, without accessories, and therefore without their
customary motives. Yet it enables us to grasp and share them fully
in this quintessence.

> Arthur Schopenhauer (1788–1860)
> *The World as Will and Idea*, 1819

All possible efforts, excitements, and manifestations of will, all
that goes on in the heart of man . . . may be expressed by the
infinite number of possible melodies.

> Arthur Schopenhauer
> *The World as Will and Idea*, 1819

It is music's lofty mission to shed light on the depths of the
human heart.

> Robert Schumann (1810–56)

(Music) reproduces for us the most intimate essence, the
tempo and the energy, of our spiritual being; our tranquility and
our restlessness, our animation and our discouragement, our vital-
ity and our weakness—all, in fact, of the fine shades of dynamic
variation of our inner life.

> Roger Sessions (1896–   )
> "The Composer and His Message," 1941

This music mads me: let it sound no more; For though it have
help madmen to their wits In me it will make wise men mad.

> William Shakespeare (1564–1616)
> *Richard II*, 1595–96

Music will express any emotion, base or lofty. She is absolutely
unmoral . . .

> George Bernard Shaw (1856–1950)
> *Music in London, 1890–94*, 1931

Music is killed by prudent reflections; the more a race is governed by its passions, the less it has acquired the habit of cautious and reasoned argument, the more intense will be its love of music.

> Stendhal (1783–1842)
> *Life of Rossini*, 1824

. . . What is music without a touch of pensive sadness in it?

> Stendhal
> *Life of Rossini*, 1824

Music is feeling, then, not sound.

> Wallace Stevens (1879–1955)
> *Peter Quince at the Clavier*

Music is indivisible. The dualism of feeling and thinking must be resolved to a state of unity in which one thinks with the heart and feels with the brain.

> George Szell (1897–1970)
> *Time*, February 22, 1963

Our music draws the listener away beyond the limits of everyday human joy and sorrow, and takes us to that lonely region of renunciation which lies at the root of the universe.

> Sir Rabindranath Tagore (1861–1941)

Music is the shorthand of emotion. Emotions which let themselves be described in words with such difficulty, are directly conveyed to man in music, and in that is its power and significance.

> Leo Tolstoy (1828–1910)

The organ of the emotions is sound, its intentionally aesthetic language is music.

> Richard Wagner (1813–83)
> *Das Kunstwerk der Zukunft*, 1850

This is the inmost secret of music, which can be felt but cannot be explicitly stated: the undulation and the contrasting natures of

wrath and love, of blissful pain, in which salamander and sylph
embrace and merge, are here united . . .

> Carl Maria von Weber (1786–1826)
> On E.T.A. Hoffmann's opera *Undine,* 1816

After playing Chopin, I feel as if I had been weeping over sins
that I had never committed, and mourning over tragedies that
were not my own. Music always seems to me to produce that
effect. It creates for one a past of which one has been ignorant
and fills one with a sense of sorrows that have been hidden from
one's tears.

> Oscar Wilde (1854–1900)
> *The Critic as Artist,* 1891

I can fancy a man who had led a perfectly commonplace life,
hearing by chance some curious piece of music, and suddenly, dis-
covering that his soul, without his being conscious of it, had
passed through terrible experiences, and known fearful joys, or
wild romantic loves, or great renunciations.

> Oscar Wilde
> *The Critic as Artist,* 1891

THE FOOD OF LOVE

Music is an incitement to love.

Latin proverb

A true music lover is one who on hearing a blonde soprano singing in the bathtub puts his ear to the keyhole.

Anonymous

> Music divine, proceeding from above,
> Whose sacred subject often times is love,
> In this appears her heavenly harmony,
> Whose tuneful concords sweetly do agree.
> And yet in this her slander is unjust,
> To call that love which is indeed but lust.
>
> Anonymous
Music Divine, 17th century

If music be the breakfast food of love, kindly do not disturb until lunch time.

James Agee (1909–55)
Agee on Film, 1958–60

A man in music, as one in love, either lives it or talks about it; seldom both.

Ernst Bacon (1898–   )
Notes on the Piano, 1963

Music is the most sensuous of arts to loving souls.

Honoré de Balzac (1799–1850)

If Music and sweet Poetry agree,
As they must needs (the Sister and the Brother)
Then must the love be great, 'twixt thee and me,
Because thou lov'st the one, and I the other.
                    Richard Barnfield (1574–1627)
                    In Praise of Musique and Poetrie, 1598

Which of the two powers, Love or Music, can elevate man to
the sublimest heights? It is a great problem, and yet it seems to
me that this is the answer: "Love can give no idea of music; music
can give an idea of love." Why separate them? They are the two
wings of the soul.

                              Hector Berlioz (1803–69)
                              Memoires, January 1, 1865

O, my Luve is like a red red rose
That's newly sprung in June:
O, my Luve is like the melodie
That's sweetly played in tune.
                              Robert Burns (1759–96)
                              A Red, Red Rose

I conclude that musical notes and rhythms were first acquired
by the male or female progenitors of mankind for the sake of
charming the opposite sex.

                    Charles Darwin (1766–1848)
                    The Descent of Man, 1871

You and the night and the music
Fill me with flaming desire.
                    Howard Dietz (1896–   )
                    "You and the Night and the Music,"
                    Popular song, 1934

I hear music when I look at you,
A beautiful theme of ev'ry dream I ever knew.
                    Oscar Hammerstein II (1895–1960)
                    "The Song Is You," popular song, 1932

With a song in my heart
I behold your adorable face.
Just a song at the start,
But it soon is a hymn to your grace.
>> Lorenz Hart (1895–1943)
>>> "With a Song in My Heart," popular song,
>> 1929

Since Mozart's day composers have learned the art of making music throatily and palpitatingly sexual.

> Aldous Huxley (1894–1963)

The creative flame finds its true nourishment only in love and in a fervent enthusiasm for beauty, truth and the pure ideal.

> Vincent d'Indy (1851–1931)

When I'm singing, I'm inside of it . . . I feel, oh, like I feel when you're first in love, when you're first touching someone . . . chills, things slipping all over me . . . a lot of times when I get off, I want to make love.

> Janis Joplin (1943–1970)

I lost my little darlin' the
>> night they were playin'
The beautiful Tennessee Waltz.
>> Pee Wee King and Redd Stewart
>> "Tennessee Waltz," popular song, 1948

Objectivity in music is rubbish . . . Have you ever had an objective love affair? And what is music but love?

>> Lili Kraus (1908–   )
>> New York *Times*, August 1, 1976

Music is love in search of a word.

>> Sidney Lanier (1842–81)
>> *The Symphony*, 1875

The musician is the complement of the scientist. The latter will superintend our knowing; the former will superintend our loving.

> Sidney Lanier
> "From Bacon to Beethoven," *Music and Poetry*, 1898

> Tonight, I mustn't think of her,
> Music, maestro, please!
>> Herb Magidson (1906–   )
>> "Music, Maestro, Please," popular song,
>> 1938

Music, as music, can never positively suggest the pornographic . . . It is amazing that novelists should harp forever upon the supposed suggestiveness of music, when it is unspeakably feeble in this respect compared with either poetry, prose or painting.

> Sir Ernest Newman (1868–1959)
> *Weekly Critical Review*, London, 1903

In the brothels, music had the same function as wine, spirits, and striptease: it helped prepare clients for the main event upstairs.

> Tony Palmer
> *All You Need Is Love*, 1976

A love song is just a caress set to music.

> Sigmund Romberg (1877–1951)

Love is a mystery which, when solved, evaporates. The same holds for music.

> Ned Rorem (1923–   )
> *Music from Inside Out*, 1967

When I play, I make love—it is the same thing.

> Arthur Rubinstein (1887–   )
> *Arthur Rubinstein—Love of Life*, film, 1975

The shy whoresons
Have got a speeding trick to lay down ladies;
A French song and a fiddle has no fellow.
William Shakepeare (1564–1616)
Henry VIII, 1612

I am advised to give her music o'mornings, they say it will penetrate.

William Shakespeare
Cymbeline, 1609–10

If music be the food of love, play on;
Give me excess of it, that, surfeiting,
The appetite may sicken, and so die.
That strain again! It had a dying fall:
O! it came o'er my ear like the sweet sound
That breathes upon a bank of violets,
Stealing and giving odour!

William Shakespeare
Twelfth Night, 1599–1600

Give me some music; moody food
Of us that trade in love.

William Shakespeare
Antony and Cleopatra, 1606

He capers nimbly in a lady's chamber to the
lascivious pleasing of a lute.

William Shakespeare
Richard III, 1592–93

Let rich music's tongue unfold the imagined happiness
that both receive in either by this dear encounter.

William Shakespeare
Romeo and Juliet, 1594–95

No, Music thou are not the "food of love,"
Unless love feeds upon its own sweet self,
Till it becomes all Music murmurs of.
                          Percy Bysshe Shelley (1792–1822)
                          Fragment: To Music

Is not music the food of love?
                          Richard Brinsley Sheridan (1751–1816)
                          The Rivals, 1775

Doubt you to whom my Muse these notes
          intendeth,
Which now my breast o'ercharged to music
          lendeth?
To you, to you all song of praise is due;
Only in you my song begins and endeth.
                          Sir Philip Sidney (1554–86)
                          Astrophel and Stella, Song I

The wine of Love is music,
And the feast of Love is song:
And when Love sits down to the banquet,
Love sits long.
                          James Thomson (1834–82)
                          The Vine

Like sex is the thing today, you know, so I try to write a little
something hinting at sex. Like one song I wrote, "Kay got laid
and Joe got paid."
                          Tina Turner, popular singer (c. 1938–   )

Music is the imagination of love in *sound*. It is what man imagines of his life, and his life is love.
                          W. J. Turner
                          Orpheus, or the Music of the Future, 1926

Oh, how peacefully then shall my bones rest, If your reed shall
make music of my loves!
                          Virgil (70–19 B.C.)
                          Eclogues, 37 B.C.

. . . What love is to man, music is to man as well as to the arts; for it is love itself, the purest, most ethereal language of the passions, containing their innumerable and constantly changing colors, yet expressing only one truth that is immediately understood by a thousand people endowed with the most widely divergent feelings.

> Carl Maria von Weber (1786–1826)
> On E.T.A. Hoffmann's opera *Undine,* 1816

THE LINGERING MELODY

Dear, they're playing our song.

Anonymous

They don't write songs like that anymore.

Anonymous

> I cannot sing the old songs
> I sang long years ago,
> For heart and voice would fail me,
> and foolish tears would flow.
>> Charlotte Alington Barnard (1830–69)
>> *I Cannot Sing the Old Songs*

Good music penetrates the ear with facility and quits the memory with difficulty.

Sir Thomas Beecham (1879–1961)
New York Times, March 9, 1961

"The Song Is Ended [But the Melody Lingers On.]"

Irving Berlin (1888–   )
Popular song title, 1927

There is nothing finer on which to hang a memory than a song.

Gene Buck (1885–1957)
President, American Society of
Composers, Authors and Publishers
(ASCAP)

Music once admitted to the soul becomes a sort of spirit, and never dies; It wanders perturbedly through the halls and galleries of the memory, and is often heard again, distinct and living as when it first displaced the wavelets of the air.

> Edward George Bulwer-Lytton (1803–73)
> *Zanoni*, 1842

> Yet though I'm filled with summer
> As choirs of singing birds,
> "I cannot sing the old songs"—
> I do not know the words.

>> Robert Jones Burdette (1844–1914)
>> *Songs Without Words*

A song that is well and artificially made cannot be well perceived nor understood at the first hearing, but the oftner you shall heare it, the better cause for liking you will discover: and commonly that Song is best esteemed with which our eares are most acquainted.

> William Byrd (1543–1623) 1611

> I can not sing the old songs now!
> It is not that I deem them low;
> 'Tis that I can't remember how
> They go.

>> Charles Stuart Calverley (1831–1884)
>> *Changed*

> You call it a waste of time, this taste
>   For popular tunes, and yet
> Good-bye to care when you whistle the air
>   Of the song that you can't forget.

>> Guy Wetmore Carryl (1873–1904)
>> *The Organ Man*

I wanna hear it again,
I wanna hear it again
The Old Piano Roll Blues.

> Cy Coben (1919–   )
> "The Old Piano Roll Blues,"
> popular song, 1949

How cruelly sweet are the echoes that start
When memory plays an old tune on the heart!

> Eliza Cook (1817–1889)
> *Old Dobbin*

Weep no more my lady
Oh! Weep no more today
We will sing one song for the
    old Kentucky home,
For the old Kentucky home far away.

> Stephen Foster (1826–64)
> "My Old Kentucky Home," 1853

Music, in the best sense, does not require novelty; nay, the older it is, and the more we are accustomed to it, the greater its effect.

> Johann Wolfgang von Goethe (1749–1832)

When people hear good music, it makes them homesick for something they never had and never will have.

> Edgar W. ("Ed") Howe
> *Country Town Sayings*, 1911

I think there must be a place in the soul all made of tunes
Of tunes of long ago.

> Charles Ives (1874–1954)
> "The Things Our Fathers Loved," song, 1905

We love music for the buried hopes, the garnered memories, the tender feelings it can summon at a touch.

> Letitia Elizabeth Landon (1802–38)

When I hear music, it seems to me that all the sins of my life pass slowly by me with veiled faces, and lay their hands on my head and say softly, My Child.

Sidney Lanier (1842–81)

In spite of myself, the insidious mastery of
song
Betrays me back, til the heart of me weeps
to belong.
To the old Sunday Evenings at home, with winter
outside
And hymns in the cozy parlour, the tinkling piano
our guide.

D. H. Lawrence (1885–1930)
Selected Poems

I know a sheaf of splendid songs by heart
Which stir the blood or move the soul to tears,
Of death or honor or of love's sweet smart,
The runes and legends of a thousand years;
And some of them go plaintively and slow,
And some are jolly like the earth in May—
But this is *really* the best song I know:
    I-tiddly-iddly-i-ti-iddly-ay.

Theodore Maynard (1890–1956)
Ballade of the Best Song in the World

Great music is a psychical storm, agitating to fathomless depths the mystery of the past within us. Or we might say that it is a prodigious incantation. There are tones that call up all ghosts of youth and joy and tenderness;—there are tones that evoke all phantom pains of perished passion;—there are tones that revive all dead sensations of majesty and might and glory,—all expired exultations,—all forgotten magnanimities. Well may the influence of music seem inexplicable to the man who idly dreams that his life began less than a hundred years ago! He who has been initiated into the truth knows that to every ripple of melody, to every billow of harmony, there answers within him, out of the Sea of

Death and Birth, some eddying immeasurable of ancient pleasure
and pain.

>   Paul Elmer More (1864–1937)
>   *Shelburne Essays*: "Lafcadio Hearn," (1904–10)

So-called light music has its own value, not really belonging to
music at all. Because, unlike serious work, it lacks musical content, it acts as a series of vials, often charmingly shaped and
coloured, for the distillations of memory. The first few bars of it
remove the stopper; we find ourselves re-living, not remembering,
but magically recapturing, some exact moments of our past.

>   J. B. Priestley (1894–   )
>   *Margin Released,* 1962

The pleasure in music recalled is virtually non-existent. Music
must be reheard to be re-experienced.

>   Ned Rorem (1923–   )
>   *Pure Contraption,* 1974

Often I listen still after the song has ended.

>   Jean-François, Marquis de Saint-Lambert (1716–1803)

Music, when soft voices die, vibrates in the memory . . .

>   Percy Bysshe Shelley (1792–1822)
>   *To ——: Music, When Soft Voices,* 1821

Music revives the recollections it would appease.

>   Madame de Staël (1766–1817)
>   *Corinne,* 1807

>   Mister Jefferson Lord, play that barber
>   shop chord.
>   That soothing harmony, it makes an
>   awful, awful hit with me.

>   William Tracey (1903–57)
>   "Play That Barber Shop Chord,"
>   popular song, 1910

To make music memorable is to play it over and over again.
> Jonathan Tunick (1938–)
> Quoted by Craig Zadan, *Sondheim & Co.*,
> 1974

> Old songs are best—how sweet to hear
> The strains to home and memory dear!
> Old books are best—how tale and rhyme
> Float with us down the stream of time!
> > Clarence Urmy (1858–1923)
> > *Old Songs Are Best*

The tune I still retain, but not the words.
> Virgil (70–19 B.C.)
> *Eclogues*, translated by
> John Dryden, 1697

> A quality
> Which music sometimes has, being the Art
> Which is most nigh to tears and memory.
> > Oscar Wilde (1854–1900)
> > *The Burden of Itys*, 1881

Sweetest melodies are those that are by distance made more sweet.
> William Wordsworth (1770–1850)

The music in my heart I bore long after it was heard no more.
> William Wordsworth
> *The Solitary Reaper*, 1807

LET ME HAVE MUSIC DYING

Music has here entombed a rich possession, but still more beautiful hopes.

> Inscription on a monument to
> Franz Schubert, Vienna, 1872

Here lyes Henry Purcell Esqre, who left Lyfe and is gone to that Blessed Place where only his harmony can be exceeded.

> Epitaph for Henry Purcell, 1695

Is it not fine to dance and sing when the bells of death do ring?

> Anonymous
> Medieval English rhyme

He sang one song and died—no more but that;
A single song and carelessly complete.

> Henry Augustin Beers (1847–1926)
> *The Singer of One Song*

My message to the world is "Let's swing, sing, shout, make noise! Let's not mimic death before our time comes! Let's be wet and noisy."

> Mel Brooks
> Interview in the New York *Times*,
> March 30, 1975

Until I die there will be sounds. And they will continue following my death. One need not fear about the future of music.

> John Cage (1912–)
> *Silence*, 1961

> Swans sing before they die—
> 'twere no bad thing
> Did certain persons die
> before they sing.
>> Samuel Taylor Coleridge (1772–1834)
>> *Epigram on a Volunteer Singer*, 1800

All Paradise opens! Let me die eating ortolans to the sound of soft music!
> Benjamin Disraeli (1804–81)
> *The Young Duke*, 1831

> Since I am coming to that holy room,
> where, with thy quire of Saints for evermore,
> I shall be made thy Music; as I come
> I tune the instrument here at the door,
> and what I must do then, think here before.
>> John Donne (1572–1631)
>> *Hymn to God in My Sickness*

Kindly watcher by my bed, lift no voice in prayer,
> Waste not any words on me, when the hour is nigh.
Let a stream of melody but flow from one sweet player,
> And meekly will I lay my head and fold
> my hands to die.
>> George Du Maurier (1834–96)
>> Adapted from the French of René
>> Sully Prudhomme (1839–1907)

I think songwriters have the greatest obituaries in the world. When a songwriter dies, the minute you read the list of songs he wrote, you start to identify with him . . . People read the obit and they respond, "Oh, my God, he wrote *that*. I remember the first time I heard that song, I was at a dance with a girl . . ."
> Abel Green (1900–   )
> Quoted by Max Wilk, *They're Playing*
> *Our Song*, 1973

Let me have music dying, and I seek
No more delight.

> John Keats (1795–1821)
> *Endymion,* 1818

What is life but a series of preludes to that unknown song whose first solemn note is sounded by death?

> Alphonse de Lamartine (1790–1869)
> *Méditations poétiques,* 1820

It is sobering to consider that when Mozart was my age he had already been dead for a year.

> Tom Lehrer (1928–   )

"They Needed a Songbird in Heaven, So God Took Caruso Away."

> George A. Little (1890–1946)
> and Jack Stanley (1890–1936)
> Popular song title, 1921

He is dead, the sweet musician!
He the sweetest of all singers!
He has gone from us forever,
He has moved a little nearer
To the Master of all music,
To the Master of all singing!

> Henry Wadsworth Longfellow (1807–82)
> *Hiawatha,* 1855

When *my* time comes, I hope there won't be so much brass.

> Mrs. E. Wallace Matthews
> While leaving in the middle of a
>   performance of Richard Strauss's
>   *Death and Transfiguration,*
>   quoted by Herbert Kupferberg,
>   *Those Fabulous Philadelphians,*
>   1969

Full lasting is the song, though he, the singer, passes.
> George Meredith (1828–1909)
> *The Thrush in February*

Let me die to the delicious sounds of music.
> Honoré Gabriel Riquetti, Count de Mirabeau (1749–91)
> Last words

And grant that when I face the grisly Thing,
  My song may trumpet down the gray Perhaps
Let me be as a tune-swept fiddle string
  That feels the Master Melody—and snaps.
> John G. Neihardt (1881–   )
> *Let Me Live Out My Years*

Songs have immunity from death.
> Ovid (43 B.C.–18 A.D.)

A young composer came to Brahms and asked if he might play for the master a funeral march he had composed in memory of Beethoven. Well, permission was granted, and the young man earnestly played away. When he was through, he sought Brahms's opinion. "I tell you," said the great man candidly, "I'd be much happier if you were dead and Beethoven had written the march."
> André Previn (1929–   )
> *Music Face to Face*, 1971

When I am dead, my dearest,
Sing no sad songs for me;
Plant thou no roses at my head,
Nor shady cypress tree.
> Christina Georgina Rossetti (1830–94)
> *Song*

Oh, I cannot help it, I should like to sing myself to death like a nightingale . . .
> Robert Schumann (1810–56)

Why then a final note prolong,
Or lengthen out a closing song.
                    Sir Walter Scott (1771–1832)
                    L'Envoi

I will play the swan, and die in music.
                    William Shakespeare (1564–1616)
                    Othello, 1604

There is no shadow of death anywhere in Mozart's music.
Even his own funeral was a failure. It was dispersed by a shower
of rain; and to this day nobody knows where he was buried or
whether he was buried at all or not. My own belief is that he was
not. Depend on it, they had no sooner put up their umbrellas and
bolted for the nearest shelter than he got up, shook off his bones
into the common grave of the people, and soared off into
universality.
                    George Bernard Shaw (1856–1950)
                    Music in London, 1890–94, 1931

As a matter of business . . . in music, as in joiner's work, you
can take the poorest materials and set the public gaping at them
by simply covering them with black cloth and coffin-nails.
                    George Bernard Shaw
                    Reviewing Dvořák's *Requiem,*
                    November 9, 1892

I would rather be remembered by a song than by a victory.
                    Alexander Smith (1830–67)
                    Dreamthorp: "Men of Letters," 1863

Bright is the ring of words
When the right man rings them,
Fair the fall of songs
When the singer sings them.
Still they are carolled and said—
On wings they are carried—

After the singer is dead
And the maker buried.
Robert Louis Stevenson (1850–94)
Songs of Travel, 1896

I believe in a last judgement that shall fearfully damn all those who have dared on this earth to make profit out of this chaste and holy art—who have disgraced it and dishonored it . . . I believe that such men will be condemned to hear their own music through all eternity.
Richard Wagner (1813–83)
And End in Paris, 1840

Yes, death is strong, but look you, the strongest, Stronger is music than death.
Franz Werfel (1890–1945)
The Beyond, 1943

My lute, awake! perform the last Labour that thou and I shall waste, the end that I have now begun; For when this song is sung and past, my lute, be still, for I have done.
Sir Thomas Wyatt (?1503–42)

SOLITUDE

Who hears music, feels his solitude peopled at once.
                              Robert Browning (1812–89)
                              Balaustion's Adventure, 1871

Respect all such as sing when all alone.
                                        Robert Browning
                                        Paracelsus, 1835

Music was invented to confirm human loneliness.
                              Lawrence Durrell (1912–   )
                              Clea, 1960

No more than any other talent is that for music susceptible of complete enjoyment where there is no second party to appreciate its exercise.
                              Edgar Allan Poe (1809–49)

Men, even when alone, lighten their labors by artless song.
                              Quintilian
                              Institutio Oratoria, c. 95 A.D.

In any corner of the earth where solitude and imagination go hand in hand, men learn soon enough to love music.
                              Stendhal (1783–1842)
                              Life of Rossini, 1824

WARRIORS FIRED WITH ANIMATED SOUNDS

If ye go to war . . . ye shall blow an alarm with the trumpets.
                                                    Old Testament
                                                    Numbers

And it came to pass as they came, when David was returned
from the slaughter of the Philistine, that the women came out of
all cities of Israel, singing and dancing, to meet King Saul, with
tabrets, with joy, and with instruments of music.

                                                    Old Testament
                                                    I Samuel

If the trumpet give an uncertain sound, who shall prepare himself to the battle?

                                                    New Testament
                                                    I Corinthians

War is having the customary depressing effect on musical
events.

                                    Monthly Musical Record, London,
                                    January 1900

Ah God, how pretty war is with its songs, its long rests!
                                    Guillaume Apollinaire (1880–1918)
                                    L'Adieu du Cavalier

All the delusive seduction of martial music.
                                    Fanny Burney (1752–1840)

For the great Gaels of Ireland
    Are the men that God made mad,
For all their wars are merry
    And all their songs are sad.
                Gilbert Keith Chesterton (1874–1936)
                Ballad of the White Horse

The best sort of music is what it should be—sacred; the next best, the military, has fallen to the lot of the devil.
                Samuel Taylor Coleridge (1772–1834)
                Table Talk, July 6, 1833

Have you not observed a Captain at the Head of a Company, how much he is altered at the Beat of a Drum? What a vigorous Motion, what an erected Posture, what an enterprising Visage, all of a sudden? His blood charges in his veins, his Spirits jump like Gunpowder, and seem impatient to attack the Enemy.
                Jeremy Collier (1650–1726)
                An Essay of Musick, 1702

When music and courtesy are better understood and appreciated, there will be no war.
                Confucius (551–479 B.C.)

The bombing of Pearl Harbor sent me out on my rounds . . . to obtain reactions from the tradesters. Most of them said it was a hell of a note.
        Dave Dexter
        (former editor of *Down Beat*) in
        Playback, 1976

The trumpet's loud clangor
    Excites us to arms,
With shrill notes of anger,
    And mortal alarms.
              John Dryden (1631–1700)
              A Song for St. Cecilia's Day, 1687

I am devilishly afraid, that's certain; but . . . I'll sing that I may seem valiant.

> John Dryden
> *Amphitryon,* 1690

> But not artist
> Hath yet discovered, by the tuneful song,
> And varied modulations of the lyre,
> How we those piercing sorrows may assuage
> Whence slaughters and such horrid mischief spring
> As many a prosperous mansion have o'erthrown.
> Could music interpose her healing aid
> In these inveterate maladies, such gift
> Had been the first of blessings to mankind.
>> Euripides (c. 485–406 B.C.)
>> *Medea,* translation by M. Wodhull

Lots of people who complained about us receiving the MBE received theirs for heroism in the war—for killing people. We received ours for entertaining other people. I'd say we deserve ours more.

> John Lennon (1940–   )
> *Beatles Illustrated Lyrics,* 1969

Sonorous metal blowing martial sounds.

> John Milton (1608–74)
> *Paradise Lost,* 1667

Without music a State cannot exist. All the disorders, all the wars which we see in the world, only occur because of the neglect to learn music. Does not war result from a lack of union among men? . . . And were all men to learn music, would not this be the means of agreeing together, and of seeing universal peace reign throughout the world?

> Molière (1622–73)
> *The Bourgeois gentilhomme,* 1670

How good bad music and bad reasons sound when one marches against an enemy.

> Friedrich Nietzsche (1844–1900)

Indulged in to excesses, music emasculates instead of invigorating the mind, causing a relaxation of the intellectual faculties, and debasing the warrior into an effeminate slave, destitute of all nerve and energy of soul.

> Plato (?427–347 B.C.)
> *Republic*

Indeed, if we will take pains to consider their compositions, and the airs on the flute to which they marched when going to battle, we shall find that Terpander and Pindar had reason to say that music and valor were allied.

> Plutarch (c. 46–120 A.D.)
> *Lives*

> Warriors she fires with animated sounds,
> Pours balm into the bleeding lover's wounds.
> Alexander Pope
> *Ode for Music on St. Cecilia's Day*, 1708

Music, even bad music, does not inspire ideological behavior. The regular beat of a march may impel men toward battle, but will it impel them away from battle?

> Ned Rorem (1923–   )
> *Pure Contraption*, 1974

Song forbids victorious deeds to die.

> Friedrich von Schiller (1759–1805)

Make all our trumpets speak; give them all breath, those clamorous harbingers of blood and death.

> William Shakespeare (1564–1616)
> *Macbeth*, 1605–6

Friends and foe submit to the song of the bard. Often when two armies meet, and swords are drawn, and lances set, the bards throw themselves between the contending parties and pacify them, as one by magic subdues the wild beast.

> Diodorus Siculus (1st century B.C.)
> *Bibliotheca Historica*, c. 44 B.C.

Explain it as we may, a martial strain will urge a man into the front rank of battle sooner than an argument, and a fine anthem excite his devotion more certainly than a logical discourse.

Henry Theodore Tuckerman (1813–71)

Bring the good old bugle, boys, we'll sing
another song;
Sing it with a spirit that will start the
world along;
Sing it as we used to sing it—fifty thousand
strong,
As we were marching through Georgia.

Henry Clay Work (1832–84)
"Marching Through Georgia," 1865

CONSORT NOT WITH A FEMALE MUSICIAN

To use a woman or a guitar, one must know how to tune them.
Spanish proverb

In Chicago alone, the (Illinois Vigilance) association's repre-
sentatives have traced the fall of 1,000 girls to jazz music.
New York American, January 1922

Men compose symphonies, women compose babies.
Time, January 10, 1975

All the daughters of music shall be brought low . . .
Old Testament
Ecclesiastes

A pretty one will distract the other musicians, and an ugly one
will distract me.
Sir Thomas Beecham (1879–1961)
New York *Post*, May 8, 1959

Music must strike fire from the spirit of a man; emotionalism is
only meant for women.
Attributed to Ludwig van Beethoven
(1770–1827)
according to Robert Schumann

Imagin with your selfe what an unsightly matter it were to see a
woman play upon a tabour or drum, or blow in a flute or trumpet,
or any like instrument: and this because the boisterousness of

them doth both cover and take away that sweete mildness which setteth so forth everie deede that a woman doth.

> Baldassare Castiglione (1478–1529)
> *Libro del cortegiano,* 1528

Were there no women in the world, no women singers, I would never have become a composer. They have been my inspiration my whole life song.

> Alexander Sergeivitch Dargomysky
> (1813–69)

There's no music when a woman is in the concert.

> Thomas Dekker (?1572–?1632)
> *The Honest Whore,* 1604

There is a spirituality about the face, however . . . which the typewriter does not generate. The lady is a musician.

> Sir Arthur Conan Doyle (1859–1930)
> *The Return of Sherlock Holmes:* "The
> Solitary Cyclist," 1905

When a squeamish lady objects to the digestive sportiveness of the slide trombone, to the leering cacherination of the clarinet, to the slap-tonguing of the saxophone, she is not necessarily expressing a musical opinion; she is exhibiting a dislike of the manners suggested by voices that violate the books of etiquette.

> Isaac Goldberg (1887–1938)
> *Tin Pan Alley,* 1930

Women and music should never be dated.

> Oliver Goldsmith (?1730–74)
> *She Stoops to Conquer,* 1773

What I love best about music is the women who listen to it.

> Jules de Goncourt (1830–70)

Of the ladies that sparkle at a musical performance, a very small number has any quick sensibility of harmonious sounds. But every one that goes has the pleasure of being supposed to be pleased with a refined amusement, and of hoping to be numbered among the votaresses of harmony.

> Samuel Johnson (1709–84)
> *The Idler*, August 12, 1758

Let our young ladies . . . address themselves to the violin, the flute, the oboe, the harp, the clarionet, the bassoon, the kettle-drum. It is more than possible that upon some of these instruments the superior daintiness of the female tissue might finally make the woman a more successful player than the man.

> Sidney Lanier (1842–81)
> "The Orchestra of Today," *Music and Poetry*, 1898

I just don't think women should be in an orchestra. They become men. Men treat them as equals; they even change their pants in front of them. I think it's terrible.

> Zubin Mehta (1936–   )
> New York *Times*, October 18, 1970

> . . . when the sweet talkin's done—
> A woman's a two-face,
> A worrisome thing who'll leave ya t'sing
> The blues in the night.

> Johnny Mercer (1909–   )
> "Blues in the Night,"
> popular song, 1941

Music is another lady that talks charmingly and says nothing.

> Austin O'Malley

Musick and women I cannot but give way to, whatever my business is.

> Samuel Pepys (1633–1703)
> *Diary*, March 9, 1666

The man who is not thrilled to the bone by the spectacle of a woman playing the flute, blowing a clarinet or struggling with intricacies of a trombone, is no man.

> Sir Malcolm Sargent (1895–1967)

Loud music is too harsh for ladies' heads, Since they love men in arms as well as beds.

> William Shakespeare (1564–1616)
> *Pericles,* 1608–9

What musician that has ever read a novel of Ouida's has not exclaimed sometimes, "If she would only lay on this sort of thing with an orchestra, how concerts would begin to pay!"

> George Bernard Shaw (1856–1950)
> *Music in London, 1890–1894,* 1931

Consort not with a female musician lest thou be taken in by her snares.

> Ben Sira
> Book of Wisdom (Ecclesiasticus)
> c. 190 B.C.

The legend relates that one afternoon while Adam was asleep, Eve, anticipating the Great God Pan, bored some holes in a hollow reed and began to do what is called "pick out a tune." Thereupon Adam spoke; "Stop that horrible noise," he roared, adding, after a pause, "besides which, if anyone's going to make it, it's not you but me!"

> Dame Ethel Smyth (1858–1944)
> *Female Pipings in Eden*

. . . the Musick of the Flute is the conversation of a mild and amiable Woman, that has nothing in it very elevated, nor, at the same time, anything mean or trivial.

> Richard Steele (1672–1729)
> *The Tatler*

Music is a woman . . . She must be loved by the poet, must surrender herself to him, in order that the new art-work of the future may be born . . . the begetter must be the artist.

> Richard Wagner (1813–1883)
> *Opera and Drama,* 1851

Women, indeed, are the music of life; they absorb everything more openly and unconditionally, in order to embellish it by means of their sympathy.

Richard Wagner
Letter to Theodor Uhlig, December 27,
1849

SING ME A SONG WITH SOCIAL SIGNIFICANCE

Under the effect of music, the five social duties are without admixture, the eyes and the ears are clear, the blood and the vital spirits are balanced, habits are reformed, customs are improved, the empire is at complete peace.

> "Yo Ki" (Memorial of Music in
> *Li Chi*, Record of Rites),
> Chinese manuscript, c. 500 B.C.

If any person has sung or composed against another person a song such as was causing slander or insult to another, he shall be clubbed to death.

> Roman law
> *Roman Twelve Tables*, 449 B.C.

Music should be a counterpoint to the time in which it is created. All this talk about "relevance" is wrong.

> Maurice Abravanel (1903–   )
> *Stereo Review*, October 1975

. . . we may compare the best form of government to the most harmonious piece of music; the oligarchic and despotic to the more violent tunes; and the democratic to the soft and gentle airs.

> Aristotle (384–322 B.C.)
> *Politics*, translation by William Ellis

If we could have devised an arrangement for providing everybody with music in their homes, perfect in quality, unlimited in quantity, suited to every mood, and beginning and ceasing at will, we should have considered the limit of human felicity already attained.

> Edward Bellamy (1850–98)
> *Looking Backward*, 1888

Music is so intimately connected with Poetry, Mythology, Government, Manners and Science in general that wholly to separate it from them would be an impossibility.

> Dr. Charles Burney (1726–1814)
> *History of Music*, 1776–89

I am a man first, an artist second. As a man, my first obligation is to the welfare of my fellow men. My contribution to world peace may be small. But at least I will have given all I can to an idea I hold sacred.

> Pablo Casals (1876–1973)
> *Time*, November 5, 1973

Musicke, unlike a laboring man's garment, is not necessary to existence, but, like a gentleman's apparel, is profitablie necessary for the comlinesse of life.

> John Case (died c. 1600)
> *The Praise of Musicke*, 1586

Rhythm is the feeling of *a* man; melody is the feeling of *Man*. Harmony is the feeling of *men*, of a man conscious of himself as an individual, living in a world where the interweaving lives of society reflect the orchestral pageant of growing and developing nature.

> Christopher Caudwell (1907–37)
> *Illusion and Reality*, 1939

My unextinguishable love for music and for all who find in its mystical power the real meaning of life assure me that . . . there will always be music in men's lives. Some poor music that may thrive for a time, some great music that may take a day longer than it should to be properly estimated, some artists to play it like angels or butchers, audiences to feed upon it, and critics who will immortalize themselves by their big, fat mistakes.

Abram Chasins (1903–   )
Speaking of Pianists, 1957

For changing peoples' manners and altering their customs there is nothing better than music.

Shu Ching
6th century B.C.

Music must be made popular, not by debasing the art; but by elevating the people.

Henry R. Cleveland
National Music, 1840

If a man be without the virtues proper to humanity, what has he to do with music?

Confucius (551–479 B.C.)
Analects

Wouldst thou know if a people be well governed, if its laws be good or bad, examine the music it practices.

Confucius

The superior man tries to promote music as a means to the perfection of human culture. When such music prevails, and people's minds are led towards the right ideals and aspirations, we may see the appearance of a great nation.

Confucius

The Americans are almost ignorant of the art of music, one of the most elevating, innocent and refining of human tastes, whose influence on the habits and morals of a people is of the most beneficial tendency.

James Fenimore Cooper (1789–1850)
The American Democrat, 1838

So long as the human spirit thrives on this planet, music in some living form will accompany and sustain it and give it expressive meaning.

Aaron Copland (1900–   )
Music as an Aspect of the Human Spirit,
radio address, 1954

One who opened Jowett's version (of Plato) at random and lighted on the statement that the best guardian for a man's "virtue" is philosophy tempered with music, might run away with the idea that, in order to avoid irregular relations with women, he had better play the violin in the intervals of studying metaphysics.

F. M. Cornford (1874–1943)
The Republic of Plato, 1941

Musical modes are nowhere altered without changes in the most important laws of the state.

Damon of Athens (5th Century B.C.)

It is safe to say that no man ever went wrong, morally or mentally, while listening to a symphony.

Justice John J. Dillon
New York Supreme Court decision,
December 31, 1964

The best, most beautiful, and most perfect way that we have of expressing a sweet concord of mind to each other is by music. When I would form, in my mind, ideas of a society in the highest degree happy, I think of them as expressing their love, their joy, and the inward concord, and harmony, and spiritual beauty of their souls, by sweetly singing to each other.

Jonathan Edwards (1703–58)
Miscellaneous Observations on
Important Theological Subjects, 1747

Give me the making of the songs of a nation, and I care not who makes its laws.

> Andrew Fletcher (1655–1716)
> *Conversation Concerning a Right*
> *Regulation of Government for*
> *the Common Good of Mankind,* 1703

Songs have overthrown kings and empires.

> Anatole France (1844–1924)

The artist must be as much above the political controversies of the day as the art which he serves.

> Dr. Wilhelm Furtwängler (1886–1954)
> *Neue Freie Presse,* Vienna,
> September 7, 1937

More power to the poets, to the writers and singers of songs and to the players of music. They are our salvation.

> Ralph Gleason (1917–75)
> Quoted in *ASCAP Today,* September 1971

Music is the most social, the most affecting, the purest of the arts; the one most deeply connected with the moral side of civilization. It stands alone in the arts as hardly capable of being distorted to minister to luxury, evil or ostentation. One can hardly imagine vicious music, or purse-proud music, or selfish music.

> Frederic Harrison (1831–1923)
> *Memories and Thoughts,* 1898

The most profound truths, the most blasphemous things, the most terrible ideas, may be incorporated within the walls of a symphony, and the police be none the wiser. It is its freedom from the meddlesome hand of the censor that makes of music a playground for great brave souls.

> James Huneker (1860–1921)
> *Mezzotints in Modern Music,* 1899

The future of music may not lie entirely with music itself, but rather in the way it encourages and extends, rather than limits,

the aspirations and ideas of the people, in the way it makes itself
a part with the finer things that humanity does and dreams of.

Charles Ives (1874–1954)

Music hath alarums to wild the civil breast.

Tuli Kupferberg
When the Mode of the Music Changes,
1968

Music is a means of unifying broad masses of people.

Vladimir Ilyich Ulyanov Lenin
(1870–1924)
Quoted by Dimitri Shostakovich

Music is a discipline, and a mistress of order and good manners,
she makes the people milder and gentler, more moral and more
reasonable.

Martin Luther (1483–1546)

I want to hear screaming and hollering and kicking and biting.
That's what the world's about today . . . Life is a bit chaotic, and
I think jazzmen should express something of the way life is lived.

Charlie Mariano (1923–   )
Down Beat Yearbook, 1967

Of all forms of the uplift, perhaps the most futile is that which
addresses itself to educating the proletariat in music

H. L. Mencken (1880–1956)
Smart Set, December 1919

One man with a dream, at pleasure,
Shall go forth and conquer a crown;
And three with a new song's measure
Can trample a kingdom down.

Arthur O'Shaughnessy (1844–81)
Ode

Music is a moral law. It gives a soul to the universe, wings to the mind, flight to the imagination, a charm to sadness, gaiety and life to everything. It is the essence of order, and leads to all that is good, just and beautiful, of which it is the invisible, but nevertheless, dazzling, passionate, and eternal form.

Plato (c. 428–c. 347 B.C.)

Can the true artist stand aloof from life and confine his art within the narrow bounds of subjective emotion? Or should he be where he is needed most, where his words, his music, his chisel can help the people live a better, finer life?

Sergei Prokofiev (1891–1953)

It is the duty of the composer, like the poet, the sculptor or the painter, to serve his fellow men, to beautify human life and point the way to a radiant future. Such is the immutable code of art as I see it.

Sergei Prokofiev
Autobiography, 1946

That music of itself is lawful, useful and commendable no man, no Christian dares deny, since the Scriptures, Fathers, and generally all Christian, all Pagan authors extant, do with one consent aver it.

William Prynne (1600–69)
Histriomastix, 1632

Sing me a song with social significance
All other tunes are taboo
I want a ditty with heat in it
Appealing with feeling and meat in it.

Harold Rome (1908–   )
"Sing Me a Song with Social
Significance," popular song, 1937

If it is art it is not for all, and if it is for all it is not art.

Arnold Schoenberg (1874–1951)

Enviable Nero, who had the strength to destroy a loathsome people to the sound of music and song.

> Franz Schubert (1797–1828)
> Diary, 1824

Where the people sing, no man is ever robbed.

> J. H. Seume
> *Die Gesänge*, c. 1800

> Though music oft hath such a charm
> To make bad good, and good provoke to harm.
> > William Shakespeare (1564–1616)
> > *Measure for Measure*, 1604

> The man that hath no music in himself
> Nor is not moved with concord of sweet sounds,
> Is fit for treasons, stratagems, and spoils;
> The motions of his spirit are dull as night,
> And his affections dark as Erebus;
> Let no such man be trusted. Mark the music.
> > William Shakespeare
> > *The Merchant of Venice*, 1596–97

I consider that every artist who isolates himself from the world is doomed. I find it incredible that an artist should wish to shut himself away from the people . . . I always try to make myself as widely understood as possible; and if I don't succeed, I consider it my own fault.

> Dimitri Shostakovich (1906–75)

There can be no music without ideology.

> Dimitri Shostakovich
> New York *Times*, December 5, 1931

Music must take rank as the highest of the fine arts—as the one which, more than any other, ministers to human welfare.

> Herbert Spencer (1820–1903)

One and the same thing can at the same time be good, bad, and indifferent, e.g., music is good to the melancholy, bad to those who mourn, and neither good nor bad to the deaf.

> Benedict (Baruch) Spinoza
> (1632–77)
> *Ethics*, Part IV, Preface

The spirit of music is great enough to include all of us, whether scholars, composers, clowns or vagabond minstrels.

> Walter Starkie (1894–)
> *Raggle-Taggle*, 1933

Men profess to be lovers of music but for the most part they give no evidence in their opinions and lives that they have heard it. It would not leave them narrow-minded and bigoted.

> Henry David Thoreau (1817–62)
> *Journal*, August 5, 1851

Nothing is so truly bounded and obedient to law as music, yet nothing so surely breaks all petty and narrow bonds.

> Henry David Thoreau
> *Journal*, 1854

Music must present the consummate formulation of the psychological tribulations of mankind, it should accumulate man's energy.

> Aleksey Tolstoy (1817–1875)
> Quoted by Igor Stravinsky, *Poetics of Music*, 1947

We sing to each other or listen to music together or make music together in the knowledge that the sharing of sound makes us all belong to each other, enables us to give all of ourselves in every way we can, with all the feeling we have inside. That's communication.

> Mary Travers (1937–), 1972
> Member of popular singing trio
> Peter, Paul and Mary

Open my ears to music; let
   Me thrill with Spring's first flutes and drums—
But never let me dare forget
   The bitter ballads of the slums.

> Louis Untermeyer (1885–1973)
> *Prayer*

The things humans do! The little creatures in the UFOs must have figured out sex by now, and our cars, but the dreaming, and the praying, and the singing . . . How to explain music to them?

> John Updike (1932–   )
> *A Month of Sundays,* 1975

Music can exist only if it reflects the inner life of humanity, not the outer life of its technology.

> Alec Wilder (1907–   )
> "The Emperor's New Clothes,"
> *Allegro,* December 1974

The people do not need music which they cannot understand.

> Andrei A. Zhadanov (1896–1948)
> Speech to the Central Committee
> of the Communist Party of the
> U.S.S.R., 1947

THE ONLY SENSUAL PLEASURE WITHOUT VICE

How can there be any bad music? All music is from heaven. If there is anything bad in it, I put it there—by my implications and limitations. Nature builds the mountains and meadows and man puts in the fences and labels.

> Anonymous
> Quoted by Charles Ives,
> *Music and Its Future,* 1931

Music, the greatest good that mortals know, And all of heaven we have below.

> Joseph Addison (1672–1719)
> *Song for St. Cecilia's Day,* 1694

Music cleanses the understanding, inspires it, and lifts it into a realm which it would not reach if it were left to itself.

> Henry Ward Beecher (1813–87)

Music is a part of us, and either ennobles or degrades our behavior.

> Anicius Manlius Severinus Boethius
> (c. 480–524)
> *De Institutione Musica*

Music is edifying, for from time to time it sets the soul in operation. The soul is the gatherer-together of the disparate elements, and its work fills one with peace and love.

> John Cage (1912–   )
> *Forerunners of Modern Music,* 1949

Indeed Musick, when rightly ordered, cannot be prefer'd too much. For it re-creates and exalts the Mind at the same time. It composes the Passions, affords a strong Pleasure, and excites a Nobleness of thought.

Jeremy Collier (1650–1726)
An Essay of Musick, 1702

Virtue is the strong stem of man's nature, and music is the blossoming of virtue.

Confucius (551–479 B.C.)

The greatest moments of the human spirit may be deduced from the greatest moments in music.

Aaron Copland (1900–   )
Music as an Aspect of the Human Spirit,
radio address, 1954

Music is the only language in which you cannot say a mean or sarcastic thing.

John Erskine (1879–1951)
Quoted in *Reader's Digest,*
April 1934

Music cannot express a judgement. It cannot describe. But it can carry this message of a human condition: of love . . . or forgiveness.

Hans Werner Henze (1926–   )
New York *Times,* June 2, 1963

Music is the only of the arts that cannot be prostituted to a base use.

Elbert Hubbard (1856–1915)
A Thousand and One Epigrams, 1900

It is the only sensual pleasure without vice.

Samuel Johnson (1709–84), c. 1776

Nothing is wrong when done to music.

Jerome Kern (1885–1945)

Sweet sounds, oh, beautiful music, do not cease!
Reject me not into the world again.
With you alone is excellence and peace,
Mankind made plausible, his purpose plain.

> Edna St. Vincent Millay (1892–1950)
> *On Hearing a Symphony of Beethoven*

Music should never be harmless.

> Robbie Robertson (1944–) of The Band
> Quoted by Greil Marcus, *Mystery Train*,
> 1975

Sunshine can burn you, food can poison you, words can condemn you, pictures can insult you; music cannot punish—only bless.

> Artur Schnabel (1882–1951)
> *Music and the Line of Most Resistance*,
> 1942

To prove affections in human beings is the only goal of music.

> Meinrad Spiess (1683–1761)
> *Tractatus Musicus*, 1746

Music hath caught a higher pace than any virtue that I know. It is the arch-reformer; it hastens the sun to its setting; it invites him to his rising; it is the sweetest reproach, a measured satire.

> Henry David Thoreau (1817–62)
> *Journal*, January 8, 1842

Virtue is our favorite flower. Music is the perfume of that flower.

> Le Ty-Kim
> 7th century B.C.

Music was created for the consummation of concord in human nature, not to be the cause of voluptuousness.

> Huai-nan Tzu (d. 122 B.C.)

THE TRUTH OF SONG

Music tells no truths.

> Philip James Bailey (1816–1902)
> *Festus,* 1839

There is no truer truth obtainable
By Man than comes of music.

> Robert Browning (1812–89)
> *Parleyings with Certain People;*
> *With Charles Avison,* VI

Music is the one thing in which there is no use trying to deceive others or make false pretenses.

> Confucius (551–479 B.C.)
> *On Music*

Mediocrity seeks out melodies which flatter the ear. I do not chase such. I want music strictly to express the word. I want truth.

> Alexander Sergeivitch Dargomysky
> (1813–69)

Comic operas do not lie.

> Isaac Goldberg (1887–1938)
> *Major Noah,* 1936

Jazz is playin' from the heart, you don't lie.

> William Geary "Bunk" Johnson
> (1879–1949)

I can tell you much more about what a man is really thinking
by listening to him play than by hearing him talk. You can't hide
anything in that horn, especially when you think you are hiding.

> Jo Jones (1911–   )
> Quoted by Nat Hentoff, *The Jazz Life,*
> 1961

. . . Verbalizations of emotions, particularly those evoked by
music, are usually deceptive and misleading.

> Leonard B. Meyer (1918–   )
> *Emotion and Meaning in Music,* 1956

We hide ourselves in our music to reveal ourselves.

> Jim Morrison (1943–71)
> Quoted in *ASCAP Today,* Winter 1975

Odds life! Must one swear to the truth of a song?

> Matthew Prior (1664–1721)
> *A Better Answer to Chloe Jealous,*
> c. 1715

I have never encountered anything more false and foolish than
the effort to get truth into opera. In opera everything is based
upon the not-true.

> Peter Ilyich Tchaikovsky (1840–93)
> Diary, July 13, 1888

No musician needs to be told that the intuitive musical experience is a vehicle of truth far superior to that of rational thought.

> Alan Walker (1930–   )
> *An Anatomy of Musical Criticism,* 1968

It's better not to compose lies, if only because it takes so many
notes.

> Ermanno Wolf-Ferrari (1876–1948)
> Letter to Hans Gál, September 6, 1934

The purpose of music is to draw toward a total exaltation in which the individual mingles, losing his consciousness in a truth immediate.

Iannis Xenakis (1922–)
New York *Times*, April 21, 1976

TONES IN TIME

Music is the best means we have of digesting time.
W. H. Auden (1907–73)
Quoted by Robert Craft in
Stravinsky: Chronicle of a Friendship, 1972

Music is immediate actuality and neither potentiality nor passivity can live in its presence.
W. H. Auden
Some Reflections on Music and Opera,
1952

Music washes away from the soul the dust of everyday life.
Berthold Auerback (1812–82)

All human activity must pass through its periods of rise, ripeness and decline, and music has been, to a certain extent, fortunate in that it is the last of the great arts to suffer this general experience.

Sir Thomas Beecham (1879–1961)

Music is in a continual state of becoming.
Aaron Copland (1900–   )
Music and Imagination, 1952

What music can possibly withstand, after the passage of years, the taint of out-of-dateness imparted by the cadences and embroidery which made it popular when new?

Eugène Delacroix (1798–1863)
Journal, 1823–54

In truth, there is nothing like music to fill the moment with substance, whether it attune the quiet mind to reverence and worship, or whether it make the mobile senses dance in exultation.

> Johann Wolfgang von Goethe (1749–1832)
> Letter to Zelter, October 19, 1829

Music is a thing which delighteth all ages, and beseemeth all states; a thing as seasonable in grief as in joy;

> Bishop Richard Hooker (?1554–1600)
> *The Laws of Ecclesiastical Polity*, 1594,
> 1597

Music quickens time, she quickens us to the finest enjoyment of time.

> Thomas Mann (1875–1955)
> *The Magic Mountain*, 1924

Music is a cumulative art. It is a chain of sounds through time, each sound taking its meaning from those that have gone before. It is not the art for amnesiacs.

> William Mayer
> "Live Composers, Dead Audiences,"
> New York *Times Magazine*,
> February 2, 1975

Music is enough for a lifetime—but a lifetime is not enough for music.

> Sergei Rachmaninoff (1873–1943)

Music exists—not on canvas nor yet on the staff—only in motion. The good listener will hear it as the present prolonged.

> Ned Rorem (1923–   )
> *Music from Inside Out*, 1967

Music is made of tones in time.

> Sigmund Spaeth (1885–1965)
> *The Art of Enjoying Music*, 1933

Music is the sole domain in which man realizes the present.
Igor Stravinsky (1882–1971)
Chronicle of My Life, 1935

The phenomenon of music is given to us with the sole purpose of establishing an order in things, including, and particularly, the co-ordination between *man* and *time*. To be put into practice, its indispensable and single requirement is construction . . . it is precisely this construction, this achieved order, which produces in us a unique emotion having nothing in common with our ordinary sensations and our responses to the impression of daily life.
Igor Stravinsky
Chronicle of My Life, 1935

EDUCATION

The music teacher came twice each week to bridge the awful gap between Dorothy and Chopin.

George Ade (1866–1944)

It is not easy to determine the nature of music, or why anyone should have a knowledge of it.

Aristotle (384–322 B.C.)
Politics

A musicologist is a person who can read music but can't hear it.

Sir Thomas Beecham (1879–1961)
Quoted by Harold C. Schonberg,
The Great Conductors, 1967

Many people say that too much study kills spontaneity in music, but although study may kill a small talent, it must develop a big one. In other words, if study kills a musical endowment, that endowment deserves to be killed.

George Gershwin (1898–1937)
Introduction to *Tin Pan Alley* by
Isaac Goldberg, 1930

I have always loved music; who so has skill in this art is of a good temperament, fitted for all things. We must teach music in schools; a schoolmaster ought to have skill in music, or I would not regard him; neither should we ordain young men as preachers unless they have been well exercised in music.

Martin Luther (1483–1546)
Table Talk, 1569

Professional musicians and music teachers—two distinct classes, by the way—. . . have in common their hatred of music.

> H. L. Mencken (1880–1956)
> "Huneker in Motley," *Smart Set,*
> July 1914

Stuffing birds or playing stringed instruments is an elegant pastime, and a resource to the idle, but it is not education.

> Cardinal Newman (1801–90)
> *The Idea of a University Defined,* 1873

And grant that a man read all ye books of musick that ever were wrote, I shall not allow that musick is or can be understood out of them, no more than the taste of meats out of cookish receipt books.

> Roger North (1653–1734)
> *The Musicall Gramarian,* 1728

Musical training is a more potent instrument than any other, because rhythm and harmony find their way into the secret places of the soul.

> Plato (c. 428–c. 347 B.C.)
> *Republic*

The teachers of the lyre take . . . care that their young disciple is temperate and gets into no mischief; and when they have taught him the use of the lyre, they introduce him to the poems of other excellent poets, who are the lyric poets; and these they set to music, and make their harmonies and rhythms quite familiar to the children, in order that they may learn to be more gentle, and harmonious, and rhythmical, and so more fitted for speech and action; for the life of man in every part has need of harmony and rhythm.

> Plato
> *Laws*

What will a child learn sooner than a song?

> Alexander Pope (1688–1744)
> *Satires and Epistles of*
> *Horace Imitated,* Second Book, 1737

Music, if only listened to, and not scientifically cultivated, gives too much play to the feelings and fancy; the difficulties of the art draw forth the whole energies of the soul.

Jean Paul Richter (1763–1825)
Levana, 1807

A musical education is necessary for musical judgement. What most people relish is hardly music; it is rather, a drowsy reverie relieved by nervous thrills.

George Santayana (1863–1952)
Reason in Art, 1905

. . . the notion that you can educate a child musically by any other means whatsoever except that of having beautiful music finely performed within its hearing, is a notion which I feel constrained to denounce.

George Bernard Shaw (1856–1950)
Music in London, 1890–1894, 1931

People would compose music skillfully enough if only there were no professors in the world.

George Bernard Shaw
Music in London, 1890–1894, 1931

The trouble with music appreciation in general is that people are taught to have too much respect for music; they should be taught to love it instead.

Igor Stravinsky (1882–1971)
New York *Times Magazine*,
September 27, 1964

Academism results when the reasons for the rule change, but not the rule.

Igor Stravinsky
Conversations with Igor Stravinsky,
Igor Stravinsky and Robert Craft, 1958

Teaching music is not my main purpose. I want to make good citizens. If a child hears fine music from the day of his birth, and learns to play it himself, he develops sensitivity, discipline and endurance. He gets a beautiful heart.

Shinichi Suzuki
Quoted in *Reader's Digest,*
November 1973

THE GIFT OF GOD

Praise Him with the sound of the trumpet;
praise Him with the psaltery and harp.
Praise Him with the timbrel and dance:
praise Him with stringed instruments and organs.
Praise Him upon the loud cymbals: praise Him
upon the high sounding cymbals.

Old Testament
Psalm 150

Praise the Lord upon the harp: sing to the
harp with a psalm of thanksgiving.
With trumpets also, and shawms: O shew
yourselves joyful before the Lord the King.

Old Testament
Psalm 98

Whom God loves not, that man loves not music.

Italian proverb, c. 1600

How greatly did I weep in thy hymns and canticles, deeply
moved by the voices of thy sweet-speaking church! The voices
flowed into mine ears, and the truth was poured forth into my
heart, whence the agitation of my piety overflowed, and my tears
ran over, and blessed was I therein.

St. Augustine (354–430)
Confessions, 397–401

Whosoever is harmonically composed delights in harmony; which makes me much distrust the symmetry of those heads which declaim against all Church music. For myself . . . I do delight in it: for even that vulgar and tavern-music, which makes one man merry, another mad, strikes in me a deep fit of devotion and a profound contemplation of the First Composer. There is something in it of divinity more than the ear discovers.

Sir Thomas Browne (1605–82)
Religio Medici, 1642

Perhaps it may turn out a sang,
Perhaps turn out a sermon.

Robert Burns (1759–96)
Epistle to a Young Friend, 1786

Among the various things which are suitable for man's recreation and pleasure, music is the first and leads us to the belief that it is a gift of God set apart for this purpose.

Jean Calvin (1509–64)
Institution, de la religion chrétienne, 1536

Song is the daughter of prayer, and prayer is the companion of religion.

François René de Chateaubriand
(1768–1848)
Genius of Christianity, 1856

Nothing so uplifts the mind, giving it wings and freeing it from the earth . . . as modulated melody and the divine chant . . .

St. John Chrysostom (?345–407) c. 400

A great race is not only that race which creates its god in its own image, but that race which also knows how to create its own hymn for its god.

Gabriele D'Annunzio (1863–1938)
Constitution of the Free State
of Fiume, August 27, 1920

Music and religion are as intimately related as poetry and love; the deepest emotions require for their civilized expression the most emotional of the arts.

> Will Durant (1885–   )
> *The Age of Faith*, 1950

Music was as vital as the church edifice itself, more deeply stirring than all the glory of glass or stone. Many a stoic soul, doubtful of the creed, was melted by the music, and fell on his knees before the mystery that no words could speak.

> Will Durant
> *The Story of Civilization*, 1935–37

> there's a movie called
> "Shoot the Piano Player"
> the last line proclaimin'
> "music, man, that's where it's at"
> it is a religious line.
>
> > Bob Dylan (1941–   )
> > *11 Outlined Epitaphs*, 1964

The sacredness of church music, the joyfulness and frolicsomeness of folksongs are the two pivots around which revolves true music. And it is from these two points that it will ever have the inevitable effect: devotion and dance.

> Johann Wolfgang von Goethe (1749–1832)

Music is love; it springs from religion and leads to religion.

> Eduard Hanslick (1825–1904)

> You sinners drop ev'rything
> Let dat harmony ring
> Up to heaven and sing
> Sing you sinners.
>
> > W. Franke Harling (1887–1958)
> > "Sing You Sinners," popular song,
> > 1930

Why should the devil have all the good tunes?
>> Rowland Hill (1744–1833)

To some of us the thought of God is like a sort of quiet music played in the background of the mind.
>> William James (1842–1910)

Music is a sacred, a divine, a Godlike thing, and was given to man by Christ to lift our hearts up to God, and make us feel something of the glory and beauty of God, and of all which God has made.
>> Charles Kingsley (1819–75)

God sent his singers upon earth with songs of sadness and of mirth . . .
>> Henry Wadsworth Longfellow (1807–82)
>> *The Singers*

Music is one of the greatest gifts that God has given us: It is divine and therefore Satan is its enemy. For with its aid many dire temptations are overcome; the devil does not stay where music is.
>> Martin Luther (1483–1546)
>> *In Praise of Music*

Except for theology, there is no art that can be placed in comparison with music.
>> Martin Luther

I have no pleasure in any man who despises music. It is no invention of ours; it is the gift of God.
>> Martin Luther

> There let the pealing organ blow,
> To the full-voiced quire below,
> In service high, and anthems clear
> As may, with sweetness, through mine ear,
> Dissolve me unto ecstasies,
> And bring all Heaven before mine eyes.
>> John Milton (1608–74)
>> *Il Penseroso*, 1632

God hath men who enter Paradise through their
flutes and drums.

Mohammed (c. 570–632)

The German imagines even God singing songs.

Friedrich Nietzsche (1844–1900)
The Twilight of the Idols, 1888

The young of all creatures cannot be quiet in their bodies or in
their voices . . . the Gods, who, as we say, have been appointed to
be our partners in the dance, have given the pleasurable sense of
harmony and rhythm; and so they stir us into life, and we follow
them and join hands with one another in dances and songs . . .

Plato (c. 428–c. 347 B.C.)
Laws

The first and chief Use of Musick is for the Service and Praise
of God, whose gift it is. The second Use is for the Solace of Men
. . . as a temporary Blessing to recreate and cheer Men after long
study and weary labor . . .

John Playford (1623–86)

Some to church repair not for the doctrine, but the music there.

Alexander Pope (1688–1744)

Fashion a hymn in the mouth. Expand like the cloud. Sing a
song of praise.

Rig-Veda, c. 1000 B.C.

Sing "Hallelujah! Hallelujah!" and you'll shoo the blues away—
Leo Robin (1900–   ) and Clifford Grey (1887–1941),
"Hallelujah," popular song, 1927

All true and deeply-felt music, whether secular or sacred, has its
home on the heights where art and religion dwell.

Albert Schweitzer (1875–1965)

I am highly susceptible to the force of all truly religious music, especially to the music of my own church, the church of Shelley, Michelangelo, and Beethoven.

George Bernard Shaw (1856–1950)

The Church knew what the Psalmist knew: Music praises God. Music is well or better able to praise Him than the building of the church and all its decoration; it is the Church's greatest ornament.

Igor Stravinsky (1882–1971)
Conversations with Igor Stravinsky
Igor Stravinsky and Robert Craft, 1958

Music is . . . the principal Entertainment of God, and the Souls of the Blessed hereafter.

William Tans'ur (1706–83)
The Elements of Musick Display'd,
1772

Listen to music religiously, as if it were the last strain you might hear.

Henry David Thoreau (1817–62)

Lord, what music hast thou provided for thy saints in heaven, when thou affordest bad men such music on earth!

Izaak Walton (1593–1683)

The illusive and fascinating effect of musical sound in a Cathedral unfortunately serves to blunt criticism and casts a veil over defects otherwise unbearable. No coat of varnish can do for a picture what the exquisitely reverberating qualities can do for music. And then the organ. What a multitude of sins does that cover!

Samuel Sebastian Wesley (1810–76)
A Few Words on Cathedral Music . . . ,
1849

Music comes before religion, as emotion comes before thought, and sound before sense. What is the first thing you hear when you go into a church? The organ playing.

Alfred North Whitehead (1861–1947)

THE SOUL OF A NATION

As the music is, so are the people of the country.

> Turkish proverb

Italian music is deficient in that which it has an excess; French music in that which it lacks.

> Jean d'Alembert (1717–83)
> Letter to Rameau

If the best thing you can be is a dead composer and the next best thing you can be is a German composer, the worst thing you can be is an American composer.

> Milton Babbitt (1916–)
> *The University of Chicago Magazine*,
> Autumn 1974

The English may not like music, but they absolutely love the noise it makes.

> Sir Thomas Beecham (1879–1961)

A musical nation is a nation of amateurs.

> Abram Chasins (1903–)
> *Music at the Crossroads*, 1972

A composer born in Finland who goes to Italy had better be careful. If he doesn't, he'll find he has composed *Il Trovatore*.

> Olin Downes (1886–1955)
> New York *Times*, October 24, 1937

Music—makes a people's disposition more gentle; e.g., "The Marseillaise."

> Gustav Flaubert (1821–80)

A nation creates music—the composer only arranges it.
> Mikhail Glinka (1803–57)
> Quoted in *Theatre Arts*, June 1958

It is wholly false to infer that music is independent of nationality. The composer bears the mark of his race not less surely than the poet or the painter, and there is no music with true blood in its veins and true passion in its heart that has not drawn inspiration from the breast of the mother country.

> Sir William Henry Hadow (1859–1937)

> One Russian is an anarchist;
> Two Russians are a chess game;
> Three Russians are a revolution;
> Four Russians are the Budapest String Quartet.
> > Attributed to Jascha Heifetz (1901–   )

Banality and self-deception are so integral a part of patriotic music that even in the few successful examples of the genre we must learn to avert our ears in embarrassment at times . . . How easy it is to produce empty rhetoric when propaganda is the muse.

> Donal Henahan (1921–   )
> New York *Times*, August 15, 1976

The English excel in dancing and music, for they are active and lively . . . They are vastly fond of great noises that fill the air, such as the firing of cannon, drums and the ringing of bells, so that in London it is common for a number of them when drunk to go up into some belfry and ring the bells for hours together.

> Paul Hentzner, c. 1605
> Quoted in *England as Seen by Foreigners*
> *in the Days of Elizabeth*, 1865

Rock-a-bye your baby with a Dixie melody;
When you croon, croon a tune, from the heart of Dixie.
　　Sam M. Lewis (1885–1959), and Joe Young (1889–1939)
　　"Rock-a-bye Your Baby with a Dixie Melody,"
　　popular song, 1918

The Italians exalt music; the French enliven it; the Germans strive after it; and the English pay for it well. The Italians serve music; the French make it into a companion; the Germans anatomize it, and the English compel it to serve them.
　　　　　　　　　　　Johann Mattheson (1681–1764)
　　　　　　　　　　　Das Neu-eröffnete Orchestre, 1713

　　　　Too-ra-loo-ra-loo-ral
　　　　Too-ra-loo-ra-li.
　　　　Too-ra-loo-ra-loo-ral
　　　　That's an Irish lullaby.
　　J. R. Shannon (1881–1946)
　　"Too-ra-loo-ra-loo-ral, That's an Irish Lullaby," popular
　　song, 1914

I am not prepared to say that there are absolutely no national characteristics in the music of great composers . . . In general, a great composer is national only when he is at his second best. At the height of his powers, when he has ceased being decorative or merely exciting, and becomes eloquent and moving, he is likely to sound merely like himself. The great American music of the future will be a music to which America will listen and respond. But it will not be the music of Sitting Bull or Booker T. Washington —or even George. It will . . . like all great music, belong to the world. And the world will not be curious regarding the name and address of the composer.
　　　　　　　　　　　Deems Taylor (1885–1966)
　　　　　　　　　　　Of Men and Music, 1937

The song that nerves a nation's heart is in itself a deed.
　　　　　　　　　　　Alfred, Lord Tennyson (1809–92)
　　　　　　　　　　　The Charge of the Heavy Brigade, 1885

The way to write American music is simple. All you have to do is to be an American and then write any kind of music you wish.

Virgil Thomson (1896–   )

I don't give a damn about "The Missouri Waltz" but I can't say it out loud because it's the song of Missouri. It's as bad as "The Star-Spangled Banner" so far as music is concerned.

President Harry S. Truman (1884–1972)
Time, February 10, 1958

The art of music above all other arts is the expression of the soul of a nation. The composer must love the tunes of his country and they must become an integral part of him.

Ralph Vaughan Williams (1872–1958)

Our music differs from German music. Their symphonies can live in halls; their chamber music can live in the home. Our music, I say, resides principally in the theatre.

Giuseppe Verdi (1813–1901)
Letter to Piroli, February 2, 1883

Italians have an instinct for melody; the French have the pride of the virtuoso; but to the Germans alone belongs true feeling for music.

Richard Wagner (1813–83)
Quoted by Wanda Landowska, *Landowska on Music*, 1969

I hear America singing, the varied carols I hear.

Walt Whitman (1819–92)
Leaves of Grass, 1855

THE SWEETEST PHYSIC IN THE WORLD

My bowels shall sound like a harp.

Old Testament
Isaiah

Music exalts each joy, allays each grief,
Expels diseases, softens every pain,
Subdues the rage of poison and the plague.
John Armstrong, M.D. (1709–79)
The Art of Preserving Health, 1744

This variable composition of man's body hath made it as an instrument easy to distemper. Therefore, the poets did well to conjoin music and medicine in Apollo, because the office of medicine is but to tune this curious harp of man's body and to reduce it to harmony.

Francis Bacon (1561–1626)
Advancement of Learning, 1605

What humiliation when someone stood next to me and heard a flute in the distance and I heard nothing, or when someone heard the shepherd boy singing and again I heard nothing. Such misfortunes brought me to the edge of despair, and I might have brought an end to my life—only my art held me back. Oh, it seemed impossible to me to quit this world until I had produced everything I felt I could produce.

Ludwig van Beethoven (1770–1827)
The Heiligenstadt Testament, 1802

Dear melodious song, the sweetest physic in the world.

Bion (3rd or 2nd century B.C.)
Love and Song, c. 120 B.C.

The exercises of singing is delightful to nature, and good to preserve the health of man. It doth strengthen all parts of the breast, and doth open the pipes.

William Byrd (?1540–1623)
Psalms, Sonnets and Songs, 1588

He who sings frightens away his ills.

Miguel de Cervantes Saavedra (1547–1616)
Don Quixote, 1605, 1615

Music helps not the toothache.

George Herbert (1593–1633)
Jacula Prudentum, 1640

Melancholy people like grave, solid, and sad harmony; sanguine persons prefer the *Hyporchematic* style (dance music) because it agitates the blood; choleric people like agitated harmonies because of the vehemence of their swollen gall; martially inclined men are partial to trumpets and drums and reject all delicate and pure music; phlegmatic persons lead towards women's voices because their high-pitched voice has a benevolent effect on phlegmatic humour.

Athanasius Kircher (1601–80)
*Musurgia Universalis sive Ars Magna
Consoni et Dissoni*, 1650

Music's the medicine of the mind.

John Logan (1748–88)
Danish Ode, c. 1788

The Physitians will tell you that the exercise of Musicke is a great lengthener of the life, by stirring and reviving of the Spirits, holding a secret sympathy with them.

Henry Peacham (?1576–?1643)
The Compleat Gentleman, 1622

He who mingles music with gymnastics in the fairest proportions, and best attempers them to the soul, may be rightly called the true musician and harmoniest in a far higher sense than the tuner of the strings.

Plato (c. 428–c. 347 B.C.)
Republic

It is integral to singers as to terminal cancer patients not to believe in their own decay.

Ned Rorem (1923–   )
The Final Diary, 1974

Any Body that is willing to take a hearty Sweat, may have the Pleasure of hearing many notable Performances in the charming Science of Musick.

Ned Ward (1667–1731)

THE OPEN-AIR ART

If musical sounds affect us more powerfully than the sounds of nature, the reason is that nature confines itself to expressing feelings, whereas music suggests them to us.

Henri Bergson (1859–1941)
Time and Free Will, 1889

There is music in all things, if men had ears.

George Gordon, Lord Byron (1788–1824)

See deep enough; and you see musically; the heart of nature being everywhere music, if you can only reach it.

Thomas Carlyle (1795–1881)
Heroes and Hero Worship, 1840

I love music passionately, and because I love it I try to free it from barren traditions that stifle it. It is a free art, gushing forth— an open-air art, an art boundless as the elements, the wind, the sky, the sea! It must never be shut in and become an academic art.

Claude Debussy (1862–1918)

There is nothing more musical than a sunset.

Claude Debussy

The hills are alive with the sound of music
With the songs they have sung
For a thousand years.

Oscar Hammerstein II (1895–1960)
"The Sound of Music," popular song, 1959

There is no music in Nature, neither melody or harmony. Music is the creation of man.

> Rev. Hugh Reginald Haweis (1838–1901)
> *Music and Morals*, c. 1871

The musician above all who is inspired by nature but without copying it, exhales in sound his life's most intimate secrets.

> Franz Liszt (1811–86)
> Quoted by Eleanor Perenyi, *Liszt*, 1974

My music is always the voice of nature sounding in tone . . .

> Gustav Mahler (1860–1911)

The composer's task is to copy nature . . . to stir the passions at will . . . to express the living movements of the soul and the cravings of the heart.

> Friedrich W. Marpurg (1718–95)
> *Kritische Musikus*, Volume I, 1750

> Orpheus with his lute made trees
> And the mountain-tops that freeze,
> Bow themselves when he did sing:
> To his music plants and flowers
> Ever sprung; as sun and showers
> There had made a lasting spring.
> Everything that heard him play,
> Even the billows of the sea,
> Hang there heads, and lay by.
>
> William Shakespeare (1564–1616)
> *Henry VIII*, 1612

He is made one with Nature: there is heard His voice in all her music, from the moan of thunder to the song of night's sweet bird.

> Percy Bysshe Shelley (1792–1822)
> *Adonais*, 1821

The god of music dwelleth out of doors.

> Edith Matilda Thomas (1854–1925)
> *Music*

A JUG OF WINE, A LOAF OF BREAD

A concert of music in a banquet of wine is as a signet of carbuncle set in gold. As a signet of an emerald set in a work of gold, so is the melody of music with pleasant wine.

> Old Testament Apocrypha
> Ecclesiasticus XXXII, 5–6

Old King Cole was a merry old soul,
And a merry old soul was he;
He called for his pipe and he called for his bowl,
And he called for his fiddlers three.

> Anonymous

Music with dinner is an insult both to the cook and violinist.

> Gilbert Keith Chesterton (1874–1936)
> Quoted in the New York *Times*,
> November 16, 1967

Music is really escapism. It's shutting yourself off from everything else, going into a cupboard and staying there. That's what drugs do and that's what music does. They go hand in hand.

> Eric Clapton, rock guitarist (1945–   )
> Quoted in *Time*, July 15, 1974

Some men are like musical glasses—to produce their finest tones you must keep them wet.

> Samuel Taylor Coleridge (1772–1834)
> *Table Talk*, 1834

Feed the musician, and he's out of tune.

George Crabbe (1754–1832)
The Newspaper, 1785

I cried for madder music and for stronger wine,
But when the feast is finished and the lamps expire,
Then falls thy shadow, Cynara! the night is thine . . .

Ernest Dowson (1867–1900)
*Non Sum Qualis Eram Bonae Sub
Regno Cynarae,* 1896

Music and wine are one,
That I, drinking this,
Shall hear far chaos talk with me . . .

Ralph Waldo Emerson (1803–1882)
Bacchus

For all time . . . music has been used for the purpose of caressing us like a warm bath, exciting us like alcohol, giving us dreams like mescal . . .

Scott Goddard
Penguin Music Magazine, 1946

Music is not a drug, but a diet.

Sir William Henry Hadow (1859–1937)
The Reader's Digest, October 1927

Song and dance, the crown of a feast.

Homer (thought to be between the 12th and 9th
centuries B.C.)
Odyssey

For its always fair weather
When good fellows get together,
With a stein on the table and a
good song ringing clear.

Richard Hovey (1864–1900)
"A Stein Song," 1898

Give me books, fruit, french wine and fine weather and a little music out of doors, played by somebody I do not know.

> John Keats (1795–1821)
> Letter to Fanny Keats, August 29, 1819

Who loves not women, wine and song remains a fool his whole life long.

> Attributed to Martin Luther (1483–1546)
> Also attributed to Johann Heinrich Voss
> (1751–1826)

Any musician who says he is playing better on tea, the needle, or when he is juiced is a plain straight liar.

> Charlie Parker (1920–55)
> *Hear Me Talkin' to Ya*, 1955
> Edited by Nat Shapiro and Nat Hentoff

Give in return for old wine, a new song.

> Titus Maccius Plautus (254–184 B.C.)
> *Stichus*

LIKE THE BIRDIES SING

A robin's song is not pretty to the worm.

Proverb

> That's the wise thrush; he sings each
>   song twice over,
> Lest you should think he never could
>   recapture
> The first fine careless rapture!
>> Robert Browning (1812–89)
>> *Home-Thoughts, from Abroad*, 1845

A nightingale dies for shame if another bird sings better.
> Robert Burton (1577–1640)
> *The Anatomy of Melancholy*, 1621

> A light broke in upon my brain,—
>   It was the carol of a bird;
> It ceased, and then it came again,
>   The sweetest song ear ever heard.
>> George Gordon, Lord Byron (1788–1824)
>> *The Prisoner of Chillon*, 1816

Nightingales sing badly.

Jean Cocteau (1889–1963)

A tune is more lasting than the voice of the birds, a song more lasting than the riches of the world.
> Padraic Colum (1881–1972)
> *Polonius and the Ballad-Singers*

An amiable nightingale showed me the most elaborate methods of applying rhythmic tune to the upward and downward rush of the wind, thus teaching me perfect counterpoint.

> Marie Corelli (Mary Mackay) (1855–1924)
> *The Sorrows of Satan,* 1895

> And somewhere a bird who is bound
>   he'll be heard,
> Is throwing his heart at the sky.
> It's a grand night for singing.
>> Oscar Hammerstein II (1895–1960)
>> "It's a Grand Night for Singing,"
>> song, 1945

"Let's All Sing Like the
  Birdies Sing."

> Robert Hargreaves and Stanley J. Damerell,
> Popular song title, 1932

We never miss the music till the sweet-voiced bird has flown.

> O. Henry (William Sydney Porter) (1862–1910)
> *The Pendulum,* 1907

> By shallow rivers, to whose falls
> Melodious birds sing Madrigals.
>> Christopher Marlowe (1564–93)
>> *The Passionate Shepherd to His Love*

"A Nightingale Sang in Berkeley Square."

> Eric Maschwitz (1901–   )
> Popular song title, 1940

Wilt thou have music? hark! Apollo plays and twenty caged nightingales do sing.

> William Shakespeare (1564–1616)
> *The Taming of the Shrew,* 1593–94

> The crow doth sing as sweetly as the lark,
> When neither is attended; and I think,

The nightingale, if she should sing by day,
When every goose is cackling, would be thought
No better a musician than the wren.

William Shakespeare
The Merchant of Venice, 1596–97

I do but sing because I must,
And pipe but as the linnets sings.

Alfred, Lord Tennyson (1809–92)
In Memoriam, 1850

SIGHT AND SOUND

Cautions are necessary with respect to Musick and Painting; the fancy is often too quick in them, and the Soul too much affected by the Senses . . .

The Ladies Library, Written by a Lady,
Published by Richard Steele, 1732

A man that has a taste of musick, painting, or architecture, is like one that has another sense, when compared with such as have no relish of those arts.

Joseph Addison (1672–1719)
Spectator, June 16, 1711

A distinguished philosopher spoke of architecture as *frozen* music, and his assertion caused many to shake their heads. We believe this really beautiful idea could not be better reintroduced than by calling architecture *silent* music.

Johann Wolfgang von Goethe (1749–1832)
Gespräche mit Eckermann, January 8, 1827

Music is architecture translated or transposed from space into time; for in music, besides the deepest feeling, there reigns also a rigorous mathematical intelligence.

Georg W. F. Hegel (1770–1831)

Contemporary music, like contemporary art, has rediscovered the charm of the irregular.

Joseph Machlis (1906–)
Introduction to Contemporary Music, 1961

The painter turns a poem into a painting; the musician sets a picture to music.

> Robert Schumann (1810–56)
> *Aphorisms,* c. 1833

The sight of such a monument is like a continuous and stationary music.

> Madame de Staël (1766–1817)
> *Corinne,* 1807

Both music and painting add a spirit to devotion, and elevate the ardor.

> Laurence Sterne (1713–68)

Where painting is weakest, namely in the expression of the highest moral and spiritual ideas, there music is sublimely strong.

> Harriet Beecher Stowe (1811–96)

Part Seven
MUSIC FOR THE MILLIONS

JAZZ

. . . jazz continues to flower cumulatively, taking on and transforming the new without ever abandoning the old. It is a fugue with a life of its own, endlessly recapitulating itself.

Time, July 5, 1976

. . . Jazz music is the indecent story syncopated and counterpointed.

New Orleans *Times-Picayune*, 1914

Hot can be cool and cool can be hot, and each can be both. But hot or cool, man, jazz is jazz.

Louis Armstrong (1900–71)

There'll probably be new names for it. There have been several names since I can remember back to the good ol' days in New Orleans, Louisiana, when Hot Music was called "ragtime music," "jazz music," "gut bucket music," "swing music," and now "hot music." So you see instead of dying out, it only gets new names.

Louis Armstrong
Quoted by Hugues Panassié, Introduction
to *Le Jazz Hot*, 1934

There's this mood about the music, a kind of need to be moving. You just can't set it down and hold it. You just can't keep the music unless you move with it.

Sidney Bechet (1897–1959)
Quoted by Nat Hentoff, *Jazz Is*, 1976

There is not a single emotion that jazz cannot encompass. Not only joy and depression, but indignation, anger, and scores of specific emotions.

> Marc Blitzstein (1905–64)
> Quoted by Nat Hentoff, *The Jazz Life*, 1961

Improvisation is adoration of the melody . . . imagination coupled with a strong sense of composition . . . Running chords doesn't interest me. What does is trying to superimpose a new melody on the original, to build on layers . . .

> Ruby Braff (1927–   )
> Quoted by Whitney Balliett, *Alec Wilder and His Friends*, 1974

The first challenge of a jazz performer is to unify the diverse response of an audience so that it becomes an entity. Co-creation exists in this timeless area of subconscious communication when the improvisor becomes the articulate voice of the group. The compassion of this inspired moment of unity is the reason for jazz and for its continued existence.

> Iona and Dave Brubeck (1920–   )
> From *Perspectives USA 15*, 1956

Jazz . . . was illiterate, instinctual, impulsive, aleatoric, unscorable, unpredictable—therein lay its charm.

> Anthony Burgess (1917–   )
> "The Weasels of Pop," *Punch*,
> September 20, 1967

Thus it came to pass that jazz multiplied all over the face of the earth and the wriggling of bottoms was tremendous.

> Peter Clayton (1927–   ) and Peter Gammond (1925–   )
> *14 Miles on a Clear Night*, 1966

I listen to a jazz band at the Casino de Paris: high in the air, in a kind of cage, the Negroes writhe, dandle, toss lumps of raw meat to the crowd in the form of trumpet screams, rattles, drumbeats. The dance tune, broken, punched, counterpointed, *rises* now and again to the surface.

> Jean Cocteau (1889–1963)
> *Professional Secrets*, Calendar, 1914–23

Jazz is the only music in which the same note can be played night after night but differently each time. It's the hidden things, the subconscious that lies in the body and lets you know: you feel this, you play this.

> Ornette Coleman (1930–)
> Quoted by Wilfrid Mellers,
> *Music in a New Found Land*, 1964

If you are playing jazz, you have to play what comes out at any moment—something you have never said before!

> John Coltrane (1926–67)
> New York Jazz Museum pamphlet,
> *About John Coltrane*, 1974

I think the main thing a musician would like to do is to give a picture to the listener of the many wonderful things he knows of and senses in the universe.

> John Coltrane
> New York Jazz Museum pamphlet,
> *About John Coltrane*, 1974

Jazz is a language. It is people living in sound. Jazz is people talking, laughing, crying, building, painting, mathematicizing, abstracting, extracting, giving to, taking from, making of. In other words, living.

> Willis Conover (1920–)
> Quoted by Leonard Feather, *The Book
> of Jazz*, 1976

> Mr. Paganini, Please play my rhapsody,
> And if you cannot play it,
> Won't you sing it,

> And if you can't sing it,
> You'll simply have to swing it.
>   Sam Coslow (1902–)
>   "If You Can't Sing It, You'll Have
>   to Swing It," popular song, 1936

What's swinging in words? If a guy makes you pat your foot and if you feel it down your back, you don't have to ask anybody if that's good music or not. You can always feel it.
>   Miles Davis (1926–)
>   *Down Beat,* November 2, 1955

> "It Don't Mean a Thing
> If It Ain't Got That Swing."
> Edward Kennedy "Duke" Ellington (1899–1974) and
> Irving Mills (1894–), popular song title, 1932

Playing "bop" is like playing Scrabble with all the vowels missing.
>   Edward Kennedy "Duke" Ellington
>   *Look,* August 10, 1954

It's jam, but arranged.
>   Edward ("Eddie") Farley (1904–)
>   When asked for a definition of swing, 1936

(Jazz is) the expression of protest against law and order, the bolshevik element of license striving for expression in music.
>   Anne Shaw Faulkner
>   "Does Jazz Put the Sin in Syncopation?"
>   *Ladies' Home Journal,* August 1921

Jazz without the beat, most musicians know, is a telephone yanked from the wall; it just can't communicate.
>   Leonard Feather (1914–)
>   *Show,* January 1962

The requirements for glamour in jazz too often include eccentricity, limited technical scope (supposedly compensated by "soul"), a personal background of social problems, and a tendency to show up for the Wednesday matinee at midnight on Thursday.

Leonard Feather
From Satchmo to Miles, 1972

Jazz I regard as an American folk music; not the only one, but a very powerful one which is probably in the blood and feeling of the American people more than any other style of folk music.

George Gershwin (1898–1937)
"The Relation of Jazz to American Music,"
American Composers on American Music,
edited by Henry Cowell, 1933

Jazz has contributed an enduring value to America in the sense that it has expressed ourselves.

George Gershwin

The "jazz mania" has taken on the character of a lingering illness and must be cured by means of forceful public intervention.

Boris Gibalin, Russian composer
Izvestia, September 28, 1958

It's about time that America takes pride in the tremendous contribution of a music whose originality and character have already captivated the European mind. It's about time that America takes pride in those who will surely rank high on the honor roll of artistic immortality: Louis Armstrong, Duke Ellington and some others. It's about time that American intellectuals adopt, as their own, a thing in which all Europe fervently believes, and find in it a source of a new and truly moving form of sensibility.

Robert Goffin
Jazz—From the Congo to the Metropolitan,
1944

It is a truism that many of the baroque recorded masterpieces in jazz are of a technical complexity which would be quite beyond the ability of their creators to play them were they faced with the notes written out as a composition.

Benny Green (1927–   )
Notes for an Art Tatum record album, 1974

Of all sophisticated forms of music, jazz is the most self-revealing, the music where there is the least room for the performer to hide who he or she is.

Nat Hentoff (1925–   )
Jazz Is, 1976

Jazz doesn't pretend.

Nat Hentoff
Jazz Is, 1976

The chief trouble with jazz is there is not enough of it; some of it we have to listen to twice.

Don Herold (1889–   )

Jazz is an art in which conception cannot be divorced from means of expression and the way in which creative thought is given form . . .

André Hodeir (1921–   )
Jazz: Its Evolution and Essence, 1956

I don't think I'm singing. I feel like I am playing a horn. I try to improvise like Les Young, like Louis Armstrong . . . What comes out is what I feel. I hate straight singing. I have to change a tune to my own way of doing it.

Billie Holiday (1915–59)

I can't stand to sing the same song the same way two nights in succession. If you can, then it ain't music, it's close order drill or exercise or yodelling or something, not music.

Billie Holiday
Lady Sings the Blues, 1956

Jazz is a kind of growing Old Testament of the Negro race and of all the lost tribes in America too—a Testament being written night after night by unknown, vagrant poets on the spot . . .

John Clellon Holmes
The Horn, 1958

Jazz it up, jazz it up. Keep moving. Step on the gas. Say it with dancing. The Charleston, The Baptists. Radios and Revivals. Uplift and Gilda Gray. The pipe organ, the nigger with the saxophone, the Giant Marimbaphone. Hymns and the movies and Irving Berlin. Petting parties and the First Free United Episcopal Methodist Church. Jazz it up!

Aldous Huxley (1894–1963)
Jesting Pilate: An Intellectual Holiday, 1926

The jazz players were forced upon me; I regarded them with a fascinated horror. It was the first time, I suddenly realized, that I had ever clearly seen a jazz band. The spectacle was positively terrifying.

Aldous Huxley
"Do What You Will," 1929

Jazz is playin' from the heart, you don't lie.

Bunk Johnson (1879–1949)

Jazz has always been a man telling the truth about himself.

Quincy Jones (1933–   )
Quoted by Raymond Horricks, *These Jazzmen of Our Time*, 1959

When we stop swinging, we're competing with Ravel, Bartók, Stravinsky and a lot of other brilliant musicians on their own ground . . . musicians who easily outdo us there. Jazz must develop its *own* language.

Quincy Jones
Quoted by Raymond Horricks, *These Jazzmen of Our Time*, 1959

Jazz has never existed in Africa, and it doesn't exist there today. It was formed from the two musical cultures; from the African, which has the highest development of rhythm in the world, and from the European, which has the greatest development of harmony in the world; and it happened in America.

> Max Kaminsky (1908–)
> *My Life in Jazz*, 1963

Jazz joins together what man has put asunder. To man the theorizer, builder, tradesman and scientist, jazz restores man the tribesman, maker of symbols and myths and dreams . . .

> Father G. V. Kennard, S.J. (1919–)
> Quoted by Nat Hentoff in *Show*,
> November 1961

To swing is to affirm.

> Father G. V. Kennard, S.J.
> From album notes to *Shelly Manne and
> His Men*, Volume 5

"Jazz," used mainly as an adjective descriptive of a band. The groups that play for dancing, when colored, seem infected with a virus that they try to instill as a stimulus to others. They shake and jump and writhe in ways to suggest a return to the medieval jumping mania.

> Walter Kingsley
> New York *Sun*, 1917

Jazz is the best of all nourishments. It feeds the creative spirit like nothing else can. It is a fantastic adventure, an exciting game of giving and taking and exchanging musical ideas with brothers and friends. When the conditions are right, it is possible to achieve a level of rapport that is nowhere else to be found in music—or for that matter—in art.

> Michel Legrand (1932–)

Swinging is like being on a tightrope or roller coaster. It's like walking in space. It's like a soufflé: It rises and rises and rises.

> Marian McPartland (1920–   )
> Quoted by Whitney Balliett, *Alec Wilder and His Friends*, 1974

There wouldn't be a soul around. Then, when it was time to start the dance, he'd say, "Let's call the children home." And he'd put his horn out the window and blow, and everyone would come running.

> Edward "Kid" Ory (1886–1973)
> Speaking about the legendary New Orleans trumpeter Buddy Bolden, quoted in
> *Hear Me Talkin' to Ya*
> Edited by Nat Shapiro and Nat Hentoff, 1955

It (jazz) is obviously a curious use of rhythmic resources. And moreover what a terrible revenge by the culture of the Negroes on that of the whites!

> Ignacy Paderewski (1860–1941)

Music is your own experience, your thoughts, your wisdom. If you don't live it, it won't come out of your horn.

> Charlie Parker (1920–55)
> Quoted in *Hear Me Talkin' to Ya*
> Edited by Nat Shapiro and Nat Hentoff, 1955

> Jazz,
> The meaning of it,
> Is as evasive as silence.
> Name one who could
> Accurately define this
> Passional art that slices
> And churns one's senses
> Into so many delicate
> barbarous
> And uncountable patterns.

> > Gordon Parks (1912–   )
> > *Esquire*, December 1975

Jazz may be thought of as a current that bubbled forth from a spring in the slums of New Orleans to become the main spring of the twentieth century.

> Henry Pleasants (1910–   )
> News summaries, December 30, 1955

The basic difference between classical music and jazz is that in the former the music is always greater than its performance—whereas the way jazz is performed is always more important than what is being played.

> André Previn (1929–   )
> To Miles Kington, London *Times*, 1967

If everyone is in a frisky spirit, the spirit gets to me and I can make my trombone sing. If my music makes people happy, I will try to do more. It is a challenge to me . . . When I play sweet music I try to give my feelings to the other fellow. That's always in my mind. Everyone in the world should know this.

> Jim Robinson (1892–1976)
> Quoted in *Hear Me Talkin' to Ya*, 1955
> Edited by Nat Shapiro and Nat Hentoff

You see, the average working man is very musical. Playing music for him is just relaxing. He gets as much kick out of playing as other folks get out of dancing. The more enthusiastic his audience is, why, the more spirit the working man's got to play. And with your natural feelings that way, you never make the same thing twice. Every time you play a tune, new ideas come to mind and you slip that one in.

> Johnny St. Cyr (1890–   )
> Quoted in *Hear Me Talkin' to Ya*, 1955
> Edited by Nat Shapiro and Nat Hentoff

> Drum on your drums, batter on your
>   banjos, sob on the long cool
>   winding saxophones.
> Go to it, O jazzmen.

> Carl Sandburg (1878–1967)
> *Jazz Fantasia*, 1920

Jazz is either a thrilling communication with the primitive soul, or an ear-splitting bore.

> Winthrop Sargent (1903–)

Jazz will endure just as long as people hear it through their feet instead of their brains.

> John Philip Sousa (1854–1932)

Jazz has nothing to do with composed music and when it seeks to be influenced by contemporary music it isn't jazz and it isn't good.

> Igor Stravinsky (1882–1971)

Polyphony, flatted fifths, half-tones—they don't mean a thing. I just pick up my horn and play what I feel.

> Jack Teagarden (1905–64)
> Quoted in his obituary in the New York
> *Times,* January 16, 1964

Bop is the shorthand of jazz, an epigram made by defying the platitude of conventional harmony; it performs a post-mortem on the dissected melody. The chastity of this music is significant. It shuns climaxes of feeling, and affirms nothing but disintegration.

> Kenneth Tynan (1927–)
> *The Observer,* May 8, 1955

Jazz is music invented by devils for the torture of imbeciles.

> Henry van Dyke (1852–1933)

It is the truth: comedians and jazz musicians have been more comforting and enlightening to me than preachers and politicians or philosophers or poets or painters or novelists of my time. Historians in the future, in my opinion, will congratulate us on very little other than our clowning and our jazz.

> Kurt Vonnegut, Jr. (1922–)
> Foreword to *The Best of Bob and Ray,* 1974

New Orleans was what I like to call "The University of Jazz." Oh, lots of musicians and bands came from places like Kansas

City and Chicago, but there was something—a certain combination of hot weather, dumps, dives, and people—that only New Orleans could provide.

> Frank Walker (1889–1963)
> Quoted in *Hear Me Talkin' to Ya*, 1955
> Edited by Nat Shapiro and Nat Hentoff

There's something of the opium eater in your jazz cultist. His enthusiasm affects him like a drug habit, removing him, it seems, from the uninitiated and less paranoid world about him and encouraging many of the attitudes of full-blown megalomania.

> Orson Welles (1915–   ), 1946

BLUES AND BLACKS

I love the blues, they hurt so nice.
>> Anonymous blues
>> Quoted by Ben Sidran, *Black Talk*, 1971

Make your Negroes pleasant and cheerful, make them dance to the beat of the drum.
>> Anonymous slave merchant, 18th century

A wave of vulgar, filthy and suggestive music has inundated the land. Nothing but ragtime prevails, and the cake-walk with its obscene posturings, its lewd gestures . . . Our children, our young men and women are continually exposed to the contiguity, to the monotonous attrition of this vulgarizing music. It is artistically and morally depressing, and should be suppressed by press and pulpit.
>> *Musical Courier*, September 13, 1899

Character and vigour earn respect all the world over, even when the character is unpleasant and the vigour misdirected. Now of ragtime, there can be no doubt that it is absolutely characteristic of its inventers. From nowhere but the United States could such spring. It is the music of the hustler and the feverishly active speculator.
>> "Ragtime as Source of National Music,"
>> London *Times*, February 15, 1913

In de ebening by the moonlight, you could hear
us darkies singing,

In de ebening by the moonlight, you could hear
    de banjo ringing;
How de old folks would enjoy it, they would
    sit all night and listen;
As we sang in de ebening by de moonlight.
                James A. Bland (1854–1911)
                "In the Evening by the Moonlight,"
                song, 1879

Soul is sass, man. Soul is arrogance . . . Soul is that nigger whore comin' along . . . and walkin' like she's sayin' "Here it is baby. Come an' get it." Soul is being true to yourself, to what is *you*. Soul is that uninhibited, not *extremely* uninhibited self-expression that goes into practically every Negro endeavor. It's exhibitionism, and it's effortless.
                Claude Brown (1937–)
                Quoted by Arnold Shaw, *The World of*
                Soul, 1970

I'd like to think that when I sing a song, I can let you know all about the heartbreak, struggle, lies and kicks in the ass I've gotten over the years for being black and everything else, without actually saying a word about it.
                Ray Charles (1932–)
                Interview in *Playboy*, 1970

I heard somebody one time say that all black people got rhythm. Bullshit.
                Ray Charles

    . . . And then they nursed it, rehearsed it,
    And gave out the news
    That the Southland
    Gave birth to the blues.
    B. G. DeSylva (1895–1950) and Lew Brown (1893–1958)
    "The Birth of the Blues," popular
      song, 1926

And so by fateful chance the Negro folk song—the rhythmic cry of the slave—stands today not simply as the sole American music, but as the beautiful expression of human experience born this side of the seas . . . It still remains as the singular spiritual heritage of this nation and the greatest gift of the Negro people.

W. E. B. Du Bois (1868–1963)

Oh, de white ban' play hits music,
    an' hits mighty good to hyeah,
An' it sometimes leaves a ticklin' in yo' feet;
But de hea't goes into bus'ness fu' to he's
        erlong de eah,
W'en de colo'ed ban' goes marchin' down de street . . .

Paul Laurence Dunbar (1872–1906)
When Malindy Sings

But hit's Sousa played in rag-time,
And hit's Rastus on Parade,
When de colo'ed ban' comes
Ma'chin' down de street.

Paul Laurence Dunbar
When Malindy Sings

In the Negro melodies of America I have discovered all that is needed for the creation of a great and noble school of music. These beautiful and varied themes are the product of the soil. They are the folk songs of America, and your composers must turn to them. All the great musicians have borrowed from the songs of the people.

Antonin Dvořák (1841–1904)

The blues is an impulse to keep the painful details and episodes of a brutal experience alive in one's aching consciousness, to finger its jagged grain, and to transcend it . . . by squeezing from it a near-tragic, near-comic lyricism.

Ralph Ellison (1914–   )

I have concluded . . . to pursue the Ethiopian business without fear or shame and . . . to establish my name as the best Ethiopian songwriter.

> Stephen Foster (1826–64)
> Letter to E. P. Christy, May 25, 1852

The blues is a feeling and a form. It is singular and plural at will . . .

> Ralph J. Gleason (1917–75)
> *Lithopinion*, No. 15, Fall 1969

It is possible to speculate that all the white musicians could be eliminated from the history of music without significantly altering its development.

> Ralph J. Gleason
> *Lithopinion*, No. 15, Fall 1969

Ragtime is something that music did to the Negro and that the Negro did to music. It began . . . in the restless feet of the black; it rippled through his limbs, and communicated itself to every instrument upon which he could lay his hands.

> Isaac Goldberg (1887–1938)
> *Tin Pan Alley*, 1930

It is possible to properly produce "Blues" effects on any instrument, although the wailings, moaning, and croonings . . . are more easily produced on instruments like the saxophone, trombone or violin. Without the necessary moan, croon, or slur, no blues number is properly sung.

> Porter Grainger and Bob Ricketts
> *How to Play and Sing the Blues Like the Phonograph and Stage Artists*, pamphlet, 1926

The Blues, the most convenient harmonic progression ever discovered . . . the most hackneyed, overplayed, obvious musical effect in the world, and yet in some curious way at times the most compelling.

> Benny Green (1927–   )
> *This Is Jazz*, 1960

The blues are ever-changing and infinite, and they probably represent the greatest concentration of feeling in pop music.

John Hammond (1910–   )
Billboard, June 24, 1967

The blues come from nothingness, from want, from desire.

W. C. Handy (1873–1958)

All I can say is that when I was a boy we always was singin' in the fields. Not real singing, you know, just hollerin'. But we made up our songs about things that was happening to us at the time, and I think that's where the blues started.

Son House (1902–   )

The music is slow, often mournful, yet syncopated, with the kind of marching bass behind it that seems to say, "In spite of fate, bad luck, these blues themselves I'm going on! I'm going to get there!"

Langston Hughes (1902–67)

A dark man shall see dark days. Bop comes out of them dark days. That's why Bop is mad, wild, frantic, crazy—and not to be dug unless you've seen dark days, too. Folks who ain't suffered much cannot play Bop, neither appreciate it. They think Bop is nonsense like you. They think it's just *crazy* crazy. They do not know Bop is also MAD crazy, SAD crazy, FRANTIC WILD CRAZY—beat out of somebody's head! That's what Bop is. Them young colored kids who started it, they know what Bop is.

Langston Hughes
Simple Takes a Wife, 1953

The blues always impressed me as being very sad, sadder even than the spirituals, because their sadness is not softened with tears, but hardened with laughter, the absurd incongruous laughter of a sadness without even a god to appeal to.

Langston Hughes
Letter to Carl Van Vechten

Anyone who sings the blues has a broken spirit . . . Being oppressed or worried about something and not knowing God, they've sought a way of trying to relieve themselves . . . the blues makes you feel moody and sad and makes you cry.

Mahalia Jackson (1911–72)
Television interview, 1957

It started with the moans and groans of the people in the cotton fields. Before it got the name of soul, men were sellin' watermelons and vegetables on a wagon drawn by a mule, hollerin' "watermellllon!" with a cry in their voices. And the men on the railroad track layin' crossties—everytime they hit the hammer it was with a sad feelin', but with a beat. And the Baptist preacher —he the one who had the soul—he give out the meter, a long and short meter, and the old mothers of the church would reply. This musical thing has been here since America been here. This is trial and tribulation music.

Mahalia Jackson
Quoted in *Time*, June 28, 1968

In music, the blacks are more generally gifted than the whites, with accurate ears for tune and time, and they have been found capable of imagining a small catch. Whether they will be equal to the composition of a more extensive run of melody or of complicated harmony, is yet to be proved.

Thomas Jefferson (1743–1826)
Notes on the State of Virginia, 1781

When you get your ass kicked that hard, it makes you go to the inner most depths of what you are all about as a human being. Now, maybe most people have not been kicked that hard, but it's still in everybody, and this music rings a bell that you can hear throughout the fucking world.

Quincy Jones (1933–   )
Quoted in *Rolling Stone*, July 1, 1976

Ghetto blacks . . . "speak jazz" (or blues or gospel) as their native tongue as Italians "speak opera."

> Frank Kofsky (1935–   )
> *Black Nationalism and the Revolution*
> *in Music,* 1970

So when the people in them times, they'd be sad and feelin' bad, and they'd sing blues; they didn't know how to sing nothin' else, but that old feelin' came to 'em. That's what they'd call the blues, that old feelin' . . .

> Huddie (Leadbelly) Ledbetter (1885–1949)

The blues is a feeling and when it hits you, it's the real news.

> Huddie (Leadbelly) Ledbetter
> *Leadbelly Anthology,* Volume II,
> Folkways Records

In his music he (the Negro) gave voice to the character and quality of his existence, to his rage and the infinite variations of joy, lust, languor, growl, cramp, pinch, scream and despair of his orgasm. For jazz is orgasm . . .

> Norman Mailer (1923–   )
> *The White Negro,* 1957

Ragtime came north with the rhythm of the coonjiners striding down gangplanks from Mississippi steamers, and of wenches in black-and-tan houses humming plaintive homicidal legends during the boredom of the afternoons.

> Edward B. Marks (1865–1945)

The Negro, with his unusual sense of rhythm, is no more accurately to be called musical than a metronome is to be called a Swiss music-box.

> George Jean Nathan (1882–1958)
> *Comedians All,* 1919

The blues? Man, I didn't start playing the blues ever. That was
in me before I was born and I've been playing and living the blues
ever since. You've got to live the blues.

> T-Bone Walker (1913–   )
> Quoted in *Hear Me Talkin' to Ya*, 1955

"The Blues Ain't Nothin' but a Woman Cryin' for Her Man."

> Mayo Williams
> Blues song title, 1924

The blues as an art form didn't come from the black man being
more miserable than the white man, but rather from his being
more honest with himself about it.

> Paul Williams (1948–   )
> *Crawdaddy*, March 1975

The most astonishing aspect of the blues is that, though replete
with a sense of defeat and downheartedness, they are not intrin-
sically pessimistic; their burden of woe and melancholy is dialec-
tically redeemed through sheer force of sensuality into an almost
exultant affirmation of life, of love, of sex, of movement, of hope
. . . Blues are a lusty, lyrical realism charged with taut sensibility.

> Richard Wright (1908–60)

ROCK

Rock appeals to the intelligence without interference from the intellect.

Chester Anderson
Quoted by Richard Neville, *Playpower*,
1970

Q. How do you rate your music?
A. We're not good musicians. Just adequate.
Q. Then why are you so popular?
A. Maybe people like adequate music.

The Beatles

The popular music scene today is unlike any scene I can think of in the history of all music. It's completely of, by and for the kids, and by kids I mean anyone from eight years old to twenty five. They write the songs, sing them, own them, record them. They also buy the records, create the market, and they set the fashion in the music, in dress, in dance, in hair style, lingo, social attitudes.

Leonard Bernstein (1918–)
Quoted in *Popular Song and Youth Today*,
edited by Louis M. Savary, 1971

It is not music to listen to, but music to move to. Rock 'n Roll is our modern version of rituals that have existed in other societies as far back as the time when primitive man shuffled and stomped around a drummer pounding on a hollow log until he fell in a state of mystic frenzy.

Charles Broeckman

A rock concert is in fact a rite involving the evocation and transmutation of energy.

> William Burroughs (1914–   )
> *Crawdaddy*, June 1975

Commercial rock-and-roll music is a brutalization of one stream of contemporary Negro church music . . . an obscene looting of a cultural expression.

> Ralph Ellison (1914–   )
> *Shadow and Act*, 1964

We're working with dynamics now. We've spent two years with loud, and we've spent six months with deafening.

> Jerry Garcia (1942–   )
> Quoted in *Popular Song and Youth Today*, edited by Louis M. Savary, 1971

You have to blame Thomas Alva Edison for today's rock 'n' roll. He invented electricity.

> Stan Getz (1927–   )

Rock is a corruption of Rhythm and Blues which was a dilution of the blues, so that today's mass-marketed noise is a vulgarization of a vulgarization.

> Benny Green (1927–   )
> Notes for a Joe Turner record album, 1976

Music today is money, that's all. It's rhythm, it's hypnosis, it's a good deal of hysteria and a lot of complaint. The words spell out the terror of the age in which the young are growing up . . . It belongs to today, but it won't belong to tomorrow. Good music and good lyrics should belong to all time.

> E. Y. (Yip) Harburg (1898–   )
> Quoted by Max Wilk, *They're Playing Our Song*, 1973

I remember when I was very young, this is very serious, I read an article by Fats Domino which has really influenced me. He said, "You should never sing the lyrics out very clearly."

> Mick Jagger (1944–   )
> Quoted in an interview in *Rolling Stone*, 1969

I declare that the Beatles are mutants. Prototypes of evolutionary agents sent by God, endowed with a mysterious power to create a new human species—a young race of laughing freemen.

> Timothy Leary (1920–   )

The kids today are quite right about the music their parents listened to: most of it was trash. The parents are quite right about what their young listen to: most of it is trash too.

> Gene Lees
> "Rock," *High Fidelity*, November 1967

Pop is the perfect religious vehicle. It's as if God has come down to earth and seen all the ugliness that was being created and chosen pop to be the great force for love and beauty.

> Donovan Leitch (1946–   )
> Quoted by Richard Neville, *Playpower*, 1970

We're more popular than Jesus Christ now. I don't know which will go first. Rock and roll or Christianity. Jesus was all right, but his disciples were thick and ordinary. It's them twisting it that ruins it for me.

> John Lennon (1940–   )
> *The Beatles Illustrated Lyrics*, 1969

In the Top 40 half the songs are *secret* messages to the teen world to drop out, turn on, and groove with the chemicals and light shows at discotheques.

> Art Linkletter (1912–   )

Rock and roll is a lovely playground, and within it kids have more power than they have anywhere else in society, but the play-

ground's walls are awfully maintained and guarded by the corpo-
rate elite that set it up in the first place.

> Michael Lydon
> "Rock for Sale," *Ramparts*, 1969

In primitive musics demonic possession denies "personal" expression; in modern rock the immense sea of sound has a comparable effect, on a vaster scale, and loudness becomes paradoxically
more silent than silence, since one is no longer aware of gradation!

> Wilfrid Mellers (1914–)
> *The Music of the Beatles*, 1973

A song can be a "hit," a "blast," a "smash," or even a "gasser";
Kinetic destruction is inherent in Kinetic success.

> Richard Meltzer
> "The Aesthetics of Rock," *The Age of
> Rock*, edited by Jon Landau, 1969

Good rock stars take drugs, put their penises in plaster of paris,
collectivize their sex, molest policemen, promote self-curiosity,
unlock myriad spirits, epitomize fun, freedom and bullshit. Can
the busiest anarchist on your block match THAT?

> Richard Neville (1941–)
> *Playpower*, 1970

Rock began as a series of grunts, got hung up with language,
and may yet evolve into a new poetry of laughter, chants and
howls.

> Richard Neville
> *Playpower*, 1970

Rock and roll might best be summed up as monotony tinged
with hysteria.

> Vance Packard (1914–)
> Testimony before a subcommittee
>   of the Interstate Commerce Committee,
> Senate of the United States, 1958

I just have to jump around when I sing. But it ain't vulgar. It's just the way I feel. I don't feel sexy when I'm singin'. If that was true, I'd be in some kinda institution as some kinda sex maniac.

> Elvis Presley (1935–1977)
> Quoted in *Popular Song and Youth Today*,
> edited by Louis M. Savary, 1971

Rock music must give birth to orgasm and revolution.

> Jerry Rubin
> *Do It!*, 1970

It (rock 'n' roll) fosters almost totally negative and destructive reactions in young people. It smells phony and false. It is sung, played and written for the most part by cretinous goons and by means of its almost imbecilic reiterations and sly—lewd—in plain fact, dirty—lyrics, and . . . it manages to be the martial music of every side-burned delinquent on the face of the earth. This rancid aphrodisiac I deplore . . .

> Frank Sinatra (1915–)
> Quoted in a lecture by Russell Sanjek,
> "The War on Rock," 1971

There's no bullshit going down with rock and roll. It's an honest form and one of the most open. It encompasses poetry, jazz and just about anything you can imagine . . . it is the highest form. It goes beyond color, gender—anything.

> Patti Smith
> *Cash Box*, January 24, 1976

When I'm onstage, I feel this incredible, almost spiritual experience . . . lost in a naturally induced high. Those great rock-'n'-roll experiences are getting harder and harder to come by, because they have to transcend a lot of drug-induced stupor. But when they occur, they are sacred.

> Peter Townshend (1945–)
> *Playboy*, June 1974

Pop music is ultimately a show, a circus. You've got to hit the audience with it. Punch them in the stomach, and kick them on the floor. Pop music will cease to be of any interest if it gets too interested in musical or lyrical obscurity, because when it comes down to it, its purpose and its value is in the creation of an immediate and overwhelming excitement.

> Peter Townshend
> Quoted by Tony Palmer, *Born Under A Bad Sign*, 1970

The American idea of youth assumes that all rebels finally join the herd. But you can't ignore us. Even if you don't like the ideas behind our music, you have to listen to it because it is everywhere.

> Frank Zappa (1940–)
> Quoted in *Rock and Other Four Letter Words*, 1968

POPULAR AND LIGHT

In the future we will have pop song cycles like classical Lieder,
but we will create our own words, music and orchestrations, because we are a generation of whole people.

> Judy Collins (1939–   )
> Quoted in *Rock and Other Four Letter Words*,
> 1968

Extraordinary how potent cheap music is.

> Sir Noël Coward (1899–1973)
> *Private Lives*, 1930

I was born into a generation that still took light music seriously.

> Sir Noël Coward
> Introduction to *The Noël Coward
> Songbook*, 1953

> . . . the chime of minstrel music, dulcimer,
> and harp with many strings, a pleasant dinning
>   makes
> To him, who heareth not distinct the note.

> Dante Alighieri (1265–1321)
> *The Divine Comedy: Paradise*, c. 1300

Sweet popular music is claptrap in the main, and in the main is
where it belongs.

> Peter De Vries (1910–   )

The only place where it's happening is on the radio and on records. That's where people hang out. It's not in book form, it's not

on the stage. All this art they've been talking about, it just remains on the shelf. Radio and records, that's the place.

Bob Dylan (1941–   )

The song people praise is always the latest thing.

François Fénelon (1651–1715)
Telemachus, 1699, translation by
W. H. D. Rouse

The song of today is machine-made, machine-played, machine-heard. It is a formula . . . It obeys every rule laid down . . . in search of speed, pep and punch. It builds up a musical literature of escape, of wish fulfillment, of vicarious sex experience, of whoopee. It is in itself a tonal aphrodisiac, providing a limited but effective vocabulary of love for a vast audience whose conceptions —and executions—of *love* are, if limited, effective.

Isaac Goldberg (1887–1938)
Tin Pan Alley, 1930

Songs Written to Order . . . words, music, emotions, notions, heart-beats, gutter philosophies, elementary wish-fulfillments, pathos, bathos . . . You pays your money—that's important—and you takes your choice.

Isaac Goldberg
Tin Pan Alley, 1930

Popular songs are those written, published and sung, whistled and hummed by the great American unmusical public, as distinguished from the more highly cultivated class which often decries and scoffs at the tantalizing and ear-haunting melodies that are heard from ocean to ocean in every shape and form.

Charles K. Harris (1867–1930)

Modern popular music is more barbarous than any folk art has been for hundreds of years.

Aldous Huxley (1894–1963)
Quoted by Alan Jenkins, *The Twenties,* 1974

The loveliest tune imaginable becomes vulgar and insupportable as soon as the public begins to hum it and the hurdygurdies make it their own.

> Joris Karl Huysmans (1848–1907)
> *Against the Grain*, 1884

I regard all pop music as irrelevant in the sense that people in 200 years won't be listening to what is being written and played today. I think they will be listening to Beethoven. Pop music is just fun. That's one of the reasons I don't take myself seriously.

> Elton John (1947–   )

And the tunes that mean so much to you alone—
Common tunes that make you choke and blow your nose,
Vulgar tunes that bring the laugh that brings the groan—
I can rip your very heartstrings out with those.

> Rudyard Kipling (1865–1936)
> *The Song of the Banjo*, 1894

The most irritating quality about the vododeo, poo poop-a-doop school of jazz song is its hysterical emphasis on the fact that the singer is a jazz baby going crazy about jazz rhythms.

> Constant Lambert (1905–51)
> *Music Ho!*, 1948

I sometimes think that the most plaintive ditty has brought a fuller joy and of longer duration to its composer than the conquest of Persia to the Macedonian.

> Walter Savage Landor (1775–1864)

Light music is a good lubricant.

> Arthur Loesser (1894–1969)
> *Men, Women and Pianos*, 1954

Music-hall songs provide the dull with wit, just as proverbs provide them with wisdom.

> W. Somerset Maugham (1874–1965)
> *A Writer's Notebook*, 1949

Keep it simple, keep it sexy, keep it sad.
> Mitch Miller (1911–   )
> On popular music, *Time*, February 23, 1950

Sir Arthur Bliss, Master of the Queen's Music, once described the B.B.C.'s pop programme as "aural hashish," but it's not *that* good.
> Richard Neville (1940–   )
> *Playpower*, 1970

I still believe in the future of love songs. After all, nobody has yet written a hit song about hate.
> Richard Rodgers (1902–   )
> Quoted in *ASCAP Today*, March 1971

"Tin Pan Alley"
> Monroe H. Rosenfeld
> Title of a New York newspaper article about the music publishing business, c. 1892

From window, door, and transom, notes and bars of ballad pour, ions of rue and longing, and they spin and tumble in the wind, they sway and swing and drum, and some seem to sort themselves, to touch and cling, to join and fly away, and soon the world will sing the thin tones of the tin tunes made on an upright eighty-eight. These shrill and facile chansonets, these valedictories for the tonguetied, these ready-to-wear regrets for the threadbare back of the common run—what do they hold that the Misereres lack?
> John Sanford (1904–   )
> *A More Goodly Country*, 1975

Some of the songs making the rounds now will be popular when Bach, Beethoven and Wagner are forgotten—but not before.
> Louis Sobel (1896–1955)
> New York newspaper columnist

Dance tunes are always right.

Dylan Thomas (1914–53)

Melodrama, cleverness, contrivance, imitativeness, pretentiousness, aggressiveness, calculatedness, and shallowness may be elements which result in a hit song but never in a great song.

Alec Wilder (1907–   )
*American Popular Song: The Great
Innovators, 1900–1950, 1972*

FOLK

A folksinger is someone who sings through his nose by ear.
Anonymous

A folksinger is an intellectual who sings songs that nobody ever wrote.
Anonymous

The only thing to do with a folk-melody, once you have played it, is to play it louder.
Anonymous

Folk melodies are a real model of the highest artistic perfection. To my mind, on a small scale, they are masterpieces, just as much as, in the world of larger forms, a fugue by Bach or a Mozart sonata.
Béla Bartók (1881–1945)

I guess all songs is folk songs. I never heard no horse sing 'em.
Big Bill Broonzy (1893–1958)
Quoted by Charles Keil, *Urban Blues*, 1966

While we sit here singing folksongs in our Folksong Club, the folk are somewhere else—singing something different.
Tony Davis
Sing Out, Summer 1963

All the great musicians have borrowed from the songs of the common people.
Antonin Dvořák (1841–1904)

There is many music. There is almost as many music as there are folk. There are a fantastic number of folk. There is therefore, many folk music.

> Mort Goode (1922–)
> Record album notes, 1960

A folk song composes itself.

> Jacob Grimm (1785–1863) and
> Wilhelm Grimm (1786–1859)

Work is the thing. The biggest and best thing you can sing about is work . . . Just learn where the work is: that's where you'll find real honest American music and songs being made up.

> Woody Guthrie (1912–67)
> "Ear Players," *Common Ground*, 1942

The best way to get to knowing any bunch of people is to go and listen to their music.

> Woody Guthrie
> *Woody Sez*, edited by Studs Terkel, 1975

Folk songs are written, like all other songs, by individuals. All the folk have to do with them is to choose the ones that are to survive.

> H. L. Mencken (1880–1956)
> "The Music of the American Negro,"
> *Chicago Sunday Tribune*, November 15, 1928

Every period which abounded in folk songs has, by the same token, been deeply stirred by Dionysiac currents.

> Friedrich Nietzsche (1844–1900)

Just as the lily, in its glorious and chaste beauty, eclipses the brilliance of brocades and precious stones, so folk music, thanks to its very childlike simplicity, is a thousand times richer and stronger than all the artifices of the learning taught by pedants in the conservatories and musical academies.

> A. N. Serov (1820–71)
> *Critical Articles*, Volume III, 1931

Folk music is the ungarbled and ingenuous expression of the human mind and on that account it must reflect the essential and basic qualities of the human mind.

Cecil Sharp
English Folk Song, 1907

The hackneyed melancholy of street music; a music which sounds like the actual voice of the human Heart, singing the lost joys, the regrets, the loveless lives of the people who blacken the pavements, or jolt along on the buses.

Logan Pearsall Smith (1865–1946)
Trivia, The Organ of Life, 1902

If I may venture to give my own definition of a folk song, I should call it "an individual flowering on a common stem."

Ralph Vaughan Williams (1872–1958)

You got to have smelt a lot of mule manure before you can sing like a hillbilly.

Hank Williams (1923–53)
Quoted by Christopher S. Wren,
Look, July 13, 1971

DANCE

We have piped unto you, and ye have not danced.

New Testament
Matthew 11:17

One should try everything once, except incest and folk-dancing.

Sir Arnold Bax (1883–1953)
Farewell My Youth, 1943

On with the dance! Let joy be unconfined.

George Gordon, Lord Byron (1788–1824)
Childe Harold, 1816

> Imperial waltz; imported from the Rhine
> (Famed for the growth of pedigrees and wine)
> Long be thine import from all duty free,
> And hock itself be less esteem'd then thee.

George Gordon, Lord Byron
The Waltz

The regular and insatiable supporters of ballet are people too sluggish of intellect to listen to a play on the one hand, and too devoid of imagination to listen to fine music without accompanying action, on the other.

Alan Dent (1905–   )
London *News-Chronicle*, 1952

"Takes Two to Tango."

Al Hoffman (1902–60) and Dick Manning (1914–54)
Popular song title, 1952

"Papa Loves Mambo"

> Al Hoffman, Dick Manning and
> Bix Reichner
> Popular song title, 1954

> To the music of Rimsky-Korsakoff
> I could never take my corset off
> And where are the sailors who would pay
> To see me strip to Massenet?
>
> Gypsy Rose Lee (1914–70)

> Charleston, Charleston, made in Carolina
> Some dance, some prance,
> I'll say nothing's finer . . .
> Cecil Mack (1883–1944) and Jimmy Johnson (1891–1955)
> "Charleston," popular song, 1923

The waltz is magnificently improper—the art of tone turned lubricious. I venture to say that the compositions of Johann Strauss have lured more fair creatures to complaisance than all the movie actors and white slave scouts since the fall of the Western Empire. There is something about a waltz that is irresistible. Try it on the fattest or sedatest or even upon the thinnest and most acidulous of women, and she will be ready, in ten minutes, for a stealthy snack behind the door—nay, she will forthwith impart the embarrassing news that her husband misunderstands her, and drinks too much, and is going to Cleveland, O., on business to-morrow.

> H. L. Mencken (1880–1956)
> *Prejudices, Sixth Series*, 1927

> Once a jolly swagman camped by a billy-bong,
>   Under the shade of a kulibar tree,
> And he sang as he sat and waited for his
>   belly-boil,
> "You'll come a-waltzing, Matilda, with me."
>   Andrew Barton "Banjo" Paterson (1864–1941)
>   "Waltzing Matilda," song, 1903

"Begin the Beguine"
> Cole Porter (1893–1964)
> Popular song title, 1935

The author's conviction on this day of New Year is that music begins to atrophy when it departs too far from the dance . . . Bach and Mozart are never too far from physical movement.
> Ezra Pound (1885–1972)
> *ABC of Reading*, 1934

Music is the meter of this poetic movement, and is an invisible dance, as dancing is silent music.
> Jean Paul Richter (1763–1825)
> *Levana*, 1807

It is sweet to dance to violins
    When Love and Life are fair:
To dance to flutes, to dance to lutes
    Is delicate and rare:
But it is not sweet with nimble feet
    To dance upon the air!
> Oscar Wilde (1854–1900)
> *The Ballad of Reading Gaol II*

O body swayed to music, O brightening glance.
How can we know the dancer from the dance?
> William Butler Yeats (1865–1939)
> *Among School Children*

FILM AND THEATER

"The Rite of Spring" is an exciting piece of music, but I don't believe that it has any future as a Broadway musical.

George Abbott (1889–)
Dramatists Guild Quarterly, Spring 1974

Movie music is noise. It's even more painful than my sciatica.

Sir Thomas Beecham (1879–1961)
Time, February 24, 1958

The only American art, the escape of everyman, discouraged by bleakness, worn by rush and machinery, into the blue of enchantment and rhythm and laughter, the art with Dionysian frenzy in it, the valid, the great American art, so far, is to be found on a blazing stage, full of shapes acrobatically dancing to the exact beat of drums and the seductively insincere moan of saxophones.

Mary Cass Canfield (d. 1966)
Grotesques and Other Reflections, 1927

Music in the theater throws a man off his guard, makes way for an ill Impression, and is most Commodiously planted to do mischief.

Jeremy Collier (1650–1726)
A Short View of the Immorality and Profaneness of the English Stage, 1698

Film music is like a small lamp that you place below the screen to warm it.

Aaron Copland (1900–)

A film musician is like a mortician—he can't bring the body back to life, but he's expected to make it look better.

> Adolph Deutsch (1897–)
> Quoted by Tony Thomas, *Music for the Movies*, 1973

He hasn't got the presumption of so many composers, who want their music to be heard in the film. He knows that, in a film, music is something marginal and secondary, something that cannot occupy the foreground except in a few rare moments and . . . must be content to support the rest of what's happening.

> Federico Fellini (1920–)
> On composer Nino Rota, *Fellini on Fellini*, 1976

No music has ever saved a good picture, but a lot of good pictures have saved a lot of bad music.

> Jerry Goldsmith
> Quoted by Irwin Bazelon, *Knowing the Score*, 1975

A song demands more of an audience than its interest and attention. It demands applause, the toughest achievement in the theater. This is what makes songwriting for the stage a mysterious and unique art form.

> E. Y. (Yip) Harburg (1898–)
> *Dramatists Guild Quarterly*, Spring 1974

Compare the music of "The Beggar's Opera" with the music of a contemporary revue. They differ as life in the Garden of Eden differed from life in the artistic quarter of Gomorrah.

> Aldous Huxley (1894–1963)

Having adapted Beethoven's Sixth Symphony for "Fantasia," Walt Disney commented: "Gee! This'll make Beethoven."

> Marshall McLuhan (1911–)
> *Culture Is Our Business*, 1970

God, it's an empty feeling watching a movie without any
music!

> Henry Mancini (1924–   )
> *As You Remember Them*, Time-Life Records,
> 1972

My sole inspiration is a telephone call from a producer.

> Cole Porter (1893–1964)
> Press interview, February 8, 1955

Suitable music played to any scene, action, event or surround-
ing seems to disclose to us its most secret meaning, and appears as
the most accurate and distinct commentary upon it.

> Arthur Schopenhauer (1788–1860)
> *The World as Will and Idea*, 1818

Film music should have the same relationship to the film
drama that somebody's piano-playing in my living-room has on
the book I am reading.

> Igor Stravinsky (1882–1971)
> *The Music Digest*, September 1946

The theater is not the place for the musician. When the curtain is up the music interrupts the actor, and when it is down the
music interrupts the audience.

> Sir Arthur Sullivan (1842–1900)
> *Musical Times*, February 1909

(I) realize where the fault in our Hollywood musical credo lies.
It lies in the simple truth that it is not possible to write real music
about an unreal emotion.

> Virgil Thomson (1896–   )
> New York *Herald Tribune*, April 10, 1949

I would like to thank Beethoven, Brahms, Wagner, Strauss, Rimsky-Korsakov . . .

> Dimitri Tiomkin (1899–   )
> Accepting an Academy Award for the
> best original dramatic musical score
> for the motion picture *The High
> and the Mighty*, 1955

I would be willing to set even a newspaper or a letter etc. to music, but in the theater the public will stand for everything except boredom.

> Giuseppe Verdi (1813–1901)
> Letter to Antonio Somma, May 17, 1854

Films are fantasy and fantasy needs music.

> Jack L. Warner (1892–   )
> Quoted in "The Sound of Movie Music," The
> New York *Times*, March 28, 1976

Part Eight
METAPHYSICS, METAPHOR, AND MISCELLANY

THE MUSIC OF THE SPHERES

The morning stars sang together, and all the sons of God shouted for joy.

Old Testament
Job

He who sings becomes straight and displays his moral influence and, when he himself comes into motion, Heaven and Earth respond, the four seasons are in Harmony, stars and planets are orderly, life is sustained in all beings.

"Yo Ki" (Memorial of Music in *Li Chi*, Record of Rites), ancient Chinese manuscript, c. 500 B.C.

The single harmony produced by all the heavenly bodies singing and dancing together springs from one source and ends by achieving one purpose, and has rightly bestowed the name not of "disordered" but of "ordered universe" upon the whole. And just as in a chorus, when the leader gives the signal to begin, the whole chorus of men, or it may be of women, joins in the song, mingling a single studied harmony among different voices, some high and some low; so too it is with the God that rules the whole world . . .

Aristotle (384–322 B.C.)

Music fathoms the sky.

Charles Baudelaire (1821–67)

Her voice, the music of the spheres,
So loud, it deafens mortals' ears;

As wise philosophers have thought.
And that's the cause we hear it not.
                                        Samuel Butler (1612–80)
                                        Hudibras, 1664

There's music in the singing of a reed;
There's music in the gushing of a rill;
There's music in all things, if men had ears;
Their earth is but an echo of the spheres.
                    George Gordon, Lord Byron (1788–1824)
                    Don Juan, Canto 15, 1819–24

And left so free my ears, that I might hear the music of the
spheres.
                                        George Chapman (?1559–1634)
                                        The Tears of Peace, 1609

O Music! sphere-descended maid, Friend of Pleasure, Wisdom's
aid!
                                William Collins (1721–59)
                                The Passions, an Ode for Music, 1750

Music is another planet.
                                        Alphonse Daudet (1840–97)

In holy music's golden speech
    Remotest notes to notes respond:
Each octave is a world: yet each
        Vibrates to worlds its own beyond.
                        Aubrey Thomas de Vere (1814–1902)
                        Implicit Faith

From harmony, from heavenly harmony
    This universal frame began:
From harmony to harmony,
Through all the compass of the notes it ran,
The diapason closing full in man.
                            John Dryden (1631–1700)
                            A Song for St. Cecilia's Day, 1687

> For the world was built in order
> And the atoms march in tune;
> Rhyme the pipe, and Time the warder,
> The sun obeys them, and the moon.
>> Ralph Waldo Emerson (1803–82)
>> *Monadnock*

It is Proportion that beautifies everything, the whole Universe consists of it, and Musicke is measured by it.
>> Orlando Gibbons (1583–1625)

> Somewhere there's music,
> How faint the tune!
> Somewhere there's heaven,
> How high the moon!
>> Nancy Hamilton (1908–   )
>> "How High the Moon," popular song, 1940

According to ancient Chinese lore the purpose of music and dance is to keep the world in its right course and to force Nature into benevolence towards man.
>> Johan Huizinga (1872–1945)

Nothing exists without music; for the universe itself is said to have been framed by a kind of harmony of sounds, and the heaven itself revolves under the tones of that harmony.
>> Isidore of Seville (c. 560–636)
>> *Etymologies*

Music is the harmonious voice of creation; an echo of the invisible world; one note of the divine concord which the entire universe is destined and one to sound.
>> Giuseppe Mazzini (1805–72)

> Ring out ye crystal spheres,
> Once bless our human ears
> (If ye have power to touch our senses so)
> And let your silver chime
> Move in melodious time;

And let the base of heav'n's deep organ blow,
And with your ninefold harmony
Make up full consort to th' angelic symphony.
                    John Milton (1608–74)
                    On the Morning of Christ's Nativity, 1629

Such sweet compulsion doth in music lie,
To lull the daughters of necessity,
And keep unsteady Nature to her law,
And the low world in measured motion draw
After the heavenly tune.

                                        John Milton
                                        Arcades, 1633

"This *must* be music," said he, "of the *spears,* for I am cursed if
each note of it doesn't run through one."
                            Thomas Moore (1779–1852)
                            The Fudge Family in Paris, 1818

The world's Musicke is an Harmonie, caused by the motion of
the starres, and the violence of the Spheares . . . Now the cause
wee cannot heare this Sound, according to Pliny is, because the
greatnesse of the sound doth exceed the sense of our eares.
                            Ornithoparcus
                            Musicae Activae Micrologus, 1516

The rotation of the universe and the motion of the planets
could neither begin nor continue without music . . . For everything, they say, is ordered by God according to the laws of Harmony.

                            Plutarch (c. 46–120 A.D.)

There is geometry in the humming of the strings. There is
music in the spacings of the spheres.

                            Pythagoras
                            6th century B.C.

Music changes meaning as it recedes in time the way stars do as they approach in space. But the meaning of stars grows clearer, while that of music grows vaguer—at least the original meaning.

> Ned Rorem (1923–   )
> *Pure Contraption,* 1974

Music is a sublime art precisely because, unable to imitate reality, it rises above ordinary nature into an ideal world, and with celestial harmony moves the earthly passions.

> Gioacchino Rossini (1792–1868)
> Quoted by Antonio Zanolini, *The*
> *Biography of Gioacchino Rossini,* 1875

Music is . . . in her health, the teacher of perfect order, and is the voice of the obedience of angels, and companion of the course of the spheres of heaven . . .

> John Ruskin (1819–1900)

I had rather hear you solicit that than music from the spheres.

> William Shakespeare (1564–1616)
> *Twelfth Night,* 1599

But hark, what music? . . . The music of the spheres! . . . Do you not hear? . . . Most heavenly music! It nips me unto listening, and thick slumber Hangs upon mine eyes: let me rest.

> William   Shakespeare
> *Pericles,* 1608–9

Cause the musicians play me that sad note I named my knell, whilst I sit meditating On that celestial harmony I go to.

> William Shakespeare
> *Henry VIII,* 1612

So great is the correspondence between music and the soul that many, seeking out the essence of the latter, have thought it to be full of harmonious accords, to be, indeed, a pure harmony. All nature itself, to speak the truth, is nothing but a perfect music that the creator causes to resound in the ears of man, to give him pleasure and to draw him gently to Himself.

> Jan Pieterszoon Sweelinck (1562–1621)
> *To the Burgomasters and Aldermen of*
> *Amsterdam,* March 30, 1603

Music is the sound of universal laws promulgated.

> Henry David Thoreau (1817–62)

MUSIC AS METAPHOR

Though I speak with the tongues of men and of angels, and have not charity, I am become as sounding brass, or a tinkling cymbal.

New Testament
I Corinthians, XIII

Hold this sea-shell to your ear,
And you shall hear,
Not the andante of the sea,
Not the wild wind's symphony,
But your own heart's minstrelsy.

Thomas Bailey Aldrich (1836–1907)

Flowers are my music.

Dr. Thomas Arnold (1795–1842)

"A Pretty Girl Is Like a Melody."

Irving Berlin (1888–   )
Popular song title, 1919

If man is the tonic and God the dominant, the Devil is certainly the sub-dominant and Woman the relative minor.

Samuel Butler (1835–1902)
Note Books

You sigh, the song begins,
You speak and I hear violins, It's magic.

Sammy Cahn (1913–   )
"It's Magic," popular song, 1948

The still sweet fall of music far away.

> Thomas Campbell (1777–1844)
> *The Pleasures of Hope*, 1799

Pleasure must vary, not be long; Come then, let's close and end the song.

> Thomas Campion (1567–1620)
> *Masque*

> Lovely forms do flow
> From conceit divinely framed;
> Heaven is music, and thy beauty's
> Birth is heavenly.

> Thomas Campion

And as an aungel hevenly she song.

> Geoffrey Chaucer (1340–1400)
> *The Knightes Tale*, c. 1386

I hope his tune will be worthy of the instrument.

> Cicero (106–43 B.C.)
> *Ad Atticum*, 50 B.C.

The Flamenco singer spits out flowers of fire, then extinguishes them beneath his heel.

> Jean Cocteau (1889–1963)

The sweetest noise on earth, a woman's tongue;
A string which hath no discord.

> Barry Cornwall (1787–1874)
> *Rafaelle and Fornarina*

He promptly made a trumpet of his arse.

> Dante Alighieri (1265–1321)
> *Inferno*, Canto XXI, c. 1300

O, Love's but a dance where time plays the fiddle!

> Henry Austin Dobson (1840–1921)
> *Cupid's Alley*

So just, so small, yet in so sweet a note,
It seemed the music melted in the throat.
John Dryden (1631–1700)
The Flower and the Leaf

I see you have a singing face—a heavy, dull sonata face.
George Farquhar (1678–1707)
The Inconstant, 1702

Music must be paramount: Prefer an uneven rhythm.
Anatole France (1844–1924)

When you work you are a flute through whose heart the whispering of the hours turns to music. Which of you would be a reed, dumb and silent, when all else sings together in unison?
Kahlil Gibran (1883–1931)

All the sounds of the earth are like music . . .
Oscar Hammerstein II (1895–1960)
"Oh, What a Beautiful Mornin'," popular
song, 1943

If cities were built by the sound of music, then some edificies would appear to be constructed by grave, solemn tones; others to have danced forth to light, fantastic airs.
Nathaniel Hawthorne (1804–64)
The American Note-Books, January 4, 1839

Fate's a fiddler, Life's a dance.
William Ernest Henley (1849–1903)
Double Ballade of Life and Fate

There's not a string attuned to mirth but has its chord in melancholy.
Thomas Hood (1799–1845)
Ode to Melancholy

Was it a vision, or a waking dream?
Fled is that music:— do I wake or sleep?

> John Keats (1795–1821)
> *Ode to a Nightingale*

Music's golden tongue Flatter'd to tears this aged man and poor.

> John Keats
> *The Eve of St. Agnes,* 1819

The music, yearning like a God in pain.

> John Keats
> *The Eve of St. Agnes,* 1819

America is a tune. It must be sung together.

> Gerald Stanley Lee (1862–1944)
> *Crowds,* 1913

> I hear music
> Mighty fine music,
> The murmur of a morning breeze up there
> The rattle of the milkman on the stair
> Sure that's music . . .

> > Frank Loesser (1910–69)
> > "I Hear Music," popular song, 1940

> I hear the wind among the trees
> Playing the celestial symphonies;
> I see the branches downward bent,
> Like keys of some great instrument.

> > Henry Wadsworth Longfellow (1807–82)
> > *A Day of Sunshine*

When she had passed, it seemed like the ceasing of exquisite music.

> Henry Wadsworth Longfellow
> *Evangeline,* 1847

> Oh, could you view the melodie
> of ev'ry grace,

And musick of her face,
You'd drop a teare,
Seeing more harmonie
In her bright eye,
Then now you heare.

> Richard Lovelace (1618–58)
> *Orpheus to Beasts*

You are beautiful and faded,
Like an opera tune
Played upon a harpsichord.

> Amy Lowell (1874–1925)
> *A Lady*

Sentimental people, in her phrase, fiddle harmonies on the strings of sensualism.

> George Meredith (1828–1909)
> *Diana of the Crossways*, 1885

Silence is but a rich pause in the music of life.

> Sarojini Naidu (1879–1949)
> *The Bird of Time*, 1912

The music's not immortal, but the world has made it sweet.

> Alfred Noyes (1880–1958)
> *The Barrel-Organ*

Laughter is the music of life.

> Sir William Osler (1849–1919)

In Heaven a spirit doth dwell
    Whose heart-strings are a lute;
None sing so wildly well
As the angel Israfel.

> Edgar Allan Poe (1809–49)
> *Israfel*, c. 1830

Silence more musical than any song.

> Christina Georgina Rossetti (1830–94)
> *Rest*

All one's life is a music, if one touches the notes rightly, and in time.

John Ruskin (1819–1900)

There's no music in a "rest," Katie, that I know of: but there's the making of music in it. And people are always missing that part of the life-melody.

John Ruskin
Ethics of the Dust: Lecture 4, "The
Crystal Orders," 1866

Architecture in general is frozen music.

Friedrich von Schelling (1775–1854)
The Philosophy of Art, 1845

The skies, the fountains, every region near
Seem'd all one musical cry: I never heard
So musical a discord, such sweet thunder.
William Shakespeare (1564–1616)
A Midsummer Night's Dream, 1595–96

You would play upon me; you would seem to know my stops; you would pluck out the heart of my mystery; you would sound me from my lowest note to the top of my compass.

William Shakespeare
Hamlet, 1600–1

And I, of ladies most deject and wretched,
That suck'd the honey of his music vows,
Now see that noble and most sovereign reason,
Like sweet bells jangled, out of tune and harsh . . .
William Shakespeare
Hamlet, 1600–1

Come, your answer in broken music; for thy voice is music and thy English broken.

William Shakespeare
Henry V, 1598–99

His tongue is now a stringless instrument.

William Shakespeare
Richard II, 1595–96

One whom the music of his own vain tongue
Doth ravish like enchanting harmony.

William Shakespeare
Love's Labour's Lost, 1594–95

Let music sound while he doth make his choice;
Then, if he lose, he makes a swan-like end,
Fading in music . . . He may win;
And what is music then? The music is
Even as the flourish when true subjects bow
To a new-crowned monarch; such it is
As are those dulcet sounds in break of day
That creep into the dreaming bridegroom's ear
And summon him to marriage.

William Shakespeare
The Merchant of Venice, 1596–97

There's not the smallest orb which thou behold'st
But in his motion like an angel sings,
Still quiring to the young-eyed cherubins;
Such harmony is in immortal souls;
But, whilst this muddy vesture of decay
Doth grossly close it in, we cannot hear it.

William Shakespeare
The Merchant of Venice, 1596–97

How sweet the moonlight sleeps upon this bank!
Here we will sit and let the sounds of music
Creep in our ears; soft stillness and the night
Become the touches of sweet harmony.

William Shakespeare
The Merchant of Venice, 1596–97

Melodious discord, heavenly tune harsh-sounding,
Ear's deep-sweet music, and hearts deep-sore wounding.

William Shakespeare
Venus and Adonis, 1593

Are we not formed, as notes of music are,
For one another, though dissimilar.

Percy Bysshe Shelley (1792–1822)
Epipsychidion, 1821

Short-swallow-flights of song, that dip their wings in tears, and skim away.

Alfred, Lord Tennyson (1809–92)
In Memoriam, 1850

There is sweet music here that softer falls
Than petals from blown roses on the grass,
Or night-dews on still waters between walls
of shadowy granite, in a gleaming pass;
Music that gentler on the spirit lies
Than tired eyelids upon tired eyes.

Alfred, Lord Tennyson
The Lotus-Eaters

It is the little rift within the lute,
That by and by will make the music mute,
and ever widening slowly silence all.

Alfred, Lord Tennyson
The Idylls of the King, 1859

The city is built to music, therefore never built at all, and therefore built forever.

Alfred, Lord Tennyson
The Idylls of the King, 1859

Thy lute, thy harp, or else thy
Heart-strings take,

And with thy musick let thy
sense awake . . .
> Thomas Traherne (?1637–74)
> *Poems of Felicity*

An ecstasy is a thing that will not go into words; it feels like
music . . .
> Mark Twain (Samuel Langhorne Clemens)
> (1835–1910)

For we desire above all—nuance,
Not color, but half-shades!
Ah! nuance alone unites
Dream with dream and flute with horn.
> Paul Verlaine (1844–96)

The long sobbings
of the violins
of autumn
wound my heart
with monotonous
languor.

> Paul Verlaine
> *Chanson d'automne*

Our life contains a thousand springs,
And dies if one be gone.
Strange! that a harp of thousand strings
Should keep in tune so long.
> Isaac Watts (1674–1748)
> *Hymns*, Book II, No. 19, 1707

Dust as we are, the immortal spirit grows
Like harmony in music; there is a dark
Inscrutable workmanship that reconciles

Discordant elements, makes them cling together
In one society.

> William Wordsworth (1770–1850)
> *The Prelude*, 1805

Where light and shade repose, where music dwells
Lingering—and wandering on as loth to die;
Like thoughts whose very sweetness yieldeth proof
That they were born for immortality.

> William Wordsworth
> *Ecclesiastical Sonnets*, 1822

The still, sad music of humanity.

> William Wordsworth
> *Lines Composed a Few Miles Above
> Tintern Abbey*, 1798

The moving accident is not my trade;
To freeze the blood I have no ready arts;
'Tis my delight, alone in summer shade,
To pipe a simple song for thinking hearts.

> William Wordsworth
> *Hart-leap Well*, 1800

PROVERBS, APHORISMS, WORDPLAY, AND
ASSORTED MUSICAL SAWS

We could make such beautiful music together.

Anonymous

Vamp till ready.

Anonymous

My baby rocks me with a steady roll.

Anonymous, traditional blues

> Little Boy Blue, come blow your horn,
> The sheep's in the meadow.
> The cow's in the corn.

Anonymous, nursery rhyme, c. 1750

> Sing a song of sixpence, a pocket full of rye.
> Four and twenty blackbirds baked in a pie.

Anonymous, nursery rhyme

> Ride a cock-horse to Banbury Cross,
> To see a fine lady upon a white horse,
> Rings on her fingers and bells on her toes,
> And she shall have music wherever she goes.

Anonymous

Bird Lives.

Anonymous
Graffito, a reference to
Charlie "Bird" Parker

Try this on your piano.

> Anonymous

Play it again, Sam.

> A line never spoken by, but usually
> identified with, actor Humphrey Bogart
> in the film *Casablanca*, 1942

The lute which affords sweet music to princes is not appreciated by weavers.

> Babylonian Talmud, c. 450 A.D.

> Here's to music
> Joy of joys!
> One man's music's
> Another man's noise.

> Anonymous toast

Great strokes make not sweet music.

> Anonymous

INTERLOCUTOR: Who was that oboe I saw you with last night?
MR. BONES: That was no oboe, suh, that was my fife.

> Minstrel joke, c. 1900

Beat your drum inside your house, and outsiders will not hear.

> Chinese proverb

The older the fiddle, the sweeter the tune.

> English proverb

If you sing before breakfast, you will cry before night.

> English proverb

In the fiddler's house, all are dancers.

> French proverb

These three are not to be trusted; a singer, a shopkeeper, and an opium eater.

> Hindu proverb

Face the music.

> Anonymous
> 19th-century Americanism

The Sweetest Music this side of Heaven.

> Motto of Guy Lombardo
> and his Royal Canadians,
> American dance orchestra

I play a musical instrument some, but only for my own amazement.

> Fred Allen (1894–1956)
> *Reader's Digest*, 1936

Just play the notes as they are rotten.

> Instructions to orchestra
> attributed to Ernest Ansermet in
> *Music All Around Me*, by Anthony
> Hopkins, 1967

A bad accompanist makes a good singer.

> St. Augustine (354–430)

Young Man with a Horn

> Dorothy Baker (1907–68)
> Title of a novel, 1938

> Yankee Doodle, keep it up,
> Yankee Doodle Dandy;
> Mind the music and the step,
> And with the girls be handy.
> Words and music by Edward Bangs, 1775

Everything ends in songs.

> Pierre Augustin Caron de Beaumarchais (1732–99)
> Last line of *The Marriage of Figaro*, 1784

"Say It with Music"

> Irving Berlin (1888–   )
> Popular song title, 1921

"Let's Face the Music and Dance"

> Irving Berlin
> Popular song title, 1936

Nobody knows the Traubels I've seen.

> Sir Rudolf Bing (1902–   )
> While General Manager of the
> Metropolitan Opera

The best music should be played as the best men and women should be dressed—neither so well or so ill as to attract attention to itself.

> Samuel Butler (1612–80)

"I know I have to beat time when I learn music."

"Ah! that accounts for it," said the Hatter. "He won't stand beating."

> Lewis Carroll (Charles Lutwidge Dodgson) (1832–98)
> *Alice's Adventures in Wonderland*, 1865

They play one tune and dance another.

> John Clarke (1609–76)
> *Paroemiologia Anglo-Latina*, 1639

When a musician hath forgot his note, He makes as though a crumb stuck in his throat.

> John Clarke
> *Paroemiologia Anglo-Latina*, 1639

Learn to say before you sing.

> John Clarke
> *Paroemiologia Anglo-Latina*, 1639

It's a pity to shoot the pianist when the piano is out of tune.

> René Coty (1882–1962), President of France
> Quoted in *Time*, January 4, 1957

I bought it for a song.

> John Crowne (1640–c. 1703)
> *Regulus*, Act III, 1694

We can face the music together.

> Howard Dietz (1896–   )
> "Dancing in the Dark," popular song, 1931

Blowing one's own trumpet.

> Diogenianus (2nd century A.D.)

No longer Pipe, no longer Dance. No longer play the Fool, no longer please some People.

> Oswald Dykes
> *English Proverbs*, 1709

If a man cannot sing as he carries his cross, he had better drop it.

> Havelock Ellis (1859–1939)

By the cigars they smoke, and the composers they love, ye shall know the texture of men's souls.

> John Galsworthy (1867–1933)
> *Indian Summer of a Forsyte*, 1918

> If you wish in this world to advance
> Your merits you're bound to enhance;
>   You must stir it and stump it,
>   And *blow your own trumpet*,
> Or, trust me, you haven't a chance.
>
> W. S. Gilbert (1836–1911)
> *Ruddigore*, Act I, 1887

One ought, every day at least, to hear a little song, read a good poem, see a fine picture, and, if it were possible, to speak a few reasonable words.

> Johann Wolfgang von Goethe (1749–1832)
> *Wilhelm Meister's Apprenticeship*, 1796

"On Wings of Song"

> Heinrich Heine (1797–1856)
> Song title, 1832

Ye harpe on the stryng that geueth no melody.

> John Heywood (?1497–?1580)
> *Proverbs,* 1546

The harper is laughed at who always blunders on the same
string.

> Horace (65–8 B.C.)
> *Ars Poetica,* c. 20 B.C.

Sheshell ebb music wayriver she flows.

> James Joyce (1882–1941)
> *Finnegan's Wake,* 1939

> Each little lyrical
> Grave or satirical
> Musical miracle!
> Frederic Lawrence Knowles (1869–1905)
> *On a Fly-Leaf of Burns's Songs*

Shostakovich small by a waterfall.

> Oscar Levant (1906–72)
> *The Memoirs of an Amnesiac,* 1965

Is everybody happy?

> Ted Lewis (1892–1957)

Loud is good.

> Frank Loesser (1910–69)

> One truth you taught us outlived
> all the rest:
> Music has Brahms to soothe
> the savage breast.
> Daniel Gregory Mason (1873–1953)
> Lines to Percy Goetschius on his
> 82nd birthday

It ain't a song-and-dance
I'm giving you either.

>Brander Matthews (1852–1929)
>*A Confident Tomorrow*, 1900

If the King loves music, there is little wrong in the land.

>Mencius (Meng-tzu) (?372–?289 B.C.)

"Whistle While you Work"

>Larry Morey (1905–   )
>Popular song title, 1937

Hidden music counts for nothing.

>Attributed to Nero in 58 A.D.

Without music, life would be an error.

>Friedrich Nietzsche (1844–1900)
>*The Twilight of the Idols*, 1888

Indeed the Idols I have loved so long
Have done my credit in this World much wrong,
Have drowned my Glory in a shallow Cup,
And sold my Reputation for a Song.

>Omar Khayyam (11th century)
>*The Rubaiyat*, translation by
>Edward FitzGerald, 1859

Ah, take the Cash, and let the promise go,
Nor heed the rumble of a distant drum.

>Omar Khayyam
>Translation and adaption by
>Edward FitzGerald, 1859

I am out of tune.

>Pindar (?518–c. 438 B.C.)

A *Dance to the Music of Time*

> Anthony Powell (1905–)
> Omnibus title to a series of twelve
> novels, 1951–1975

Thou singest like a bird called a swine.

> John Ray (?1627–1705)
> *English Proverbs*, 1670

The greatest strokes make not the best music.

> John Ray
> *English Proverbs*, 1670

Why is life different when the singing stops?

> James Reeves
> *The Idiom of the People*, 1958

It got to a point where I had to get a haircut or a violin.

> President Franklin Delano Roosevelt (1882–1945)
> *Reader's Digest*, May 1938

I am quite at your service to play second fiddle in all your laudable enterprises.

> Alain René Le Sage (1668–1747)
> *Gil Blas*, 1715–35, translation by
> B. H. Malkin, 1809

Rascals have no songs.

> J. G. Seume
> *Die Gesänge*, c. 1800

I know a man sold a goodly manor for a song.

> William Shakespeare (1564–1616)
> *All's Well That Ends Well*, 1602–3

I have a reasonable good ear in music; let us have the tongs and the bones.

> William Shakespeare
> *A Midsummer Night's Dream*, 1595–96

Harp not on that string, madam; that is past.

> William Shakespeare
> *Richard III*, 1592–93

The time was once when thou unurg'd
    wouldst vow
That never words were music to thine ear . . .

> William Shakespeare
> *The Comedy of Errors*, 1592–93

I'm going to pay the piper and call the tune.

> George Bernard Shaw (1856–1950)
> *Major Barbara*, 1905

What Histories might ever make my fame yield so sweet a music to my ears . . .

> Sir Philip Sidney (1554–1586)
> *Arcadia*, 1590

God giveth speech to all, song to the few.

> Walter Chalmers Smith (1824–1908)
> *Olrig Grange*, 1872

. . . Canned music.

> John Philip Sousa (1854–1932)
> Article in *Appleton Magazine*, 1906

The love of music seems to exist for its own sake.

> Herbert Spencer (1820–1903)

It needs more skill than I can tell
To play the second fiddle well.

> Charles Haddon Spurgeon (1834–92)
> *The Salt-cellars*

Always those that dance must pay the music.

> John Taylor (1580–1653)
> *Taylor's Feast*, 1638

If a man does not keep pace with his companions, perhaps it is because he hears a different drummer. Let him step to the music which he hears, however measured or far away.

> Henry David Thoreau (1817–62)
> *Walden*, 1854

It takes no more energy to write *fortissimo* than to write piano, or universe than *garden*.

> Paul Valéry (1871–1945)

We sing to deaf ears.

> Virgil (70–19 B.C.)
> *Eclogues*, 37 B.C.

One never knows, do one?

> Thomas "Fats" Waller (1904–43)

A careless song, with a little nonsense in it now and then, does not misbecome a monarch.

> Horace Walpole (1717–97)
> Letter to Sir Horace Mann, 1774

And sings a solitary song that whistles in the wind.

> William Wordsworth (1770–1850)
> *Lucy Gray*

ENCYCLOPEDIA OF QUOTATIONS
ABOUT MUSIC

INDEX OF NAMES AND SOURCES

ENCYCLOPEDIA OF QUOTATIONS
ABOUT MUSIC

Ballad(s)
  b. singer's shrilling strain, 163
  b. strikes mind and softens
    feelings, 154
  bitter b. of slums, 240
  love a b. even too well, 157
Ballet
  bel canto is to opera what
    pole-vaulting is to b., 167
  insatiable supporters of b., 315
Band
  my b. is my instrument, 85
  strike up the b., 86
  won't do business if not got b.,
    116
Banging
  b. and slamming and booming and
    crashing beyond belief, 178
Banjos
  b. rattled, 89
Bank
  cried all the way to b., 118
Barbarous
  more b. than any folk art, 308
Barber shop
  Play That B. Shop Chord, 212
Bard
  friends and foes submit to song of
    b., 224
Baritones
  b. are born villains, 170
Baseball
  more Americans went to
    symphonies than to b. games,
    113
  sensible as b. in Italian, 175
Baseness
  no b. in those who sing, 160
Bass(es)
  b. roar blasphemy, 131
  b., the beast can only bellow,
    162
  earth made the b., 10
  grunt out b. as number of hogs,
    167
Bath
  take a music b., 186
Battle
  if trumpet uncertain sound, who
    prepare to b., 221
  march impel men toward b., 224
Bawdy
  sing me b. song, 169

what b. house is to cathedral, 176
Bawl
  weep, not b., 193
Bawling
  medium for b. in public, 134
Beast
  charms to sooth savage b., 182
  music's force tame furious b., 188
  turns self into b. with musick of
    own making, 129
Beat
  b. me daddy, eight to the bar, 99
Beating
  he won't stand b., 344
Beatle(s)
  B. are mutants, 303
  everyone analysing B. songs, 139
Beautiful
  anything describable as b., 149
  b. moments but awful quarter
    hours, 57
  b. music, do not cease!, 243
  b. music less relished by ignorant,
    129
  Beethoven is not b., 49
  make such b. music together, 341
  most b. experience is mysterious, 7
  most b. organ of music, 170
  to terminate in love of b., 22
  what b. language music is, 41
Beauty
  combination of sounds with view
    to b., 3
  creation of supernal b., 22
  form produces b., 58
  thy b.'s birth is heavenly, 332
Becoming
  continual state of b., 247
  music is a b., 20
Beer
  embodied spirit of b., 108
Beeritone
  hark to red-faced b., 160
Beethoven
  B. can write music, thank God, 41
  B. contributed to advent of long
    hair, 47
  B. embraced the universe, 45
  B. Fifth Symphony may be
    Fate—or Kate—knocking, 23
  B. Fifth Symphony most sublime
    noise, 47
  B. is greatest composer, 57

Brutalization
  b. of Negro church music, 302
Bugle
  blow, b., blow, 93
  bring the good old b., boys, 225
Bugs
  fiddle b. of sweet-potato vine, 102
Bullfight
  concert is like b., 113
Bullshit
  no b. going down with rock, 305
Business
  easier to make b. man out of
    musician, 118
  going into starvation b., 118
  won't do b. if not got band, 116
  worldly pursuit known as musical
    B., 116
Butcher
  I want to know a b. paints, 115

Cake
  c. in oven—not fully baked, 92
Calculation
  c. which the soul makes, 16
Calling
  c. rather than profession, 116
Cancer
  c. patients not believe in own
    decay, 267
Candlestick-maker
  c. acquaints soul with song,
    115
Canned
  c. music, 349
Capture
  you can never c. it again, 11
Care(s)
  c. lessened by sweet song, 186
  c. that infest the day, 187
  killing c. and grief of heart, 188
Carefully
  only twelve tones, treat them c.,
    48
Caress
  c. set to music, 204
Caressing
  c. us like warm bath, 271
Caruso
  so God took C. away, 216
Cat
  music of c. hung up by tail, 129

Caterwauling
  belligerent c. can sell anything,
    138
Cat-gut
  no c. swoon out so much soul, 102
  rubbing hair and c. together, 103
Cathedral
  effect of musical sounds in
    Cathedral, 259
  what bawdy house is to c., 176
Celebrate
  c. events with music, 46
Cello
  c. is like beautiful woman, 83
Censor
  meddlesome hand of c., 235
Century
  c. of aeroplanes, 69
  composer c. ahead of his time, 71
Chansonets
  shrill and facile c., 310
Chaos
  hear far c. talk with me, 270
  know something about music—but
    this is c., 136
  music creates order out of c., 19
Charleston
  C., C., made in Carolina, 316
Charm(s)
  c. alone for peaceful minds, 188
  c. can build wand'ring sense, 183
  c. of the irregular, 276
  c. to sooth savage beast, 182
  c. to soothe savage breast, 130,
    183
  music c. every living thing, 183
  music hath c. to make bad good,
    238
  music that would c. forever, 190
Charming
  c. the opposite sex, 202
Charmingly
  talks c. and says nothing, 228
Chaste
  music was c. and modest, 68
Chattel
  c. with a soul, 110
Cheap
  c. music set to noble words, 151
  how potent c. music is, 307
  only c. and unpunished rapture, 27

Duty
  d. toward music to invent it, 61
Dying
  instead of d., gets new names, 281
  let me have music d., 216
Dynamics
  we're working with d. now, 301

Ear(s)
  addresses itself to the e., 17
  e. always lead you right, 65
  e. disapproves but tolerates, 130
  e. for music different from taste, 131
  genius and e. deny what we are seeking, 55
  if men had e., 268
  inner e. sole judge, 65
  music is eye of e., 11
  never words were music to e., 349
  not listening with e. of period, 4
  penetrates e. with facility, 208
  sings through his nose by e., 312
  taught us to see with our e., 194
  those who have no e. for music, 134
  world lacks e. of taste, 134
Earth
  joins Heaven and E. with threads of sounds, 49
  music that is down to e., 9
  sounds of e. like music, 333
Eccentric
  other arts offer e. pleasures, 192
Echo(es)
  e. from invisible world, 6
  set wild e. flying, 93
Ecstasy(ies)
  dissolve me into e., 257
  e. of logic, 7
  e. will not go into words, 339
Edifying
  music is e., 241
Edison
  blame E. for rock 'n' roll, 302
Educate
  e. a child musically, 252
Educating
  e. proletariat in music, 236
Education
  he had no singing e., 130

musical e. necessary for musical judgement, 252
  resource to idle, not e., 251
Eight
  beat me daddy, e. to the bar, 99
Electric
  e. guitars are abomination, 110
Electrical
  e. soil in which spirit lives, 6
Elements
  e. which result in hit song, 311
Elevates
  e. and ennobles whatever it expresses, 12
Elevating
  music made popular by e. people, 233
Elevator
  impulse to ring for e. man, 99
Eloquence
  this e. is quite beyond me, 104
  where harmony, no need of e., 34
Elusive
  more e. and mysterious it becomes, 6
Emasculates
  e. instead of invigorating, 224
Embrace
  symphony must e. everything, 52
Eminence
  not rise to e. who is merely good singer, 119
Emotion(s)
  beauty of form and expression of e., 3
  created out of e. to move e., 197
  e. modern music arouses, 71
  e. not equally sharp and profound, 63
  generate flow of pure e., 197
  made sonorous own e., 63
  music arouses various e., 193
  music is shorthand of e., 199
  music will express any e., 198
  no e. jazz not encompass, 282
  not possible to write real music about unreal e., 320
  organ of e. is sound, 199
  vehicle of e. and thought, 20
  verbalization of e., 150

Emotional
  e. first and intellectual second, 197
  most e. of the arts, 256
Emotionalism
  e. only meant for women, 226
Enchant
  singing should e., 166
Enchanters
  sounds the e. made, 153
Enchanting
  e. *fata morgana*, 4
Enchantment
  strok'st mine ears with e., 195
Enemy(ies)
  critic e. on provocation of bad
    performance, 126
  e. those who debase music, 92
  people make music together not e.,
    87
  when one marches against e., 223
Energy
  e. with which manipulated, 45
  evocation and transmutation of e.,
    301
English
  E. excel in dancing and music, 262
  E. may not like music, 261
  E. pay for it well, 263
  E. terrible language for vocalizing,
    146
  only creditable incident in E.
    history, 119
Enjoy
  don't mess about it; just e. it, 4
Enjoyed
  e. that in spite of singing, 178
Enjoyment
  finest e. of time, 248
  music susceptible of complete e.,
    220
Enlightenment
  sing for own e., 87
Ennobles
  elevates and ennobles whatever it
    expresses, 12
  e. or degrades behavior, 241
Entertaining
  sorry if only succeeded in e., 48
Entertainment
  principal e. of God, 259
Eolian

E. doth appease tempests of
    minds, 21
Epic
  rather written best song than
    noblest e., 156
Epilepsy
  sound of flute will cure e., 109
Equilibrium
  e. between composition and
    conscience, 89
Error
  life would be an e., 347
Escapism
  music is really e., 270
Esthetic
  I have no e. rules, 53
Eternal
  exaltation of mind derived from
    things e., 4
  what music expresses is e., 29
Eternity
  e. of nothing was deadliest, 177
  into e. itself, beyond the veil, 11
  vanity of fixing both eyes on e.,
    125
Ethiopian
  pursue E. business without fear,
    296
Etiquette
  voices that violate book of e., 227
European
  originality and character captivated
    E. mind, 285
Eve
  E., anticipating Great God Pan,
    229
Everyday
  e. music, 9
  limits of e. joy and sorrow, 199
Everyman
  escape of e., 318
Everything
  e. is music for born musician, 24
Evidence
  music must be e. for living, 18
Evil
  fundamental e. in music, 87
  great pains to turn out e. work,
    177
  not e. ruining earth, but
    mediocrity, 91

f. not instrument with good moral effect, 108

f., variously perforated hollow stick, 108

heard f. in distance and I heard nothing, 265

man who plays violin a bore to man with f., 88

music of zither, f. and lyre, 90

soft, complaining f., 108

sound of f. will cure epilepsy, 109

tutor who tooted a f., 107

what is worse than f., 107

when you work you are a f., 333

Foes

friends and f. submit to song of the bard, 224

Folk

all songs are f. songs, 312

almost as many music as f., 312

every period which abounded in f. songs, 313

f. are somewhere else, 312

f. melodies are real model, 312

f. music, thanks to childlike simplicity, 313

f. song composes itself, 312

f. songs written by individuals, 313

frolicsomeness of f. songs, 256

only thing to do with f. melody, 312

singing f. songs in f. song club, 312

try everything once except incest and f. dancing, 315

Folklore

melodies more authentic than f., 65

Folksinger

f. is intellectual, 312

f. sings through nose by ear, 312

Food

f. for your soul, 184

f. of us that trade in love, 205

give me books, f., french wine, 271

if music f. of love, play on, 205

is not music f. of love?, 206

music is like f., 4

music thou art not "f. of love," 206

no passion but finds f. in music, 196

Foolish

music so f. I am amazed, 72

Fools

originality may reveal itself in face of f., 15

Footlights

her place is before the f., 165

Foreign

f. and unknown to other tongue, 29

Form

art in which f. and matter are always one, 66

f. is balance between tension and relaxation, 63

f.—outer shape dictated by work's inner organic life, 63

f. produces beauty, 58

f. remains supreme, 57

hot longing for f., 71

no f. without logic, 58

only when f. clear will spirit become clear, 59

Fortissimo

no more energy to write f., 350

Foundation

Bach is f. of piano playing, 96

Bach used in f., 49

Fragrance

music is f. of universe, 18

Freaks

race of f. arise in race of artists, 91

Free

f. it from barren traditions, 268

mind and soul must be f., 48

music is f. speculation, 28

music was born f., 8

you got to stay f. inside it, 82

Freedom

f. from meddlesome hand of censor, 235

price of f. for all musicians, 89

French

F. are the wittiest, 139

F. enliven it, 263

F. have pride of virtuoso, 264

F. music (deficient) in lacks, 261

F. song and fiddle has no fellow, 205

F. write poor (tragedies), 175

there is an old F. air, 155

Frenchman
  F. admires you, 65
Friend(s)
  ain't got f. without song, 188
  f. are those who give good
    performances, 92
  f. and foes submit to song of bard,
    224
  music is f. of labor, 185
  no f. like music, 185
Frightens
  f. away his ills, 266
Frog
  who does that F. think he is, 124
Frozen
  architecture is f. music, 336
Fugue
  demonstration of universal truth
    by f., 60
  f. is acute phase of disease of
    dullness, 138
  f. music in which voices come in
    one after another, 41
  f. with life of its own, 281
  why should I write a f., 46
Fundamental
  f. evil in music, 87
Funeral
  augmenting grief at f., 160
  f. march in memory of Beethoven,
    217
Fury
  allaying f. and passion with sweet
    air, 189
  engender f., kindle love, 191
Futile
  f. theorizing about music, 13
Futility
  impudent f. to endeavor to
    translate music, 8
Future
  composer of the f., 68
  concerts in England have no f.,
    112
  direction for musical art of f., 72
  f. of music not with music itself,
    235
  making love to f., 47
  no f. as Broadway musical, 318
  nostalgia for the f., 24
  not fear about f. of music, 214

Garden
  magnificent g. of music, 124
  room in g. of song, 116
Gate-crasher
  contemporary composer is g., 117
Gem
  song considered perfect g., 9
Generals
  G. singing Word of Command,
    172
Genius
  g. and ear deny what we are
    seeking, 55
  if g. pleases, everything is possible,
    24
Gentleman
  great composer if not such a
    perfect g., 134
Gentler
  music g. on spirit lies, 338
Geometry
  g. in humming of strings, 328
German(s)
  G. imagines God singing, 258
  G. music and bad music, 136
  G. strive after it, 263
  next best thing G. composer, 261
  only the G. can love you, 65
  our music differs from G. music,
    264
  to G. belongs true feeling for
    music, 264
Gift(s)
  among g. God has sent, 17
  g. of God set apart, 255
  g. of sweet song, 165
  g. of the imagination, 9
  greatest g. God has given us, 257
  greatest of divine g., 38
  no invention of ours, g. of God,
    257
Giftless
  what a g. bastard, 62
Girls
  fall of 1,000 g. to jazz music, 226
Glamour
  requirements for g. in jazz, 285
Glasses
  men like musical g., 270
Glistening
  it is g. music we seek, 196

Gloomy
g. night of life, 23
Glorious
great and surpassingly g., 26
Gluck
I sympathize with G., 62
Gluttony
imprudence, intemperance, g., 135
God
agreeable harmony for honor of
G., 5
All G.'s Chillun Got Rhythm, 35
among gifts G. has sent, 17
Bach is Bach, as G. is G., 42
believed G. himself delighted, 139
creates g. in own image, 255
German imagines G. singing, 258
gift of G. set apart, 255
G. giveth speech to all, 349
G. has few whom he whispers in
the ear, 83
G. has given cheerful heart, 48
G. hath given to some wisdom,
105
G. is in the house tonight, 100
g. of music dwelleth out of doors,
269
G. sent singers upon earth, 257
G. tells how music should sound,
79
G. the dominant, 331
greatest gifts G. has given us, 257
I am the instrument of G., 3
music is almost definition of G.,
17
music praises G., 259
no invention of ours, gift of G.,
257
of G.'s prerogatives, song fairest,
158
ordered by G. according to laws of
harmony, 328
principal entertainment of G., 259
service and praise of G., 258
sons of G. shouted for joy, 325
speech of G. himself, 15
thought of G. like quiet music,
257
'tis G. gives skill, 103
whom G. loves not, 254
yearning like G. in pain, 334

Godlike
music is sacred, divine, G., 257
Gods
by song gods are pleased, 156
g. appointed to be partners in
dance, 258
Gold
no g. for sounding, 119
Golden
g. orb of perfect song, 154
music's g. tongue, 334
Good
g. composer slowly discovered, 54
g. music not bad as it sounds, 141
it is better to be short and g., 53
music was G., but it didn't sound
right, 129
Governed
wouldst know if people well g.,
233
Government
compare g. to piece of music, 231
Graces
nameless g. no methods teach, 23
Gravity
natural force, like g., 35
Greed
I can definitely recognize g., 117
Greeks
G. created superb tragedies, 175
Grief
allays each g., 265
eases g.'s smarting wound, 188
seasonable in g. as in joy, 248
Grieved
half of music is to have g., 197
Grimace
only pianist who did not g., 100
Grunts
rock began as series of g., 304
Guillotine
piano is a veritable g., 96
Guitar
g. has moonlight in it, 110
invention of electric g., 111
my g., I sing of thee, 110
my wife, my g. and me, 110
to use a woman or g., 226
Gunpowder
almost as dangerous as g., 131

I l. to play for people, 99
I l. to write music, 53
imagination of l. in sound, 206
incitement to l., 201
instrumentalities of l. and peace,
      182
is not music food of l., 206
l. ballad even too well, 157
l. be great twixt thee and me, 202
l. but a dance, 332
l. can give no idea of music, 202
l. in search of word, 203
l. is a mystery, 204
l. men in arms as well as beds, 229
l. music more than own
      convenience, 79
l. of music to exist for own sake,
      349
l. playing so much I would do it
      for nothing, 99
l. song is just a caress, 204
make list of music you l., 42
making l. to future, 47
music is l., 256
music thou art not "food of l.,"
      206
my l. is like a red red rose, 202
one in l. either lives it or talks, 201
reed make music of l., 206
thing of world I l. most, 22
to sing is to l. and affirm, 161
to terminate in l. of beautiful, 22
try singing "l." or "death," 146
unextinguishable l. for music, 232
violin should be played with l., 105
what is music but l., 203
when I play, I make l., 204
wine of l. is music, 206

Loved
   only l. when one falls asleep with
      it, 26
Loveliest
   l. tune becomes vulgar, 309
Lover(s)
   balm into bleeding l.'s wounds,
      224
   L. chanting out Billetdoux, 172
   woes of hopeless l., 108
Loving
   most sensuous of arts to l. souls,
      201

Low
   l. woman who sings, 160
Lubricant
   light music is good l., 309
Lugubrious
   vocal music l. and gloomy, 170
Lullaby
   that's an Irish l., 263
Lust
   call love what is but l., 201
Lute
   lascivious pleasing of l., 205
   little rift within the l., 338
   l. affords sweet music to princes,
      342
   l. strung with poets' sinews, 92
   my l., awake!, 219
   Orpheus with his l., 269
Lydian
   lap me in soft L. airs, 187
   L. doth sharpen wit of dull, 21
Lyre
   music of zither, flute and l., 90
   teachers of the l., 251
   verses are children of the l., 145
Lyric
   songs, my l. minions, 155
Lyricism
   near-tragic, near-comic l., 295
Lyricist
   to be a l. you've got to be a
      euphoric masochist, 148
Lyrics
   l. should be heard, not seen, 146
   never sing l. out clearly, 303

Machine(s)
   apotheosis of m. age, 70
   m.-made, m.-played, m.-heard, 308
   multiplication of m., 72
Mad
   make wise men m., 198
Madder
   m. music and stronger wine, 271
Madman
   m. talking to himself, 56
Madrigals
   melodious birds sing m., 274
Maestro
   music, m., please, 204
Magic
   it is with music as with m., 48

for every n., another n. melts it, 97
formed as n. of music are, 338
n. I handle no better than many,
    99
Nothing
    love playing so much I would do it
        for n., 99
    music *per se* means n., 82
    not conceive of music that
        expresses n., 5
    n. but songs wanting here, 158
    talks charmingly and says n., 228
Notices
    consequently I got pretty good n.,
        50
Nourishments
    jazz is best of all n., 288
Novelty
    music does not require n., 69, 210
Nuance(s)
    n. alone unites dream with dream,
        339
    n. and subtleties make charm of
        music, 84
Nuisance
    not composing becomes positive n.,
        49
Nurse
    music is n. of soul, 181

Obituaries
    songwriters have greatest o., 215
Objectivity
    o. in music is rubbish, 203
Objects
    music, not made up of o., 6
Oblivion
    genius of interpretation is o., 85
Oboe
    o. is an ill wind, 107
    That was no o., suh, that was my
        fife, 342
Obsolete
    contemporary composer is o., 71
Obvious
    never strain to avoid o., 42
Occult
    music is o. metaphysical exercise,
        26
Ocean
    music is an o., 15

Old
    melody never grows o., 35
    o. King Cole was merry old soul,
        270
    o. songs are best, 213
Opera(s)
    absurdity of o., 174
    any subject good for o., 176
    bel canto is to o. what
        pole-vaulting is to ballet, 167
    comic o. do not lie, 244
    equally dull was o. season, 112
    good o. never written, 173
    in o. details out of place, 173
    kind of o. that starts at 6 o'clock,
        176
    learn from o. that there are two
        sexes, 174
    music in o. like poetry, 173
    nobody really sings in o., 174
    no good o. plot sensible, 173
    not mind language o. sung in, 172
    o. based on not-true, 245
    o. exotic and irrational, 175
    o. has no business making money,
        115
    o. is like an oyster, 175
    o. is when guy gets stabbed, 174
    o. lifted to realm of drama, 177
    o. like husband with foreign title,
        172
    o. nothing but public gathering
        place, 178
    o. not what it used to be, 174
    o. performer apes an ape, 173
    o. tolerable in language he not
        understand, 172
    o. tune upon harpsichord, 335
    to o. one goes for want of other
        interest, 178
Opiate
    music is beautiful o., 19
Opinion
    what is my o. against that of
        millions, 51
Opium
    singer, shopkeeper and o. eater,
        342
    something of o. eater in jazz
        cultist, 292